Thank you for your purchase. I am pledging 100% of the author royalties for this book to the Shoe4Africa Foundation.

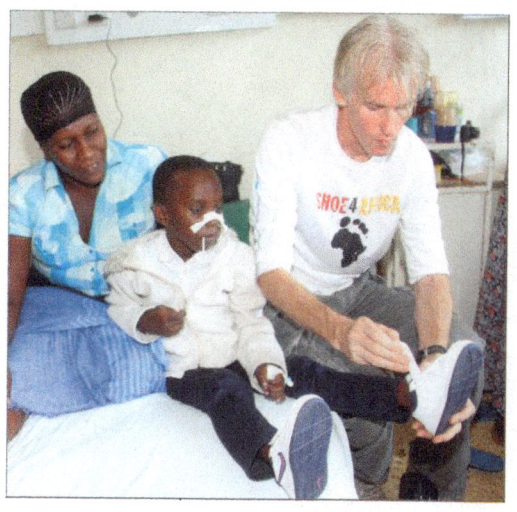

A patient at the Shoe4Africa Children's Hospital receives a pair of donated shoes.

No part of this publication may be reproduced, distributed, or transmitted in any form or by any means, including photocopying, recording, or other electronic or mechanical methods, or by any information storage and retrieval system without the prior written permission of the publisher, except in the case of very brief quotations embodied in critical reviews and certain other noncommercial uses permitted by copyright law.

ISBN: 9798517603302
Copyright © 2021 by Toby Tanser. All Rights Reserved.
Cover Design: Farago.com

Written (mostly) in American English and edited with (free) open-source tools.

Contents

Prologue 1

Chapter 1. The Berk 3

Chapter 2. Who Do You Want To Be? 10

Chapter 3. The Trigger Moment 30

Chapter 4. Into Africa 45

Chapter 5. Camp Life & Street Death 54

Chapter 6. Kibera, Koitalel, and Crocodiles 63

Chapter 7. Shoes To Africa, An Aéroport Experience, And A Swedish Angel 78

Chapter 8. Wordsmith, Windrunning, And A Way Forward 93

Chapter 9. Cracking The Cranium, And The Message Of The Millennium 99

Chapter 10. NYC. Veni, Vidi, Velcro; I Came, I Saw, I Stuck Around 127

Chapter 11. A Smelly Shoes Charity 142

Chapter 12. Women Run Iten, And The Manhattan Marathon 151

Chapter 13. The Kenyan Clashes 167

Chapter 14. Love. Peace. Unity. 191

Chapter 15. East & Central Africa's 1st Public Children's Hospital? 203

Chapter 16. Kibera Revisited With 5,800 Friends ... 221

Chapter 17. The Benefits Of Begging In Manhattan 225

Chapter 18. Now A School? 233
Chapter 19. From The Sea To The Stars......................... 242
Chapter 20. Stoning In Turkana....................................... 285
Chapter 21. Problems, Problems, And Solutions............ 295
Chapter 22. With A Little Help From A JCB Digger 303
Chapter 23. Love Is. A Nandi Elder. And Poison............ 306
Chapter 24. Flat Out On Fifth.. 316
Chapter 25. No Finishing Line... 332
Epilogue. Ever Onward... 336
An Inventory Of Acknowledgements 343
About The Author... 346
Quotes 348

www.runningwithdestiny.com

PROLOGUE

At the age of fourteen, one breezy day, I free soloed alongside my brother Liam on the craggy, vertical incline of Stanage Edge—a rock climber's paradise in the aptly named Peak District of England. Free soloing first allows you to utilize equipment to attempt a preferred route before later scaling without ropes. But possessing no harnesses, hooks, or helmets, we simply climbed—was it possible? We would find out.

Stuck halfway up the short rock face, I froze, unable to proceed, up or down. The people on the rough below, like toy figurines, were no help since I was too high. Balancing above and conducting the ascent, Liam yelled I must reach up to a finger ledge beneath his foot,
"Stretch, Toby!" I tried—but my short arms failed. For a dreadful chunk of time, lasting forever, I could not budge. Five minutes, ten minutes? With a trembling body, I desperately clung to what I recognized was my life.
Pinky-blue feeble hands hugged the hard gritstone, and those nimble quivering fingers would be the players to determine my fate. Cramps crept like a virus into every toe, and blood rushed from a face that would promptly start blubbering.
Exposed, figuratively and emotionally, I recognized my limited options. For what absurd reason was I here? As a challenge, but against what? A lifeless and cold rock?

My mind began wandering. How would the falling feel? Would I gain speed, blackout before, or upon impact? The stone bed below promised nothing but a painful conclusion to the story.

Liam repeatedly screamed encouragement,
"You can do it. You can do it." How I did so, not being as strong or sinuous as him, I do not understand. But completing the climb offered no sense of achievement or joy. It was during this time in

my life I decided I wanted to live for a worthwhile purpose, not for a personal experience.

If you run with your dreams, you can fly with your mind.

Chapter 1. 1995

THE BERK

The non-risk taker does not grow. You just get older. – Joan Root

'What on earth am I doing?' I should not have been asking this question when boarding a plane to Nairobi on the 11th of November 1995. Ten days earlier, I knew all the answers. Leaving Sweden's frosty winter for Africa's embracing sunshine suggested commonsense, but the emerging detail that no person or place expected my arrival remained a slight concern. Nevertheless, in my mid-twenties, I was at the ideal age for an alluring adventure. I did not know much about East Africa, but who the heck did? What I understood came from digesting the mainstream news. The region hit the headlines for diseases, droughts, despair, and other depressing issues.

Well, as a sportsperson, I would not have to face such realities. Instead, I daydreamed about the thrilling escapades ahead—training with the world's best athletes in Kenya. Traveling to Africa had been a brash decision and certainly not my idea. One person was to blame for both proposing and then presenting a compelling case to cancel—a wiry eccentric russet-haired Irishman, Noel Berkeley.

The Berk, as he proudly dubbed himself, and I met last year on the 4th of July 1994, in the Swedish city of Gävle, competing in a 5000-meter (3.1 miles) race on the Grand Prix circuit. Nerves jangled, the pungent smell of liniment tinged the warm air, and a gaggle of twenty athletes from close to as many countries anticipated a fiery competition. Toeing the line, and seconds before the gun, the starter scuttled down the list of entrants. Each athlete flailed an arm to acknowledge his presence for a swift roll call. The elderly Swedish gent donning a feathered fedora and an olive corduroy jacket faltered over the pronunciation of The Berk's surname, "Burrr-Koh-Lay," he mumbled.

The Berk had, to my astonishment, violated protocol by stepping forward—taking the Swede aside—and began delivering a brief lesson on the strokes of Irish intonation. "Ah, you'll not be butchering my name like dat my fyn fella."

Who pulls a stunt like that? What a goofball! I decided to introduce myself to the fellow *after* the race.

That was precisely how our firm friendship, which stands to this day, began.

A year later, phoning from Dublin, he casually declared he would like to marry a Swedish woman—could I procure the bride? He planned to lodge with my girlfriend and me at our apartment in Bromma, Stockholm, for two weeks and fancied the idea of landing a Scandinavian beauty.

"I'll come to train and kill two birds with one stone." His humor was unrivaled.

The Berk turned out to be a marvelous houseguest. Few of my friends like commencing the day by baking fresh scones. Then, following breakfast, without fail, we ran together. I worked hard at athletics, not Noel. At the session, say 20 x 400 meters (437 yards) of sprints, after a measly two or three efforts, he would pipe up, "Aye, tat'll be enough for the day." But not possessing a bantamweight frame born for distance running as this Olympic leprechaun, I would force Noel to complete the workout. Albeit as he whined and grumbled as if he were a red pig about to be shunted into the slaughterhouse. Hence, before The Berk flew home without a wife, he had deduced although I flopped as a fixer, I might retain another usable talent.

Noel declared, at the season's close, we must travel to Kenya for a stint of warm-weather training to avoid the ice and the chills of Northern Europe. Like the Americans in the game of hoops or the Brazilians belting the leather ball, the Kenyans reigned supreme in long-distance running. Noel suggested traveling to Africa to discover the reasons why.

Too late, I had already booked a month by the Sandia Mountains in New Mexico. Electricity was a commodity I enjoyed, and clean water? Count me in. Who wished to holiday in a country where the average citizen earned a dollar a day, and people died of dysentery? But Noel was not a man who took no for an answer, "I'm well-known in the running community. Everyone knows T' Berk. Leave your wallet at home because you will be well looked after. Those famous runners? I know them all."

According to Noel, I would have a blast as his training partner. Then, incidentally, he announced our destination—Eldoret. What a bizarre coincidence that innocent word jolted a childhood memory. Mike and Liz, the agemates of my parents, when returning from a mission trip to Kenya, had once presented me with a green satchel. Narrating their adventures, they referred to a town called Eldoret. You may wonder how I might recollect such an obscured memory. Initially, I scowled at this recycled gift. Which third-born likes hand-me-downs? And cotton satchels are for little girls—eight-year-old boys desire brand-name sports bags. Maybe if Mike observed my misery, he might offer a better gift, like a toy pistol? But seeing my crestfallen face Mike attempted to enhance the bag's value by mentioning poultry,

"Can you imagine someone transported a hen in this bag?"

My face dropped further, imagining the yellow stains coating the lining. Ungrateful, spoilt, and a brat summed up my behavior, but as a devout crusader, Mike persevered.

He mentioned the names of random local towns, and I heard the word Eldoret. What? The ears pricked up—did he say El-door-Et? Eldoret sounded distinctly like Eldorado, a location featuring extensively in my cowboy comics. Did I know two visitors to the African Eldorado? How cool, Kit Carson, frontiersmen, and cowboys were my heroes.

Dashing to a pile of Encyclopedias and travel books, I scoured the pages searching for these African cowhands. But I discovered Kenyan cowpunchers garbed themselves in scarlet robes instead of leather chaps, and they replaced a silver-handled Colt 45 with long spears, short swords, and bore decorative shields. Those striking pictures became my wardrobe into Africa. Like Alice in Wonderland, I stepped out of my hometown and forgot I favored Kit Carson. I pondered, if I were extremely pleasant, would Mike return and carry the full weaponry upon his next vacation? Arise, Chief Toby of the Maasai, from Eldoret.

Right away, I obsessed about the school's African project, which I had all but ignored. Each year Clifford Infants adopted one cause to sponsor, and an announcement at our morning assembly stated that every child must sign up to help. Seats became rearranged in our classroom, the blinders yanked down, and we huddled in the darkness, watching a short film to reveal the issue the faculty had voted to support. The title began displaying African children, poorly clothed with potbellies, dashing around a sandy field. Everyone giggled when the half-naked mothers chased after those kids. The camera panned to a timber shack, where a gathering of adults reeled off the hymn that we routinely bellowed out at school. The film approached its climax when a pink-faced man, wearing a frock, distributed sacks of grains to the smiling moms.

Our teacher, teary-eyed and clearing her throat, informed us it was a Christian duty to support these children. Why did she weep, as nothing frightful happened in the film, right? Did I overlook something? Composing herself, she explained those African kids suffered from chronic malnutrition, a disease of not devouring enough food. This fact looked highly doubtful as the kids' bellies bulged bigger than mine. She declared our school pledged to purchase a tractor to enable a scheme to cultivate vegetables. Again puzzling—every kid I knew despised eating greens! Those Africans should celebrate a vegetable shortage.

With the hot topic being how to help people, I must raise a hand and demand a television. Yes, I remained the one child in the world—well, at least in our school—whose parents did not own a television. I possessed proof of neglect. My best friend Kamu recently emigrated from India and had described vast poverty, but inside his house, I spied two television sets. Forcing the issue was useless, "Zombies," my mother cried. "People who gawp at tellies turn into zombies!" But since the rest of the world possessed televisions, this failed to be a credible argument. I was a charity case myself.

The school project requested kids to contribute non-perishable foods for a raffle. What an effortless task. Utilizing my African bag and accepting the role of the Chief of the Maasai provider to the poor, I snuck into the family pantry. Upon the principal mission, I stole copious tins of Campbell's Mushroom Soup, deliberately selecting the flavor my mother adored and that I despised. Stumbling on a solution to enhance the diet was an unexpected boon.

In the ensuing week, I made a second and third run. To surpass all, I won a blue ribbon for being the school's top tin donor.

So, for this particular reason, the town's name with its happy-bag memories sealed the deal. A peculiar coincidence—that is all. My anthroposophical-inclined parents would have considered the fluke predestination, but, as I always countered, then provide the proof.

Nonetheless, bags or not, Kenya did boast an irresistible romantic charm, and as my sponsors would cover the flights, I decided to join The Berk in November. I committed to an outlandish six-week training camp in the heart of exotic Africa to visit this town bearing a cowboy name. Nairobi Airport in November would be our rendezvous, and the plan was to venture to Eldoret for a holiday of a lifetime. Not viewing majestic lions and fleet-footed gazelles, like sensible tourists, but instead hanging on to the coattails of the mythical dark-skinned masters of the distance running world. Teammates at my club thought the idea hilarious. Nobody went to train with the Kenyans. Yes, go and observe the champions, but crossing swords in workouts alongside these fierce warriors? Are you nuts? Aid workers or entrepreneurial explorers turned to Africa—not athletes. No one on the team had ever been to Africa, let alone considered the continent a destination for active sports. The consensus was I would back out and never travel. Therefore, my determination doubled; I must enjoy a successful trip and return as a faster athlete. There is nothing sweeter than proving doubters wrong. From this moment, I made it a priority to wave at any Kenyan I encountered on the racing circuit perchance we should meet in the town of Eldoret.

Then one evening in November, ten short days before our flight, the phone rang—it was The Berk. For once, he dragged his feet, beating around the bush, and rambled rather than communicating on an expensive long-distance call. "What's up, Noel?" Surely this conversation could wait. "Are there any pending tasks?" I queried. He shifted gears, "Not really, but just to let you know, I will not be traveling to Kenya. Have a pleasant trip. Bye." The receiver went dead. What? My heart skipped three beats, realizing I would be flying to the vast continent of Africa all alone. I did not possess a single address, phone number, or one solitary friend to connect with, and the shock hit hard. How could I meet those famous runners?

Noel canceled with valid reasons, and a year later, I overheard his father fell ill. But too proud to plead for his help and miffed at being dumped, I sought to recall our various conversations. Forgetting the complicated names of the Kenyan athletes that all appeared to start with the letter K or Kip kippers, he had harped on about an Irish priest, Brother Colm O'Something, who taught in a secondary school. Noel spoke of Colm as if he represented a revered God, of course, a God ranking one notch below himself. Why a priest held a kinship with Kenyan running, I did not know. And whether Colm was receptive to welcoming me, who was neither a brother, a teacher, coach, nor Irish, lurked as another question.

Buckling up in the cheap seats of the Air France plane, shielding my eyes from the aerosolized insecticide a flight attendant sprayed abundantly along the aisles, my sole intention was that this journey should help me to become a champion runner. I would prove the cynics wrong. Back out, me? Yet, waiting for the takeoff, I began regretting my perpetual lack of preparation. I am a do-er—I do not plan. Impulsive is the term, but a girlfriend tagged it differently, lazy. But why didn't I try to contact Brother Colm or put arrogance aside and question Noel for at least a couple of his Kenyan contacts? What exactly am I letting myself in for?

Noel 'The Berk' Berkeley (right) relaxes at a track meet with the Ethiopian Olympian, Fita Bayissa, and me.

CHAPTER 2. 1970s-80s

WHO DO YOU WANT TO BE?

Choices are the hinges of destiny. – Edwin Markham

Disorganized development in the 1970s-80s described my upbringing. The odyssey of this adventure begins with the act of grinding out a Marlboro cigarette and embarking upon a run at the age of twenty-one. However, before the smoking flash in the next chapter, I want to crank back the clock and explain how and why the sport of running emerged as the instrumental driver of everything—good, bad, and ugly—that happened throughout my story.

Growing up in the North of England, in a city plagued by unemployment, crumbling coal, and sinking steel industries, I had a far from mundane childhood. We—a family of six and two dandy cats—lived in a five-bedroomed Victorian house, built in 1901, in a tree-lined suburb of Sheffield. The entrance of our home displayed an intricately decorated green stained-glass door sheltering under an arched stone porch extending a visitor a spiritual welcome. Our household lived modestly, exhibiting no signs of wealth or extravagance, but I never once felt poor. Purchasing secondhand clothes, rarely visiting restaurants, or partaking in any frivolous activities, my parents spindled money well. Christians by birth and baptism, the tenets of religion structured my youth, though neither I nor any family member attended church services save for weddings or funerals.

Indoors, the spacious building imbued the ambiance of a community center more than a home. My mother, who blankly refused to bolt our front door, battered bent nails into stone, to hammer in a welcome sign, *'Come for a week come for a day, come for a visit and do not go away.'* And sadly, people took this invitation verbatim. On a rare occasion, if guests were few, my mother would recruit like the navy. God help the salesperson or evangelist who ventured to knock at our door—they would never escape. And the beggar pleading for pennies patrolling the high street? She would bundle her conscripts in a car seat and whisk the prisoners' home for afternoon tea discussions.

Our doors only closed for school or national holidays when we transformed into intrepid tourists. Initially, scouting every inch of the British Isles and the year before I entered the teens, in the 1980s, braving overseas excursions. But unlike conventional families who utilized hotels and airplanes, our household traveled and lived inside a cramped VW van. With a crafty intent, my mom hand-painted the vehicle in camouflage—soil-colored wheels, green paneled skirting, and a blue top so we could blend in with nature.

Steering clear of nasty campsite fees, surviving like gypsies, we lurked in the woods neighboring the cities hallmarked for visits during the daytime. It was not uncommon for us to be woken by shotgun-wielding landowners rapping on the windscreen, shooing us from the forests. My parents joked not to worry because, as travelers, we would never be repeating offenders. One night, lost in traffic and low on petrol, we pulled over on a random street in Paris, unable to locate a suitable hideaway. The following morning steps away from the van, I discovered the Moulin Rouge! My French teacher would marvel at this sighting.

What I adored most about traveling was every day brought surprises and diverse situations, as if I continually unwrapped unexpected new gifts.

Europe was a hoot—foods, linguistics, sights, people—even

boring episodes exploded into thrilling adventures. My parents were culture vultures; every object of beauty in the urban centers or the countryside should be gazed upon and photographed—the older, the better. We zigzagged with the passion of a slalom skier; no monument or spectacle escaped our eyes. When you travel by road, you ferret for any excuse to stop and stretch your legs, and even viewing an old stone monument would become an occasion.

Much to my delight, a couple of times, I discovered town centers adorned with ornate fountains where affluent locals flung unwanted coins into the waters. Pretending to wash my hands, which always caused my mother to beam, I could artfully scoop out extra pocket money.

The destinations and durations of these delightful holidays would never relate to schedules or school calendars. No, the funds that remained and the morning whims of the family elders guided our steps. These were the days before the euro, and my dad never left a country without exhausting every shilling of the local currency. We truly embraced the phrase living in the moment, and each holiday created a storybook of exhilaration before resuming a mirrored life back home.

I should have begun this chapter by introducing my parents. Mr. Tanser, donning a Santa Claus-styled beard, stood as thin as a toothbrush at six-foot-tall (1.82 m). His figure contradicted the name my mother christened him. "Go and ask your Fat Dad," she would say, or "Where's your Fat Dad?" The title sounded so nonsensical that today I wonder, was there an actual story behind this nickname? He was a peace-loving hippy father, and only once did I see him fly off the handle. I am ashamed to say that incident occurred when I was nabbed stealing a toy smurf from a store—my morality and sense of value sorely lacked during my childhood.

Although my father was a popular man, few kids enjoy hearing how lucky they are to have "a cool" papa. Compliments like that were misguided. Nice, he was, but neither he nor my mother was chill. Wearing paisley print clothes suited to the swinging sixties, strapped in a pair of brown buckled open-toe sandals, his dress code hardly matched the typical attire of a sensible parent.

For a vocation, he worked as the Head of the Music Department at a secondary school. Music directed his life—he ate musical notes for breakfast then hummed, sang, or whistled throughout each day. Following school hours, he tutored privately on a variety of instruments. All of which lived inside our house, including a piped church organ rescued from a street flea market and an Indian sitar formerly belonging to Ravi Shankar. A tuba, double bass, bagpipes—you name it, he owned it.

My mother, who dressed likewise in discarded fashions, also held teaching qualifications. She acted more flamboyantly than my father and uttered three words for each one of his. Brown-haired, standing at 5' 8" (172 cm) and of slender build, today I still cringe remembering how, throughout the summer months, she would jaunt barefooted to the local shops. Such behavior caused me acute embarrassment and grievous shame. Her time-consuming passion was uplifting a theater and philosophy center where, like my father, she was a founding trustee.

Tintagel House and the Merlin Theater, named after the legendary Cornish saga, sat on an opulent green twenty-six acres of land, half a mile from our home. Constructed in 1850, the house stood as an imposing mansion entombed in creeping ivy, full of unique rooms and cellars stuffed with intriguing artifacts. Was I mislaid at birth, placed in the wrong cot at the hospital, and here remained my proper home? At this center, I discovered a true identity—a lost prince living in a stately castle.

The mansion was amusement enough, yet a 300-seat theater, constructed in 1969, had been added for an exciting playhouse. Even the garden outbuildings contained fascinating objects, oily engines, and mechanical toys. The complex was Chris Boulton's brainchild after he had received a generous inheritance from two American aunts. Chris's parents, Guy & Dotty, were fascinating folks who had socialized in the same circles as Winston Churchill's family and had the finery and ornaments to prove it.

My memories of Chris are transient as he died when I hit six years, but I remember him dressing in a tailored dark suit, which made him stand out at the theater. He sported a bob of wavy mousey hair and wore horn-rimmed round spectacles. Diminutive in size, having suffered from contracting polio as a three-year-old, I immediately found him relatable. I informed my parents, "He is nice. He is little, like me." Those words tickled Chris pink.

Devoting hours to advancing the center from its infancy, my mother willingly worked without any financial reward. Whether it meant producing plays, acting, set design, or painting—even buying then sewing costumes from jumble sales—she commanded the brigade. Organizing festivals, starting craft fairs, initiating clubs—she undertook every job. Like any true captain, she carried us along for the ride. Be it selling cakes at the craft fairs, strumming Irish jigs and Scottish reels on my banjo at the festivals, or painting canvases for the stage scenery, I insisted on partaking in all activities. When my dad's lessons concluded in the evening, he too headed over to compose and produce music for the productions or sit in upon Monday to Friday meetings at Tintagel House.

My mother, disliking the local kindergarten but wishing to set about the work, would offload me at Tintagel under the watchful eye of Chris's wife May. Producing no offspring of her own, May teased she must adopt me as her grandchild. Plied with plates of treacle flapjack and as much sweetened orange juice as I could swallow in her kitchens, this made for an angelic arrangement. My only job was stoking the fire and fetching buckets of coal from the cellars. "Do not let the flames die out lovey," May would call as if the task were of world importance. And by accepting this chore, I was certain I contributed as a vital cog in the works.

Down in the cellars, I discovered suitcases of musty sepia photographs from fifty years ago. I would delve through boxes upon boxes gazing at the wondrous scenes. My favorite pictures were from the roaring twenties when Guy & Dotty hobnobbed alongside high society and drove a Bugatti around Saint-Tropez—their faraway lifestyle fascinated me like a toddler in a toyshop. On the same floor of the kitchens, an oak-paneled library storing hordes of books and more photos from the four corners of the world, a music room containing original scores written in the 1920s & 30s, would provide me with more chapters of entertainment. As a kid, I lived every day inside worlds of reality and imagination. It is true to say my childhood wove into the fabric of this dynamic center.

   My parents, working and attending endless meetings, allotted little time for me. Knowing I played safe somewhere inside the compound, I was allowed to grow like a wild weed. Tintagel House provided an indoor corridor leading into the theater, and before long, my adventures began inside the playhouse. The costume and props rooms became favorite hangouts, but every space retained intriguing elements. Hidden tunnels smelling of dust, fly galleries cobwebbed in ropes like the deck of a pirate ship, and the lighting control room, with hundreds of knobs and levers, all provided unique adventures. A canteen for the performance intermissions permitted me to sneak out snacks whenever my appetite required sustenance.
   It was at the theater where I suffered my first severe accident, rolling my tricycle down the auditorium steps as a four-year-old. I still bear a scar from that incident to this day.

   Invariably, I became entangled in amateur dramatics. With a mother directing senior and junior productions, I perpetually landed the best kid's roles, male or female, skinny or stout. Overacting every performance, I lapped up any cheer I could wring from the audience. I invented schemes to embellish the characters outside of the script to garner extra applause. Seldom at the theater do you play yourself, and as a child, there is a blurry line to switching back to behave in reality. And whose reality? There is no better way to learn about yourself than by playing another person. The stage invites you to select a character, happy or sad, ambitious or villainous, then romance your mind, wading deep into your chosen mood. Like a shot of steroids to a child's imagination, the theater sparkled as the magical element of my youthful education.

Visitors hosted at the philosophy center were as illustrious as Major Ramachandra, who had served as a batman to Gandhi. People lauded his theorizing, but I marveled how he never stopped scoffing umeboshi plums, which he carried in a transparent glass jar. Dressed in flowing white robes bearing a faint trace of incense, escorting me upon hikes, he looked significantly out of place on the drab gray streets of Sheffield. Grasping a knotted staff in his right hand, which he claimed ordered his direction, he brought Tolkien's Gandalf to life.

The Major's participation in the Salt March meant little to me as a child, but every one of his tales involved a stirring adventure. Ramachandra traveled alongside thirty followers and a bearded magician who surprised us all by sucking up a brimming glass of water through his nostrils and draining the cup. The wizard could even place his calloused feet on glowing fiery coals without flinching.

To an impressionable boy, Ramachandra and his devotees glittered as inspirational wonders. A Major sounded distinguished as if people should announce his title like a boast—none of my friends knew such a high-ranking commander. Ramachandra, and others, made an exotic life so touchable—if he traveled the world enjoying such adventure, so should I. He left a penetrating impression, challenging me to broaden my horizons with two words. If I talked about any aspirations, he would reply,

"Why not?" It played as his mantra—why not indeed? If ever stuck in the pendulum of choice, Ramachandra, like a turbaned genie, appears, "Why not?" he says…so much better than those wretched 'What ifs.'

Countless adults claim their school years were their finest but not me. Schooling, as a teenager, was boring. Actions happened daily at the theater, and each week, new visitors dropped by or entire troupes arrived to hire out the premises—what institute could top that for an education? School life, to me, seemed slow and stale. Overcrowded classrooms, uninspiring teachers, and a program to mix kids from diverse citywide neighborhoods—dividing friendships—produced a recipe for disaster in the underfunded high school I attended. Furthermore, junior tutors, imagining they landed a lifelong career, became threatened by unemployment following government budget cuts. Strikes by the National Union of Teachers happened frequently. Betrayal and bitter resentment resonated as employment opportunities began to shrink and livelihoods vanished.

The elder scholars shouldered their own issues as corporal punishment ended—the classroom-control method of walloping kids with a willow cane became outlawed. Yet the seniors at least still clung to the relief of the school-university-one job per lifetime plan, providing grinding pressure for us to cement firm choices to transfer a student to a happy retirement. A career? I did not have a clue about the ensuing week as my dreams changed like a weathervane. But no, I must specialize and select subjects to aim towards a specific university degree; this provided the route to secure a stable job. When I retaliated, explaining I must first learn how to best embrace life, seek out simple truths and structures before homing in on any career choice, the instructor groaned, "Unemployment levels in Sheffield slump at one in ten. Unless you pick a profession, you are doomed. What about the army?" His conclusion was, 'Toby lacks commitment and disappoints.'

Labeled as a lost cause, skipping school became the trick. Forging absence slips was effortless. When the headteacher insisted on scheduling a parental phone call, I discovered disconnecting a blue wire inside the house telephone prevented the ringer from sounding. Before long, I realized my parents did not care whether I attended school or not. My final school report recorded the absent days outnumbered the present. Years later, I inquired why, as a child, I enjoyed such freedom. My mother replied, "So you could become your own person." She recognized, if allowed to wander, I might discover true purpose. "Your father and I tried raising you by the principles expressed by Khalil Gibran – *'Your children are not your children. They are the sons and daughters of life's longing for itself.'*"

I disliked the establishment, not the learning. English Literature, Classical Studies, and History remained my preferred subjects, but if I identified one area where I excelled, it would be Physical Education. All sports were entertaining, but soccer played out as a favorite. How I loved dribbling and punting the ball against our garden fence, striking in the last-minute clincher saving Argentina from defeat in the World Cup finals. Why the white and blues? Because the local club had acquired a South American star, Alejandro Sabella. It was something of an abnormality back then for a second division team to snag a foreign hero. The club had signed an unknown Argentine, a seventeen-year-old called Diego Maradona, but that deal fell through after the kid's manager demanded additional cash. Accordingly, Sabella should be the city's savior—the radio commentator pummeled his name passionately at every opportunity, "Saaaaabeeellllaaaaa!"

Like most kids in sizeable families, I struggled to uncover an identity. Since no one in our house pursued any sport, I anticipated this as an arena where I might shine. With all the musical instruments scattered around our home, I had initially tried proving my worth through music. Yet I possessed the patience of a flea—I hungered and expected to become a virtuoso in less than a month. Therefore, at the age of twelve, it was no wonder I embraced the sport of running when I achieved moderate overnight success.

When enrolling in high school, I enlisted on the soccer squad, but a friend failed to make the cut. With his name omitted from the gym noticeboard, he implored me to join him on the cross-country team. No way, I had just scored a try-out for the Junior Blades, Sheffield United's development squad for young boys. To run ranked as a monstrous demotion from being a footie star, yet he reasoned since the two sports took place on alternating weekends, what did I have to lose? Initially, I flatly refused, but he pestered so persistently I thought, why not try one event?

The sport was not an easy sell. Point blank, running was far less prevalent than it is today—if you observed someone sprinting along the streets in the 1980s, it would not be for sports. The consensus suggested, running ruined your joints, and the pounding was unhealthy for growing bones. Runners seldom looked happy, not like footballers. Runners were misfits with drooling mouths and lanky bodies—I was already too skinny. No schoolboy desired to be thin. I mean, I enjoyed running hither and thither on a soccer field, or to get from A to B, but as a primary sport? No way.

Above all, my parents loathed inactivity. Our family axiom promoted volunteering, standing up, saying yes—anything—you never know what beginnings will lead to but, expressing a no is a non-starter. Full of confidence, I would attempt any task. If a person had done it, why not me. Therefore, no surprise, I conceded to his pleas and entered the city schools' colt's cross-country event.

Being young in my school year, I must battle against kids nearly two years older; therefore, I entertained modest expectations. Yet standing among hundreds of other misfits, who presumably had failed at soccer, I was quietly confident I would deliver a decent performance. My goal? Prove I could run faster than my friend, then shimmy back to the soccer squad.

My memories are brief of this first race. A gun fired, elbows flew out, legs tripped, and a frantic scramble began for a three lung-busting miles (4.8 km) dash over the parkland. Panting, plastered in mud, sweating, and blurry-eyed, the event proved to be exhausting—that is how much I remember. Past the finishing post, I made a beeline straight to our school sports instructor, Hedley Matthew. He was standing, dressed in a red waterproof tracksuit under a golf umbrella, and waited alongside a huddle of other clipboard holding teachers. His facial features expressed that I had performed above his expectations; I glowed with a sense of achievement.

I had scored in the top twenty overall, third for my year—the best by an athlete from our school. During the van ride home Mr. Matthew, who led all the school sports, encouraged us to work together, to train throughout the week, and he sowed a seed that suggested I could distinguish myself as a runner, "If you put in the work, I know you will see outstanding results." Outstanding? I was sold!

Like many kids, the sport of running developed naturally, grafted into my DNA. To my advantage, I did not carry an ounce of fat on the bones. Not by choice, but I grew as a vegetarian, and most of our food sprouted as locally farmed organic produce. Even our medicines were homeopathic and plant-based, as the family commanders believed chemicals acted as poisons and activity offered a cure for most ailments.

My earliest childhood memory replays me galloping around our garden in circles leaping over a rope. Photographs prove I adored the activity. Everywhere I went, somehow running became inserted. Although owning a car, trips within what my parents deemed a walking distance had to be on foot—that stood as a family rule. And bear in mind my mother possessed the legs of a seasoned antelope. But impatient, antsy, and eager to move on, running made logical sense. Like on Sunday hikes, if I ran, I could raid the picnic basket first and seize the choicest foods before others arrived. However, it was the mental aspect of running that lit a fire. I found my thoughts flowed faster, and I daydreamed, sang, and felt inspired as I ran. Being a sore loser, I also appreciated the accountability of running; unlike soccer, all the results, good or bad, came down to one person. Furthermore, running was an activity that fought against the task of growing up; to play in school hours and gain recognition for the achievements was an indescribable boon.

Invigorated by Mr. Matthew, I began jogging at the lunch hours and joined the Hallamshire Harriers. The Harriers were a city-based running club steeped in history—the first man to break the four-minute barrier for the 1500-meter event in 1908 had been a member.

The Moscow Olympics took place that year, and Jón Didriksson, who dated my second cousin, qualified for the 1500-meters. As a family, we trooped over to spectate at my grandparents' house, but when Jón faltered in the heats, that concluded the viewing. "Why watch others play games? You do not even recognize the people." My parents were not sports fans, and dad's words—albeit tongue in cheek—sounded reasonable.

However, at Hallamshire, I discovered one member plucked the gold medal in Jón's event. When he visited the clubhouse, bedlam erupted, and I barely got a chance to shake his hand. But then, running through Bingham Park, my friend and I—out exercising—spotted the country's idol in beautiful isolation. Instead of entering the adjacent Endcliffe Park, he stopped by a blue car, awarding us a chance to chase him down. By good luck, as he fumbled with his keys, we caught the champion. Seb Coe was a gentleman, pausing to allow two kids to feel on top of the world.

The following day, guessing he must grind through plenty of socks, we purchased a double pack—dropping the gift off at his house, which stood close to the hospital where I was born. Seb was not home, but his father, Peter, answered the door and presented us with signed postcards of Seb winning a race.

That night, at mealtime, I blurted out the scintillating announcement—I had met an Olympic champion. Seb transcended athletics, and the whole nation adored the star. My mother smiled, and after cleaning her lips with a handkerchief, she revealed the athlete had attended classes at Abbeydale Grange School, where my father had taught. My bubble burst. I quit talking sports—I wanted athletics as a private sanctuary where I could shine alone.

Success came quickly, and within a year, I ran for the county, competing at the English Schools Championships. I relished the recognition, and at school assemblies, welcomed the weekly shout-outs for my achievements. I took on the responsibility of team captain, and after recruiting other kids, we earned third place in the cross-country league. To sweeten the deal, I closed the series with an unexpected individual bronze.

For the following track season, we improved and claimed the championships. Our team outperformed themselves, and there is an immense joy I found when the exhausting physical efforts you endure pay off. Recruiting the players for each discipline and urging them to practice throughout the preseason had paid dividends. Hoisting the trophy, half my size, aloft in the stadium would be a buzz. Then, shortly before the awards, Mr. Matthew pulled me aside, "Toby, may I ask a favor—can James go up on the podium with you? He has been having a rough time, and his mother is here. She will be chuffed." That showed his character—constantly encouraging and uplifting others—an unselfish man who gave up every single weekend to support us kids. It was the smallest ask, and I should not say no. But I blush to say I did say a no figuratively.

Mr. Matthew was, by far, my favorite teacher because of his enthusiasm, positivity, and larger-than-life presence. Walking out of his office, you would always feel the world stood there for you to conquer. What other teachers at our school taught morning and afternoon and gave up their lunch breaks and weekends? None. What other teachers demanded we produce our best efforts? None. Caught on the spot, I could not process the idea that he cared for everyone, not just me. On the verge of tears, I pretended to be agreeable to his noble idea. Instead, I scurried out of the stadium to the bus stop before the prize ceremony began. At this immature age, I could not handle the disappointment. Not recognizing what an incredible opportunity I threw away, I quit running. However, Mr. Matthew's influence would guide me for years to come.

Mr. Matthew did perform magic; Nick, his son, became Britain's greatest squash player.

Quite soon, I completely forgot about running when, blaring like a trumpet rippling across the battlefield, I discovered, heard, and saw my new distraction. One man who lodged at Tintagel House would roar through town on a vintage Matchless 500cc single-cylinder motorcycle. Even as the bike propped on a kickstand, the machine bore wings. An intricate joker mural adorned the pearl-shaped petrol tank, and the booming thumper engine, buffed and chromed, sparkled in the sunlight. The owner, Chris Rooke, clad in scuffed blue jeans and a Marlon Brando leather jacket, definitely shone as the ladies' pick—naturally, I should traipse in his footsteps. At the age of thirteen, instead of aiming for the attire, I plunged for the wheels.

Motorcycling, I found, is the mechanical form of running fast; twisting the throttle, I enjoyed the same surge of adrenaline, the rush of excitement when completing my sprints. Bolstered by a recent windfall, I concluded I, too, should own a bike. Therefore, my brother Liam and I took an afternoon to peruse the secondhand aisles of the dealerships searching for a cheap bargain. After comparing models, we pushed home a vintage 1962 black and chrome Honda CD 125 Benly.

Returning home, my parents almost suffered heart attacks and demanded I return the wheels prior to striking a compromise. Being too young to ride legally, I must stay inside the acreage of the theater complex. However, before long, the open roads proved too great a temptation to resist. More than a noisy iron motor gliding on sleek spoked wheels, that machine enabled a young dreamer to be a captain of his destiny and venture wherever he desired.

Today, I blush to admit the purchase money came from improprieties. Around my tenth year, I started collecting empty bottles. When children hunted in the theater's rambling gardens for a single deposit bottle to return, I slinked to the cellars storing crates of already returned glass. I thought this idea was genius until caught in the act. The theft had become necessary to purchase chocolate bars. My parents hotly refused to buy candies, arguing our pantry stored an ample supply of choice foods. The 1960s hippies, snacking on licorice roots and carrot sticks, were out of touch with a modern kid's needs. Needless to say, I must fend for myself. When an adult clamped a padlock on the cellar door, I developed an alternative method of larceny.

An old confectionery vending machine stood outside the local corner shop. If I kept twisting the device lever, using acrobat skills, the chocolate bars continued falling. One day, arched backward in a crab, I was nabbed. Mr. Bromley, the proprietor, reset the handle, and after one turn, the mechanism locked.

But now I discovered I could superglue a cotton thread to a

coin, and the weight triggered a lever to release a bar. Then, yanking up the cord allowed another bar to drop. Predictably, Mr. Bromley soon ceased stocking his vending machine. I must invent fresh solutions. Quite soon, the answer arrived wrapped as a business proposition, 'Would you like to earn money?'

A new shop opened in the neighborhood, and, naturally, I poked my head through the door. The center offered home brewing kits, and the owner wondered, could I collect empty wine bottles for his customers? Beautiful, he hit on my solitary work experience. Under the night's shadows, I skulked to the supermarket and purloined two trolleys. After tethering the wagons, I inserted cardboard boxes into the undercarriage. Wearing a cumbersome rucksack, I aimed for a populated district of hotels and restaurants yet enjoyed no luck. All the establishments donated their drained bottles to the St. John's Ambulance Brigade, who earned cash by recycling the glass.

Unperturbed, I switched directions. Behind the offices of St. John's, I discovered a goldmine. The next morning, under a mountain of bottles, the shopkeeper's eyes bulged,

"I am sorry. Twenty or thirty maybe, but not hundreds."
Gutted, after the moonlighting, my blood tingled at the thought of returning the pilfered product.

"What about giving me store credits?" I bartered. And that is how I launched into my first business selling homemade wine to underage kids. The sales enabled the purchase of the motorcycle.

The same income, supplemented with two paperboy delivery rounds, aided an escape out of England. Around the age of sixteen, I stopped attending school altogether and planned a holiday in Amsterdam. William Shakespeare quit at thirteen—I figured I had a head start. And ironically, it was studying Othello when the straw broke the camel's back. The teacher recommended purchasing a book with previous exam questions to revise for upcoming tests in a Creative English class.

"Where is the creative part? Locating the bookshop?" I chimed. A crack I found hilarious but had me tossed from the room.

"Go, leave if you suppose you are so intelligent," she sneered, "Discover your answers elsewhere but stop disrupting this class." She lit a lightbulb—why not travel to unearth myself?

Three summers back, on our annual European vacation, we spent a week in Amsterdam. What a fascinating city—exploring museums, I read starving artists had thrived in a romantic life of poverty before becoming rich and famous. Cogs cranked, plans formalized, and shortly, I hitchhiked to London with another school reject, Simon. Upon arrival, forging my father's signature, I collected an expedited passport. Then, after scouting the High Street shops, we snapped up $25 return tickets to board the economy-line ferry bus.

Holland represented a wake-up call—money was tight, almost invisible. School friends presumed I chased the marijuana scene. Yet, I assured them I had zero interest in recreational drugs. Sure, who had not sampled pot at a party, but my throat itched when I inhaled the drug. Besides, dope smokers were the most inactive people I knew. They lounged about gazing into thin air, giggling, and discussing nonsense. I surmised these folks were the last people I should hang around. My buzz? Nicotine—like all cool motorcyclists, the Marlboro Man and Chris, my vice involved sucking on cigarettes. No, I intended to be a Dutch master. After peering at Picasso's pencil outlines, I became confident of matching those abstract shapes he had somehow managed to peddle off to prosperous collectors.

The problem was, I could not afford the sketch pad. Impoverished and budgeting one sandwich per day, no hole on the belt strap prevented my trousers from falling as I downright starved in the Dutch capital. Renting flea-hopping bunks on a barge hostel moored off Prins Hendrikkgade, we presumed a rainstorm of employment ideas would miraculously shower down upon us. Despite acquiring fiscal numbers and signing on to the city's registrar, nobody even granted us an interview, let alone a job. I realized that opportunities were fewer for foreigners. Mustering up seven words in Dutch and possessing no unique skills, bar fire-eating, and unicycle-riding did not help matters.

Frustrated, Simon departed on the homebound bus, but fellow travelers took pity on me, revealing ways how I could scavenge coins. I began loitering at the Central Station, cornering tourists, and procuring a minuscule commission guiding backpackers to inexpensive hostels in the De Wallen (red-light district). Any client booking a night meant I ate for two days. Borrowing a damaged goods guitar from a fellow barge resident, I strummed Ziggy Stardust songs on the street. Once a Dutch shop owner stormed out as I crooned Life on Mars,

"Hoi, I have a request, I'll pay you five guilders to play Over the Hills and Far Away." I told him I did not know that tune. He shook his head,

"Nee, I am paying you to go and play where I can't hear you." Was I that bad?

To stave off dogged cravings, I tried chewing and swallowing the juices from the cheapest rolling tobacco till my gums bled as for the next few hours, stomach cramps would trample over any hunger pangs. Another ploy could be visiting various religious groups serving free food. What a deal, listen to a thousand chants of Hare Krishna Hare Rama, and then stuff my face as if the next destination would be the electric chair.

When friends or I overbooked our hostel, I slept in Vondel Park or might sprawl on the city benches beseeching passersby for unwanted food. If I could afford one bottle of Grolsch beer, it stood as a luxury, and I would lick the rim for hours to make a night last at the Bulldog or the Melkweg nightclub where I chilled alongside the dropouts and drifters. Lacking money, struggling with malnourishment, and unsure of a mattress for each night, Amsterdam was hardly a barrel of laughs. Today, reflecting, I understand I was learning the skills of begging, the prime requirement for a charity job.

When I did return to England, my parents had decided to relocate to Stroud—that fortress and security of home-living vanished. Choices: I must follow as a child to a town where I did not wish to go or climb on stilts to become an adult. The decision to end schooling birthed the start of living alone. Rather than travel south, I leeched government housing support and leased a sleazy bedsit on Broomgrove Road.

My new home was a dump, a typical bachelor pad. Things did not start well—in the first week, thieves broke in and stole my guitar, camera, cash, and other possessions. If I wanted to discover a feeling of being really alone, well, that would happen the moment I recognized the busted door lock. I felt small, fragile, and violated, but I guess starting at rock bottom, life could only improve. Broke and never willing to solicit my family for help, I wondered, had I made the correct choice?

The other tenants were as irresponsible as me. When the kitchen flooded, we arranged bricks on the floor as stepping-stones—the house perpetually reeked of greasy food and clogged plumbing. A university campus across the street became a tremendous resource, and each week the bedsit boys burglarized pots and pans. I prided myself the deed was not theft, as the following week, we returned the utensils and exchanged the dirties for a clean set. I never washed dishes and resorted to wrapping wooden cooking spoons in plastic bags rather than picking up the dish soap. Employment was casual—dispatch riding and delivering parcels on a motorbike, tree chopping, deejaying, or varied theater work. Once I enrolled in an archeological course until I discovered finders were not keepers. My confidence was, any job offered, I could undertake. Say yes and learn whilst receiving compensation. I skipped around collecting sufficient funds, intending to travel to Europe, either on a motorcycle or by hitch-hiking, to enjoy a life of pleasure and adventure.

Whether at midnight tangled in a howling gale or lost on the most desolate of roads, luck was with me when hitching. Rolling blonde hair beyond my shoulders helped, as, from a distance, people mistook me for a girl. Only once did I suffer a frightening experience sitting by a vodka-chugging grouchy truck driver. Bottles rolling back and forth like grenades under the brake pedal of a speeding eighteen-wheeler can be quite unnerving.

When hitching, I rarely waited longer than ten minutes for rides, and the ones I secured led to openings like a meal and a place to pitch the tent. On occasions, even a bed for the night was on offer. With friends scattered around Europe—like my sister Lisa in Switzerland—I meandered wherever the ride took me. Lisa also carried strains of runaway blood—she had skipped university, married a descendant of the original Lord Brocket (wedding at the Brocket chapel near Brocket Hall), and currently lived at a center helping adults with disabilities near Geneva.

Never in a hurry or mapping out a plan, I adored this nomadic lifestyle of roaming as an endless holidaymaker. Carting essential camping gear—a tent without a groundsheet—my parents had instructed me well. Meals could be as raw as cold baked beans scooped out of the tin or spaghetti held under hot water till the pasta softened, yet today those memories—young, free, and freedom bound—to me, are priceless. A lack of clarity and zero responsibilities provided the perfect food for my soul.

Making friends fast, I strode into cafés and initiated discussions with strangers. Approach and be approachable; bluff and believe everyone desired to engage in conversation. More often than not, the odds worked in my favor, and I won a cheerful reply. I learned to ask for what I needed and found the majority of people wanted to help by the goodness of their human nature.

Even breaking the law as a traveler played to my advantage. It is illegal to hitchhike on the motorways. However, if I stood on the major highways, the first car approaching would typically screech to a halt and inform me so. Then a second sentence came, 'Jump in before the police see you.' Quickly, I understood implementing techniques others did not use worked best. Roadworks and no place to pull over? I rearranged the bollards to make a personalized lay-by, necessitating all cars to slow. Never once did this method fail. Yet, I became burdened with guilt thinking about the following vehicles forced to crawl through the cones. Fortunately, the remorse passed swifter than the traffic behind me.

Ordinarily, after a couple of months, I would slink to England to reboot—only on one occasion did I stay away for too long. The summer's amber glow shifted to October's overcast, and the clothes I wore were ill-fitting. Sauntering into a campsite near the

Swiss border, expensive places that I avoided like the plague, I searched for a British registration plate. Pitching a tent, I blocked the car's departure then scribbled a note which I pinned onto the windscreen wipers, 'Any chance you might be heading in England's direction?' Then, I enjoyed a siesta. Two Australian honeymooners—Carolyn and Peter Ragen—roused my sleep with heartening news. Over the next couple of days, they ferried me to Putney, London. In a nutshell, my teen travels suggested that if you bolster the courage to leap, then life arranges a mysterious way of working out a road map.

Back in England, I would hit repeat, but the echoes began sounding like a hollow slap against a shallow wall. One scheduled year of coasting rolled into a fabulous four. The theater remained a constant foundation of diverse leads, but also the center rusted into a backdrop of fading interest—definitely time to fold this chapter. The bottom line, my path did not lead to the place I wished to find myself in twenty years. As I rotated in circles, the world, like a vibrant comet, sped onward. Every person has a calling, and this life did not match my ambitions. Something was missing, and I did not know what.

My Mom and 'Fat Dad' leaving to an Aldermaston anti-nuclear march.

CHAPTER 3. 1990

THE TRIGGER MOMENT

I will go anywhere, as long as it is forward. – David Livingstone

At the age of 21, I slumped in the departure lounge of a failing relationship. The numeral 21 signified more of a weight stone than an age—I skipped through the years like a needle might glide through silk. Each New Year, an elder friend phoned, half-singing the Lennon/Ono sentence, *'Another year over, and what have you done?'*

How those words stung, as if he accentuated the fact, I had achieved diddly-squat. But what had I done? I could scribble my resume on a postage stamp. Frustrated, I felt a vocation, task, or quest would materialize. But when and how?

༄

One crisp winter afternoon on a day like many others, my girlfriend gawked at her portable television in our living room. The recent signing of a lease on an oversized three-bedroomed house loomed as a reminder of the mistakes I was making in life.

She channel-surfed for a movie as I delved inside the pages of a gripping book. The window's brown curtains, dangling like an elephant's ears from the ceiling to the floor, blocked out all of the glorious sunshine, and the air drowned in the smog of wispy-white cigarette smoke. Cracking open my fifth can of Guinness, out of the corner of my eye, I glimpsed an athlete competing in an international road race. I cannot say I knew Carl Thackery, though I recognized his form and figure right as the channel changed. "Go back, that is Carl," I exclaimed in disbelief, almost dropping a burning cigarette.

She was equally surprised, but for another reason. How could Toby, a lethargic layabout who tilted his motorcycle beside the front door to prevent a step of unnecessary walking, recognize an accomplished athlete? Toby, a loafer who guzzled nothing but caffeine and alcohol by the bucketful and whose diet of two packs of Marlboro Reds, fried junk food, and a pouch of rolling tobacco for snacks, represented a cardiovascular disaster in the making.

"Oh, come on, you associate with him?" She cried, extracting a cigarette from her lips to let out an honest burst of laughter. I described my brief foray into the sports world. With Seb Coe living in Loughborough, the prominent senior at Hallamshire was Carl Thackery. He dominated the local races. However, the fact that Carl had developed into a national class competitor came as an utter shock.

The juniors and seniors at Hallamshire, as a rule, exercised separately, but one weekend none of my age mates appeared. New to both the club and the distant neighborhood, I would not waste an hour-long commute without completing a training session. Consequently, I secretly latched onto the rear of the lanky elders' group, honored to be running alongside the club top dog. Four miles in (6.4 km), a couple of men became irritated at my presence. Shifting pace, they tried losing me. I know—I heard their snide comments three strides back. In pain, I craved to slow, but if so, I would be awfully lost. My physical limits expired, though I discovered, the mind—or the soul—possessed more power than the legs. The brain could coerce the muscles to continue working beyond the limbs' lamentable cry of exhaustion. Against all reason, I hung onto the group for eight torturous miles. For this lesson, I never forgot Carl—or at least the back of his head.

Now, my eyeballs wired themselves to the screen. Carl meantime faded unceremoniously from the picture, and indeed the competition. Two of the men dueling for the gold medal gripped my attention, and I witnessed a scrappy street brawl.

Mile by mile, I crept inside the event—no longer did I watch a rivalry—but instead, I was breathing like a competitor.

A slightly built Tanzanian, Simon Robert Naali, attired in a white and lime singlet, ran to attack by surging and hustling his opponents. He fought a larger framed, sturdy Kenyan donning a blazing red singlet, Douglas Wakiihuri. Simon, if you followed his steely gaze, wished to drill his opponents into the tarmac. Douglas, exuding confidence, locked his sights to a distant lip on the horizon. Although both propelled themselves forwards, it was as if they battled in a boxing ring, punching, and jousting. Who would prevail and outlast the other? I became mesmerized watching this weird no-contact combat of legs and arms flying but wrestling through thin air.

For the last six long years, I had attempted every trick, idea, and scheme to quit cigarettes. Most people at the theater smoked—it was our uniform. Inhaling clouds of gunk into my lungs, hankering for Marlboro's distinctive nicotine, was how days started and ended. Chewing carrots, placing bets, setting dates—nothing worked as I failed to quit. I portrayed a pathetic addict. Yet, now transfixed by the screen, unintentionally, one fist clenched and crumpled the flimsy packet of smokes. My body had decided; enough. Maybe the shock of identifying an ordinary person doing the extraordinary prompted these actions? Carl demonstrated how I could transform and re-ignite my life.

When the program concluded, now decked out in a T-shirt and Bermuda shorts, I bounded onto Junction Road. Clad in a pair of tatty tennis shoes, I headed towards Endcliffe Park.

Gulping in the crisp air, and striding with the incline in my favor, allowed my limbs to loosen up. I relaxed my arms as the muscles automatically flicked the body forward. As the heaviness lifted, a stifled soul breathed, adrenaline flowed, and I identified a pathway how I could climb out of this rut. I must rewind—why did I stop running?

*(L) Before starting running again, I did not resemble your typical athlete.
(R) Tintagel House was my home away from a home for my junior years.*

❧

Vikings, the precise word, shrieks an invitation to action and adventure. My mother's side of the family claims its origins in Iceland. A relative, Disa Halldórsdóttir, explained our family's earliest ancestors originated from the Viking inhabitants of Blönduós, a speck of a fishing village on the rugged northern coast. "If you are a Blönduós Víking, you will have double-jointed thumbs," Disa declared when bending my hands as I scrambled to set down a coffee cup. She grinned, *"Þú ert sannur Víkingur!"* (You are a genuine Viking). Well, as I have read, all good Vikings sail out on crusades.

The lifestyle wrench I sought took me much further than Junction Road, actually, all the way to terminal three of Heathrow Airport. I knew, if I wished to catapult into a new chapter, I would require a radical change of scenery. Learning from the follies of Amsterdam, I flew to a country with reliable connections. A recently divorced family member called Ásgeir, dwelling in a spacious house, kindly offered lodgings till I regained my bearings. Owning a helicopter, cars, and a motorcycle, he sounded like Vogue magazine's ultimate bachelor. And because Uncle Ásgeir possessed a trawler, I presumed I might grapple the seas, like Captain Ahab of Moby Dick.

In July 1990, after an uneventful flight, the wheels of our 747 skidded down at the Keflavík Airport twenty-four miles (38 kilometers) from the world's most northern capital city, Reykjavík. Although the clock stated eleven p.m., the midnight sun lit up a rugged wilderness, colorless lava fields, and a skyline devoid of even a solitary tree. I bet this scenery comprises the closest one can come to an on-earth moon landing. Bussing into Reykjavík, which translates as smoky bay, the center appeared smaller than I expected any capital should be. The night was serene, scant traffic patrolled the roads, and a weird sulfurous egg odor sifted inside the night air. The stark difference sparked the question, 'What am I doing here?' Truthfully, I could not envision myself as a fisherman, but something exciting would work out. Being here, I anticipated nothing less than an exceptional, explosive adventure.

The bus discharged all passengers at a central hotel and possessing no local currency, and with all shops closed, I undertook the fifteen-minute hike to Mávahlíð, a street translating as seagull slope. As my heels clicked on the clean concrete, I did not spy a soul, and my eyes marveled at the tidy, neat order. Not a scrap of garbage littered the streets, unlike my English neighborhood.

Arriving at Ásgeir's house past midnight, so much for the quiet and calm—his building rocked. A gathering of rowdy friends camped at his kitchen table, encircling a cluster of semi-drained Grant's whiskey bottles. A mug of scotch, the size of a conventional coffee cup, was thrust in my direction by a woman wrapped in a bloodied white apron. The lady was carving up dead salmon, who poked like carrots, from a barrel of ice, trophies of the day's fly-fishing excursion. Carrying my guitar, it at once came in use with requests for me to provide sing-along entertainment. Ásgeir, with a bear hug strong enough to crush a wooden chair, arrived at one a.m. and how I pitied the neighbors as he dragged out an accordion to accompany the guitar playing. As the morning opened her curtains, people continually rapped at the front door to join the party. My God, I thought when I finally sank into a waterbed, slapdash drunk, past six a.m.—and that shindig played on a Sunday night? I dreaded a Friday. I discovered Icelanders relished a rollicking party.

One of the midnight revelers was Kristinn Hrafnsson, a second cousin and a budding journalist. He became a close friend, living in our building rooftop apartment. A gruff coffee-chugging, bohemian socialist, he could rarely be seen awake, or at least outdoors, before the dusky afternoon hours. Perpetually dressed in a five o'clock shadow and carting a collection of shopping bags under each eye, he resembled a character from a Balzac novel aimlessly lost above the Nordic circle. He and his platinum blonde blue-eyed girlfriend Helga escorted me to the city center's bars and clubs, offering a liquid introduction to the vibrant nightlife of Reykjavík.

Upon our second outing, whilst stumbling home along Skólavörðustígur at five a.m., I spied a poster advertising a running race. Invigorated by the midnight sun, countless *brennivíns* (Icelandic: burning wine 70-80% proof), and noting the upcoming date in two weeks, I proclaimed a bold challenge. The last to the finish must pony-up for the post-race beers. Kristinn, never having sighted me sneaking out the house at dawn for occasional exercise jaunts, concluded the bet a slam dunk win.

Beers aside, I thought he might abandon his habit of smoking should he accept the challenge. I wanted to share the gift I had recently discovered. Babbling, revealing a runner's endorphin euphoria following a rigorous run, sounded ludicrous—non-runners would never entertain such gobbledygook. Only after running does this peculiar magic make any sense.

But flopping into bed half an hour later, the wicked spirits of alcohol wiped my memory clean. I completely forgot the race poster, let alone any intoxicated wager. Though destiny had not— Helga worked for *Íslandsbanki* (Iceland's Bank), the event's title sponsor. An internal campaign urged and prodded the staff to participate, and on Monday morning, she enrolled the drunkards. The Reykjavík Marathon was, and until now is, the highlight of the country's running calendar and received a shedload of national media. If there is one race to run in the country, this is it.

※

With a smudge of the last night's liquor coating our tongues and tinting our breath, Helga, Kristinn, and I briskly hurried to town on the morning of the event. The pale lemonade sun, although bright and cheerful, offered not a single ray of warmth. Unquestionably the day prompted movement—furthermore, the clock ran against us.

In the city center, I discovered thousands of people ready for the races. Runners, ranked like soldiers but armed in bright neon clothes, lined up stretching, jumping, and jogging in place to keep their blood circulating. Barricades and blocking tape plastered the streets with the sponsor's signage. This set-up looked unique—I had witnessed my share of track or cross-country competitions, but to observe a metropolis closed for athletics was extraordinary. Hi-tempo music blared from the loudspeakers in every direction, and you could not help but absorb the positive energy.

Arriving late, Kristinn blurred into the hubbub—maybe he went seeking a toilet? With ancillary events to the full marathon, I had no idea which distance we should run. Helga was no fool—she knew neither of us could complete a 26.2-miler (42.2 km). She had handed us a color-coded bib, so I went to stand with the other green-bibbed runners. Not shy, I slotted in at the fore of the crowd, as I intended remaining ahead of the enemy at all times. Now I would inquire regarding the specific distance. But as I dithered, a cannon fired, and three or four thousand runners surged into action. Not speaking Icelandic proficiently or wishing to hassle the laboring athletes when in need, you ask the police.

Sprinting, I chased after the departing row of patrol bikes assembled like a presidential cavalcade, fifty meters in front of the runners. Annoyingly, when I lengthened my strides, the riders sped away. I had not grasped the cops, sat on their chunky Harley-

Davidson motorcycles, took instructions to lead and escort the participants. They must ride clear and not compromise the athletes. But pursuing the police distanced me from the competitors and, most importantly, my nemesis Kristinn. Although I never caught the bikes, I caused a clean break and was currently heading the field.

I surprised everyone, myself included. But how long could I maintain this pace? Glancing over my shoulder in the distance, I saw a group chasing in pursuit though they were not gaining any ground. What fun, and who cared if in ten minutes I had to walk?

One rider continually blasted his siren as if to announce, 'Here approaches someone of importance!' Enthusiastic crowds skirting both sides of the streets cheered and yelled as if I performed as a popstar— *"Afram, Afram"* (Go, go). Although exerting effort, there seemed no limits to my energies. My heart was beating like a Cuban festival drum—ticking as a rapid metronome, not as a worrying sign of impending failure.

The miles clicked by, and excitement fueled every step. Before long, the route coiled back to the staging area that housed both the start and the finish.

7.5-km (4.6 miles) turned out to be the perfect distance—my fantastic day could have crumbled if the course dragged on, but unbelievably I won in front of a cheering animated crowd. To finish over a minute and a half ahead of the next competitor spelled out for a brilliant ending.

A six-foot man assuming a broad smile approached—he was a Nike sports rep, "You crushed the course record, crushed it. Can you come to our headquarters tomorrow morning? We would like you to represent our brand."

Nike?? If I hit a high as I breasted the tape, this man's words catapulted me into the stratosphere. Did he address me? Toby, the fitness jogger and ex-smoker whose tar blackened fingers and wheezy cough were a social disgrace? My goal was thrashing Kristinn and procuring free beer. Why would anyone offer me sponsorship from the most prestigious sports brand on this globe?

Whilst I struggled to regain my breath and digest the proposal, a coach from a sports club approached, "Hey, what about scoring for us in future races?" He promised travel expenses and a training camp overseas to escape from the harsh Nordic weather. I should collect receipts, and a stipend would be forthcoming. The national television station reporter, standing in line, now requested an interview—could he pull me aside for an exclusive? Photographers shoved cameras in my face as journalists questioned, what other races had I won and who was this longhaired athlete disrupting the field?

Kristinn, who endured a slightly different experience than me, eventually reached the finishing line, and in the evening, we celebrated. A journalist tracked us down, penning a story as we quaffed our beers. 'Veðjaði kollu og sigraði í hlaupinu' became the Monday morning's headline (Bet a pint of beer and won the race).

Veðjaði kollu og sigraði í hlaupinu

Toby Tanser frá Sheffield á Englandi sigraði með miklum yfirburðum í skemmtiskokki karla og var hátt í tvær mínútur á undan næsta manni.

Amma Tobys er íslensk og kom Toby hingað til lands í síðustu viku til að heimsækja ættingja sína. Á þriðjudaginn sat hann yfir kaffibolla með frænda sínum Kristni Hrafnssyni og kom þá hlaupið til tals. Kristinn segir Toby hafa viljað taka þátt en ekki lítist á að hlaupa einn og því hafi þeir frændur ákveðið að skella sér í hlaupið í sameiningu.

— Við veðjuðum einni kollu af bjór um hvor okkar yrði fyrri í mark. Ég verð að segja að það kom mér verulega á óvart hversu fljótur frændi minn reyndist, þótt hann hafi skokkað reglulega síðan hann hætti að reykja um árarmótin. Sjálfur varð ég númer 155 en þó örugglega efstur af reykingamönnum! sagði Kristinn Hrafnsson.

Frændurnir Toby Tanser og Kristinn Hrafnsson skála fyrir sigri Tobys á Kristni — og öllum öðrum! MYND: JH.

The following day, I applied for a work permit, and a chest X-ray was compulsory. The nurse scolded me, "Quit the habit as you own the congested lungs of a 66-year-old smoker."

"I'm an athlete!" I countered, jabbing a hand towards the glossy sports bags I received at the Nike offices. She repeated, "Quit smoking." Unfolding the newspaper, I placed a finger on the sports page revealing the results with my name at the top of the list. Visible shock spread over her face as if she encountered a ghost. Only after rereading the paper, she muttered, "Ég trúi því ekki." (I do not believe it). Well, neither did I.

Rumors say Kristinn too nixed the nicotine, albeit donkey's years later. He continued his colorful life, at one time collaborating with Bobby Fischer, the puzzling chess champion, and recently as the spokesperson for Wikileaks.

Throughout my Icelandic years, a clip displaying me galloping down the home stretch aired as a part of the intro to the evening sports news. Why the snippet included me, I do not know, but it was an honor. The script played as if to remind me of who I could become and where I might head in the future. The shadow of Toby sucking a cigarette slouched like a gluepot in the corner of a smoky pub, pouting words instead of actions, embodied the man I had left behind. Thank goodness for that random race poster and Helga's employment at the right bank.

Due to the sport, opportunities flourished—invites from around the island to attend an annual series of fifteen road and cross-country events called *stiggakeppni* (point's races) provided a fantastic way to wander and explore. For the three years I competed in this unique series, I stood undefeated. Never would I have guessed I might scramble over the slopes of Mt. Hekla days before the volcano erupted or be physically blown into the Greenland Sea when trotting in a torrential storm under the electric lime blaze of the northern lights. Dazzling memories, I will not forget. New doors opened as playing a sports personality, albeit in a pint-sized country, was like drawing four aces in a hand of poker. As a known athlete, I established beneficial connections—sporting and otherwise.

However, although Iceland upgraded my path, the location had far from ideal running conditions. An inclement cold nip and gusty winds that could knock a man backward were a year-round staple. Seemingly eight days out of ten, rain, like pellets of grit, would scar your face and blind the eyes when stepping outdoors. The slim shadings of daylight for most months offered little compensation for the summer's weeks of the piercing midnight sun. During the prolonged winters—spring and fall—we received a scant four to five hours of bleak midday illumination.

Most races kicked off at noon for this reason, which became awkward because I had accepted part-time employment in a restaurant. The uninspiring job made every run sweeter, but I flirted with the risk of squandering this position for skipping out to race at peak weekend work hours. Fortunately, most contests were short in distance, set on a course of ten kilometers (six miles) or less.

At the last possible moment, I snuck out the rear door and rushed to the event venue. Shamelessly, if late, I stripped off on the starting line to prevent the competition from preceding. Completing the race at top speed, I dashed across the finish and plunged into the passenger seat of a waiting car. A trusted friend, Stefan Friðgeirsson, who had kindly taxied me there, catapulted me back to the tedious routine of mindless manual labor.

Cringing, I recollect, on one occasion—a half marathon—I messed up badly. Early in the morning, coughing and spluttering for better effect, I called work pretending to be sick.

"I can (groan) barely crawl to the bathroom, let alone (sigh) stagger to work," I cried. Unfortunately, only in the first mile did I spot the live broadcast truck. The restaurant owner exhibited no jubilation at my remarkable recovery.

Various people I met spoke of attractive opportunities abroad for athletes. Since arriving in Iceland, I dated a Swede, Marielle Westlund, and she played the following card on my journey. Keen to venture to a country with prospects for both of us, she suggested, "Let's go anyplace and try something new." Anywhere offering opportunities, I mused.

"Sweden?" She hinted. Why not. We packed our lives into a bundle of hope and flew 1,272 miles (2,000 km) east in search of unknown adventures.

Marielle's parents, Iris & Sten-Olof, brought wondrous energy and warm hugs to Stockholm's Arlanda Airport. Piling us into a beige Volvo 240, internationally known as the iron brick, we headed north for a five-hour drive to Överhogdal, a village where the reindeer easily outnumbered the inhabitants. Their residence nestled inside a huddle of wooden chalet-style structures dotted along one roadside. Two structures, a garage cum convenience shop and a church, famous for a 1000-year-old Viking tapestry discovered in the vestry, constituted the community's center.

Upon arrival, the Westlunds' house oozed with comfort and congeniality for the visitor. The welcoming scent of freshly ground coffee wafted with the appetizing smell of oven-warmed wholewheat bread; I immediately felt right at home. The building, constructed of timber and painted burnt red, bordered huge wild-roaming gardens that led to never-ending pinewoods. Horses and ponies cantered around pens inside the compound, and moose hunting hounds added to its picture-perfect, country-life setting. Överhogdal, 160 of us, demonstrated the beautiful unity of collective living.

Though yet again, conditions were not ideal for running. Bears, wolves, and elks were the start of the problems. One meter (three-foot) of deep snow ensured training hard became nigh on impossible. Rather than run, I leaped and tumbled into mounds of the foul weather that had pummeled Northern Sweden since our arrival. Trying to retain fitness by jogging in frozen slush, praying a stray bullet from one of the legal moose hunting teams would not cuff this moving target did not represent a fun way to keep competitive.

As an alternative, straddling Iris's bicycle, I pedaled the twelve miles (19.3 km) to Ytterhogdal, where I discovered one treadmill in a gym. After exercising for an hour, gnawing hunger propelled me home in haste. Now, non-animal issues arose. Snow-plow trucks carved a single lane in each direction, allowing no room for a push-bike, and fast-moving eighteen-wheelers would barrel at top speed, unable to react swiftly on the icy tarmac. And unfortunately, Europaväg 45—my route— happened to be a principal road in Sweden. It was imperative to listen for traffic, then dismount, and toss the two-wheeler in the mounds of snow before diving in the bushes for cover. This system of training performed a wonder for the upper-body workouts but half-killed the nerves.

Presently we relocated to the capital after an athletics team offered us an apartment and a stipend in the suburb of Solna. The organization recruiting, Stockholm Spårvägens, led as Sweden's premier club on the tracks, roads, or country, and fortunately, I consistently scored on the squad, winning several national championship medals. Running transpired to be a delightful vocation. Invites to domestic and international races allowed an abundance of travel opportunities, and I applied for citizenship, imagining Sweden as a harbor.

Unknowingly, running had spiraled from a pleasant pastime to a rigid obsession. Take, for example, the occasion when I fractured a toe. Icing the foot for rehab, once numbed, I marveled how the pains vanished. Why not jog barefoot in the snow, wearing one shoe? When this failed—as the thaw brought even more excruciating aches—I tried lodging a pebble in the non-injured shoe to distract the hurt. The scheme worked as I discovered the body concentrates on the sharper pain. Tottering like a lame duck in a dance class, I jumped from a hobby-jogger to an eccentric misguided lunatic.

In Sweden, I discovered the runners trained with sophistication compared to my old technique of legging it to the Reykjavík harbor four times a week and sprinting back. Pouring over the pages of the Runner's World magazines in Iceland, I had performed whatever advice the editors suggested. A scientific approach it was not, but because I enjoyed numerous victories, it proved effective.

However, adopting the Swedish practiced methods brought noticeable improvements. Furthermore, training alongside the tight-knit team, attending group sessions, and traveling to club camps in Southern Spain was exciting fun. When I dipped under fourteen minutes on the track for the 5000-meters (3.1 miles) wearing a pair of old cross-country studded shoes, the club coach indicated, I displayed *'potentiella,'* and should undergo an assessment called VO_2 max. In this exam, machines calculate oxygen expenditure whilst exercising at a near-maximum effort. What I might achieve with the information I obtained remained a mystery. But since an expert, Bengt Saltin, a world-renowned exercise physiologist, conducted the tests, I leaped at the opportunity.

In the summer, international athletes flocked to Sweden as a base for competitions and training. World-class runners, requiring fitness facilities close to the European race circuit, lodged in Stockholm and frequently entered local events to monitor their form. One day, scrambling in the penultimate mile of the Rösjöloppet race, an African shouldered me. Accelerating as we navigated a tight turn, his nudging forced me into the fencing. Angry and willing to use my weight advantage to shove him sideways, I recognized the offending figure as Simon Robert Naali. Surreal, no longer did I spectate from the couch, but now I appeared as a player in the game.

After finishing, pulling aside the bone-thin Tanzanian, I gushed, recounting the cigarette incident. The day improved when Simon indicated I must join him for training sessions. Pinching myself, I wondered, is this crazy? The international medal-winning sports stars did not mingle with ordinary people. Running unlocked a world of opportunities, and like a storybook, each page revealed an inspiring adventure. At every race, I encountered intriguing characters—like The Berk.

At the end of the season, the results returned from Saltin's lab. Anne-Britt Olrog wrote the data scored the highest recorded figures in their facility, 87.5%. (As a guideline, Lance Armstrong logged a VO_2 max of eighty-five.) She cited the digits were beyond promising, and for a beginner, nothing short of exceptional. Essentially, I possessed a Ferrari engine but required a few consecutive years of endurance training to develop sufficient muscle strength to support the framework upholding that motor.

"Runners at your standard are not former chain-smokers with only a couple of years of training. Please introduce specific sessions, stretching, and add massage. Most important, engage a personal coach and map out a long-term plan. Be patient because if you follow this advice, you will develop to become an outstanding runner. You have *fantastisk talang* Toby."

Ooh, what an unexpected boost to read Ms. Olrog's words. Her terminology was identical to Mr. Matthew's. Okay, now I would really commit myself, and traveling to Africa would reveal how the premier athletes lived and what methods I might adopt to become a champion. Our club coach was appropriately qualified, yet as I scrambled to learn Swedish, I grasped just scraps of his wisdom. Presently I would see and hear from myself the way forward from the Kenyans.

Instead of viewing Simon Robert Naali (#15) from the smokers' couch, I was competing (#10) against the Tanzanian.

Chapter 4. 1995

INTO AFRICA

Not all those who wander are lost. – J. R. R. Tolkien

E. V. Gordon and J. R. R. Tolkien bonded as dear companions. Collectively they formed the Viking Club, whose purpose centered upon discussing the old Icelandic sagas enjoyed over a beer in the company of their students. One fortunate scholar to be employed as Gordon's successor was granddad Afi. Countless decades later, Afi gifted me—a young child—a book called The Hobbit. I asked, "Is this fact or fiction" and "are you woven into the story," having befriended the author. My grandfather, owning a spherical bald head and bushy black overgrown eyebrows, offered a sly wink,
 "I am not handing you a book—this is a path to discover your journey."
 Devouring the paperback to unwrap a personal quest, as I understood it, you merely set off trusting your heart, and fascinating experiences present themselves. People you encounter when traveling will offer guidance as the needs arise. Could it be that straightforward? Just trot off and trust your heart? As a youngster, I presumed these words reflected the gospel truth. Only now, relaxing in my airplane seat and Nairobi bound, did I muse upon how lucky the individuals were who gained that chance to table the book and embark upon their adventure. I knew I must seize this incredible opportunity and run with it.

Stiff-legged and shuffling off the plane following the nine-hour flight, I stepped into Nairobi's Jomo Kenyatta Airport. Breathing in, the typical jet fuel stench that lingers around landing bays like a moldy carpet welcomed me to Kenya.

Along with the anticipation of adventure followed a fair dose of trepidation. The truth, I had not given much thought to the logistics since Noel's abrupt announcement. I came from a family that acted upon the spur of the moment. My dear mother, on a whim, had attempted to end apartheid by becoming the white Rosa Parks. Finding herself in South Africa in the 1980s, she utilized segregated public transport and adopted the stance of sitting alongside the Africans. Her homespun plan backfired—those in the vicinity confessed to being uncomfortable at the behavior. "But I did try," she countered. Trying your best in life is what counts.

Some individuals acquire books, learn a language, rummage, and research details before considering a flight ticket. Coming from the opposing school, only after stepping on the soil did I initiate any investigations. Describe it as the economy of effort class—besides, in 1995, search engines meant looking for motorcars. And now, when walking inside the gates of Kenya, I wondered, what is the official language? Am I to encounter problems communicating like on last month's trip to Istanbul, Turkey? Fortunately, English is the primary language taught in schools before Swahili.

With last-minute planning, I had not even bothered exchanging money to the local currency—I shuffled dollars like a drug smuggler, stuffed into hidden pouches inside my jacket. The entire world understood the mighty dollar, at least everyone who has ventured anywhere near an airport. Besides, any hotel could exchange dollars for whatever currency the Kenyans carried.

Inside the international airport, designed and probably last painted in the 1970s, I hurried to beat the queue and navigate the immigration control. The pace of the foot traffic thwarted me at every turn. Little moved swiftly, least the personnel who jotted down the entry forms of all the passengers in triplicate.

At the baggage claim, I may have been the first to enter, but I would be the last to leave as none of my checked luggage arrived. This was not how I envisioned the grand African entrance. Worse yet, when encountering Kenyan athletes on the circuit, they all bemoaned of a lack of running stores in the country. How could I survive without replenishing the equipment? Run barefoot? Are you kidding? I needed my Nike's! Finding a complaint desk, I joined a lengthy line of disgruntled passengers to file a lost luggage slip.

Leaving the arrivals hall, a magnificent clear starry night reminded me of my departure from the gloomy clouds of the frozen north. The equatorial calendar offers the opposite season of Europe's—welcome to the embrace of the Kenyan summer. Despite the late hour, the warm night wind bore unknown smells of exotic lands and promised immediate excitement.

My eyes surveyed the road for the taxis. Yellow cabs in NYC, black in London, what color for Kenya? Piled up in the parking lot, I observed stacks of dilapidated non-metered private beat-up salon cars. Were these authentic taxis?

Drivers swarmed to me like moths around a flame, and men tugged both arms and jacket, pleading I hired their vehicle. Looking like the night's final customer, I became hot property. Goodness, what to do, and whom to select? I resorted to no better plan than evaluating the chauffeurs by the teeth philosophy Amma, my Icelandic grandmother (herself sporting falsies), adopted to adjudicate trusty characters. As toothy smiles chase optimistic attitudes, she may be onto something.

"So, where to boss?" inquired the chosen fang-man. An excellent question, where to indeed? Runners detest crowding, "Is there a park or area known for exercising, and if so, any chance of an inexpensive hotel close-by?" I wondered.

"Yeah, there's a place I see runners—let's go." He replied. As we departed, under the grumble and splutter of an untuned engine, I thought I heard him mutter, "Let us drive to the Shady." The word caused me to reflect on the decision to enter this cab.

Shady? It dawned upon me the taxi-man could be an ax murderer. Pictures of my dissected body in a Nairobi jungle might be the gory news of tomorrow's papers—Went running with the Kenyans, did not run fast enough. Yikes, best not dwell on such notions. Instead, I gazed out of the window, hoping to spot an elephant.

We pulled up at the hotel past 12:30 a.m., the name The Shade suited the joint perfectly. After a couple of long blasts on the horn, a hefty iron gate, surrounded by a thickset privet hedge hiding any viewing of the buildings, opened a sliver. A towering man in a gray trench coat strode forward, and wielding a club gripped in his hand, offered anything but a friendly welcome. I alerted the driver; was he aware of our impending doom?
"The stick, is it for decoration or an emblem of the hotel perhaps?" I asked, extremely concerned for my safety. The driver sniggered, "It's a *rungu*. This man will direct you to the hotel's reception." Apparently, the threatening chap worked as the night watchman and clutched a Maasai cudgel, called a *rungu*. If he represented the good guy, what would the bad look like?
Cudgel man escorted me to a sparse room brightened by a naked light bulb, and I had to rattle the door handle to arouse the snoring receptionist. Dorcas, wrestling a grossly undersized red nylon pantsuit, appeared unhappy at my impromptu arrival, retorting her regular guests had the courtesy to call in advance. She shoved a dog-eared sign-in book across the counter as I inquired,
"Any runners residing near here? Maybe a chance of an introduction at breakfast?"
Frowning, fretting, and whining under her breath regarding tardiness and manners, she gave no hope or encouragement. How disappointing, did the taxi man fib, and this off-beat hotel was a cousin's joint where he snaffled a commission? Why exactly did I travel to Africa? I should never have boarded the plane. Noel's cancelation was the hint—why did I not follow suit?

My quarters stood separately from the main building block—another ominous sign. The accommodation resembled a hut, but not like the quaint safari cabins I had admired in *National Geographic visits the Mara*. The hovel matched the type of structure purposed for gardening tools—dingy and dark. Opening the door, I spied an uncomfortable-looking junior bed vaulted knee-high over a barely swept concrete floor. Against the back wall, I spied a stained sink and a porcelain toilet lacking a seat. I noted a piped showerhead protruding above from a cracked wall at eye level. Was this to body wash or to clean the lavatory? Perchance both! To the side of the potty lay a large rusty iron grate; I could just imagine the bugs and odors ruining my stay.

"Self-contained suite!" Dorcas beamed, passing over a door key attached to a key fob the size of a house brick. Her other hand groped ominously inside her nose. Basic accommodations, but for ten dollars, breakfast included, I could not complain.

When Dorcas left, and after bolting the door, I tore off my clothes and stood under the shower nozzle, desperate to scrape off the grime accumulated after the last day's travel. Despite turning and turning the brass tap, unbelievably, no water flowed. Instead, measly cold droplets dripped from the rusty spout. I thought of calling grumpy Dorcas, but with no telephone in the room and her despondent attitude, perhaps not. Completely wiped, I collapsed on the thin foam mattress. At least I would be secure with Mr. Munster outside.

⚘

An attacking mosquito zipping inside the room stirred the morning sleep. Panic! Why did I not purchase the anti-malaria tablets that a friend had insisted would safeguard a person's life? I presumed mosquitoes buzzed around swamps and jungles—not hotel rooms. Leaping out of bed to dress, I noticed I was too late. Three puffy welts punctured my hand. Goodness, how big was the tiny geezer's stomach? Did this mean I had already contracted a fatal tropical disease? Was I now a blackwater fever carrier? That is the last straw—I decided to fly home. No luggage, no runners, no water, no shoes, and now infected with the bubonic plague? A plethora of problems suggested adios Africa. After revamping the gear in Sweden, I could jet to our club's traditional Spanish training camp near the charming coastal town of Marbella. Functioning power-showers inside a luxurious beachfront condominium, a change of clothes, no toxic insects, and running shoes? That sounded like a prudent upgrade to adopt.

However, before taxiing to the airport, I wanted to go for a run. No, I needed to go running—that is my routine, and I missed yesterday's session due to journeying. Despite lacking a change of clothes, I could purchase a T-shirt and underwear from a roadside store following the exercise. Fortunately, I always traveled in old running shoes.

Outdoors, the sweltering heat promised a challenging run. Cripes, it was muggy. My mind drifted to breakfast and putting the flight plans in motion. I dreamt of Spain and looked forward to joining the Stockholm boys. As I departed, I had a choice—left or right. Years ago, I learned a little play-on-words, 'Go right, you don't go wrong.' Hence, a tad superstitious, I hung a right onto a heavily trafficked road. I pressed the stopwatch to ensure I did not exercise a second over forty minutes, which I considered the minimal amount for a diary entry. Had I turned left, then I may have flown home that afternoon.

Running on the dirt by the edge of the tarmac, a *matatu* (passenger minibus) decelerated to match my pace. The conductor, hanging from the side door of the vehicle, yelled to solicit trade, "Where to *bwana* (mister)?" I ignored him, having no wish to stop jogging. He laughed at my behavior, "Hey man, are you too stingy to dole out five shillings (5-US cents) for a ride?" How the commuters inside the brightly colored bus screamed and whooped at his daft humor. "*M'zungu,* (foreigner) spend your pennies," he cried, "Yes, we have vehicles in Africa!" The bus refused to leave and lagged at my tempo, so hoping to defuse the situation, I explained,

"Actually, I'm a runner, an athlete."

"He is a runner?" Now the conductor and his passengers burst out in a chorus of hysterical laughter. Every man of this trade I would find is well-versed at jiving with the customers.

As the van finally pulled away, smothering me in a cloak of dust and clouds of choking diesel fumes, I ran on, pretending the ribbing fell like water off a duck's back. In a jiff, another vehicle slotted into place, and the next comedian struck up his spiel.

Plentiful on the roads, these privately owned public transport vehicles spoiled the day. The ones I encountered were gaudy ancient minibuses and crammed to the gills with passengers, patrolling the streets like a bevy of bugs around a month-old corpse. Far from the tourist trails, I must have looked an odd sight. Not every day do you see a thin white man dressed in jeans clomping up the road, beetroot-faced, and wheezing in the elevated altitude.

Woefully, this route was the commuter's congested direct line in and out of Nairobi. What awful luck—had I not missed yesterday's training, I would have scooted back to the hotel. But two days of inactivity meant a significant dent in the weekly mileage. Focus Toby, I set my head down as yet another *matatu* driver slowed to poke fun and mock the alien.

Peeking at my stopwatch and convincing myself the constant jeering did not bother me, I aimed to run back to the hotel and end this pity party. That was it. The African adventure could be over— nothing but sour experiences. Then, on the nineteenth minute, when I scanned for a suitable swing-round marker, I almost screamed aloud with joy. One hundred meters (109 yards) ahead were twenty, feasibly thirty, of the legendary Kenyan runners. Like prancing stallions, they paraded across the road, obstructing the traffic, and then galloped down a bushy path. Whoa, for real, is this a chance to join the Kenyans on my first run?

What a random stroke of luck. Dashing forward, I raced to latch onto the group. Surprisingly, the athletes neither acknowledged my presence nor gestured me away, and I seized this as an invitation to tag along. Weird indeed, but who cared. Look at me, living a dream on my maiden African morning.

After a couple of miles of running, cresting a hill, the men ground to a stop before a spacious field. Several enormous weather-beaten tents stood pitched as a camp, the size one might find at a traveling circus. What I now observed looked too good to be true. Streams of skinny athletes sauntered around the tents, garbed in a variety of tracksuits or T-shirts. The runner closest, Tanui, grinned and extended a hand, "*Kar-i-bu* (welcome) to our camp. And who exactly are you?"

I had mistaken the silence for unfriendliness. Unlike my Swedish teammates and I, who cackled like fishwives, these men preferred to concentrate on the task at hand, leaving the socializing to the post-training. Upon catching my concern, Tanui chuckled, "No, we are friendly. But in training to race and when competing, there is no chitchat." Ok, lesson learned.

The athletes urged me to join them and dig into a prepared brunch. Fortuitously, I had stumbled upon arguably the greatest distance running group on the globe. Here the Navy, Air Force, and Army runners dwelt. They numbered three to four hundred of Kenya's swiftest men, and as any fan knows, that indicated the finest athletes in the world. In the mid-nineties, independent management or the shoe company teams had not penetrated Kenya as they do today. The customary route to becoming an international champion was via this camp. And yes, I instantly recognized the man pouring the cup of tea from a feature in the Runner's World magazines.

Talk about a runner's high—world and Olympic stars wandered to the left and right, as common as books in a library. Moreover, I was welcome to join these titans' training sessions, and an army truck shuttled to the airport to collect my luggage, making the day complete. Not only had I the offer to train alongside the talented men, but the opportunity was to run with the *greatest* of the Kenyan runners. Any thoughts of returning to Sweden vanished immediately. At this location, I would receive tips and training advice to improve my skills. My humble task remained to look, listen, learn, and leave.

Camp Kenya pics, and one of the men I met on my first morning in 1995. Moses Tanui was the first athlete to break the one-hour barrier for the half marathon competition. Here, in 2018, we stand at the site of his old café in Eldoret where I was handed a life changing proposal.

Chapter 5. 1995

CAMP LIFE & STREET DEATH

Only through experience of trial and suffering can the soul be strengthened, ambition inspired, and success achieved. – Helen Keller

Karen Blixen's memoir, published in 1937, recounted the story of a Danish Baroness residing in Kenya, living under the blue shadows of the N'gong Hills. Each chapter, penned as if her nib flowed straight from her heart, invites the reader to explore the lands and understand the perspectives of the local characters most often ignored by the writers of that era. Few have ever described the blood, body, and bones of this region better.

Following an assortment of jarring life experiences spanning seventeen years, she leads us with profound sadness and tragedy, like the book is entitled, Out of Africa. Broken-hearted and bankrupt, she retreated to Denmark in 1931, never to return. Of Kenya, she wrote, "You woke up in the morning and thought: Here I am, where I ought to be." In England, stuck in the steel city, it had not been hard to slip inside the pages of her manuscript and visualize her setting.

At the camp, I discovered the location to be N'gong, and the foothills looming before us—which we utilized for hill-running repeats—were the same ones inspiring Blixen's magnificent writing. This base, although a recent addition to the military sports program, looked as dated as of the old book. The living conditions were Spartan and sketchy. If Kenyan secrets existed, they must be well-hidden.

The giant canvas tents contained rows upon rows of functional but uncomfortable metal bunks. Strings tethered tautly between the inner-tent poles supported lines of weather bleached running clothes—ready for the morning work. Personal space was limited, and each man owned a crude tin-metal chest used instead of a wardrobe for their few possessions. No gym, treadmill, or even an exercise bike stood at the camp. As for sporting equipment, all I unearthed was a car tire for jumping exercises and a wrought-iron bar, as long as a broom handle, with concrete blocks at each end, improvising for dumbbells. And for entertainment, without electricity, I could tell we were not here for the high life. On the rare occasion, a newspaper appeared, after splitting the spine with a razor, people sat in a circle and held single pages, then passed the sheet to the right after reading.

N'gong did not represent a state-of-the-art training center—damp clothes and dried sweat pinged your nostrils, dirt lay underfoot—yet ironically, the venue produced the Kenyan world-beaters. At the least, I expected the runners would enjoy the services our Swedish club provided. But instead, I discovered primitive methods. Like when an athlete complained of a foot blister, the doctor cleaned off his soup spoon in an open flame and proceeded to press the red stainless steel against the flesh. Even the resident physiotherapist played the eccentric as he healed athletes by reciting a rousing verse of the bible and advising men to add extra prayers—devotions for a stress fracture? What kind of plan is that to duplicate?

Days in N'gong began by slipping into shorts, a T-shirt, and an overlay of a tracksuit. Though as soon as the sun climbed to eye level, I should prepare for a roasting. The Kenyan fashion promoted overdressing for training runs and not entirely without reason. Each layer ensured the workout would be more arduous. Thus, when stripping off to shorts and a singlet for a competition, the sensation became liberating—heavy clothing restricts movement, suffocates the skin, and hinders the body's cooling system.

How I suffered in the spanking heat, dressed like a deranged Eskimo, and it was not just clothing; every element seemed designed to maximize discomfort. It felt like we trained all day long—six days a week, three times a day, with a seventh single-day long run being the welcomed reprieve. If I sought immersion in athletics, I trod water at the bed of the deepest ocean.

Guessing the daily program to be hi-tech, progressively structural, and individualized, I was in for a surprise. In Sweden, the team coach handed us schedules matched to splits for the kilometers, and we should complete a route with precise timing and monitor gradual improvement. Not so in Kenya. Nobody in our group asked about pace, and approximate distances worked fine. Start slowly to finish like a charging racehorse—follow the pack and do not ask questions. To my agony, whatever the coach prescribed of time spent exercising, the athletes consistently ran longer than he specified, much longer. What a paradox—simplicity and less science produced optimal outcomes.

In Sweden, tests measured exercise economy, and muscle balancing machines were available. Air-conditioned gyms, saunas, and dietary breakdowns with pages of analysis aided sports folk. I had even heard of runners hiring shrinks hoping to gain a psychological edge. Our team coach, Ulf, handed out sports drinks during training sessions, and each of the squad's coaches specialized in short, mid, or long distances.

Meantime, in Kenya, one coach controlled about one hundred runners competing in varied distances. William Tanui, the Olympic 800 meters champion, was training alongside marathoners. Everyone joined the weekly long runs when the Kenyan coach dropped us twenty miles (32 km) from the camp and ordered us to run home. Thirsty, injured, or tired? Too bad, walk the distance.

Who would have guessed, these bare basics, camping like boy scouts in tents befitting circus animals, produced the winning formula? Worse yet, scouts at least enjoyed showers—here we had plastic buckets and frigid river water. Athletes did slip-on sports shoes, but most had not shodden a pair until their late teens.

Bred from a culture with paths to enable an easier life, I consistently noticed the opposite in Kenya. One time, the first Kenyan athlete to break the 2:10 barrier for the marathon requested a pair of shoes, "When you travel to Sweden, can you send me size thirteen?"

"But Joseph, your foot is smaller than mine. You must be an eight, not a thirteen."

"Yes, but imagine, if I trained in thirteens, how fast I will be on race day when I slip on an eight," he responded.

My covert mission became hunting out one aspect of our day that enabled my life to be easier. Even the location strategically tortured our lungs. The camp sat at an altitude of 1889 meters (6,200 feet) because less oxygen is available at loftier heights. The 'air' in your body breaks down glucose, creating fuel for the muscles. Therefore, runners struggle when breathing hard at these elevations. Later, I learned that training at a high altitude is advantageous since the body naturally then produces extra red blood cells, meaning you fly when returning to the lowlands. But at that time, it became the next hurdle to burden the day.

High in the hills, there could have been less oxygen, but I did stumble upon incredible views. Between sessions, we enjoyed strolls, and apparently, ambling as a tortoise worked as a part of the plan to run fast.

One morning out hiking, watching the eagles soar, a coach pointed to a dim blotch on the horizon. "Look at Kil-i-man-jar-o," he said, cracking the word to emphasize the fourth syllable. "The translation is the hill of shining greatness."

I strained my eyes whilst digesting his words, "How can it be as Kilimanjaro sits in Tanzania."

"Yes, Tanz-a-ni-a." He sighed, "But as far as your eyes can travel is the same soil which places you in what you call Tanz-a-ni-a. We named it Africa because, before Europeans, we possessed land without borders. Kenya and Tanzania are concocted entities you invented—so please consider our land Africa. Recognize the buffalo grazing? Do they realize a division?"

Taking offense, I stepped in, "My people?" Is he accusing me of supporting colonialism? I did not wish to discuss politics—who bothered what he believed. Instead, I made a mental note to include conquering Kilimanjaro on my bucket list. The coach meanwhile continued, "No blame," he smiled, "Our chief, Jomo Kenyatta, instructed us to forget the past and unite. The country's slogan is *Harambee* meaning 'All pull together.' As a nation, this is how we live—look at the camp, we succeed as one. Have you seen a single Kenyan athlete training alone? Lose your focus on the individual—when you work as a team, you gain the strength of a community. Having no social security system in Kenya, this is how we have learned to survive."

Those unifying words gave me much thought. No one but me challenged the methods or complained about the lack of facilities. Do not overthink—run free on these beautiful never-ending trails without thought or question. Simplicity served as an easy lesson to absorb. I synchronized with this rhythm of continuous exercise and an over-the-limit commitment to forget all else in the name of becoming a champion athlete. My life became enchantingly uncomplicated, and the days filled with splendor.

I marveled to admire scenes so foreign to my Swedish life; giraffes, gazelles, and wandering zebras meandered daily into our running routes. The mellow animals felt secure in our company, barely paying attention to anyone's approach. Man, beast, and nature all merged to create an indelible memory. The athletes had adopted an organic way of combining training and living—we should slide in as a piece of the scenery without disturbing or disrupting the surroundings. In this magical and majestic setting, I lived in paradise. Yet, after three weeks, I searched for a distraction.

To break from the monotony of clambering in and out of my running clothes, I planned a day trip to Nairobi, East Africa's largest capital. I now understood the term cabin fever. Although not in my wildest dreams could I have pictured a more idyllic training camp, I yearned to talk to ordinary people. Maybe travel to town, chat with the ladies, make friends, and discover what the city had to offer.

Nairobi had originated as a depot workshop built on a marsh by the railway's general manager, George Whitehouse, in May 1899. After eight years, the swamp, drying up, developed into the capital of the East Africa Protectorate. When Britain established the colony of Kenya in 1920, Nairobi remained its administrative center.

☙❧

Acquiring no other options in N'gong town, I nervously stepped inside a dreaded *matatu* for the fifteen-mile (24 km) city-bound journey. I received instructions on which number bus I must board and what fare to pay. Our vehicle, christened with gory-colored spray paint, bore the name Masterblaster, as all *matatus* wear a unique handle for ease of identification. The ride looked like a wreck; I imagined a coffin transported on four threadbare wheels.

Beginning our journey, worryingly, passengers uttered prayers, clasped hands, and fingered rosary beads as the van departed. Was this the standard? I cringed, noting the poorly welded metalwork panels allowed sightings of the road below. Maybe, I should not look down because viewing the tarmac moving is pretty unnerving, yet glancing forwards made matters worse since the madman perching behind the wheel careened and weaved over the road as if he owned the highway in both directions. Potholes the size of Texan bathtubs, as common as polka dots on a fancy shirt, provided entertainment for the chuckling driver—he lurched from left to right like a slalom skier. Traffic lights? None worked—the driver informed me that the dysfunctional poles stood as African street decorations. Junctions and roundabouts? These presented the game of the bullish vehicle wins. Oh lord, what an experience. This journey, I later discovered, depicted an ordinary day of *matatu* travel in the nineties.

By the grace of God, I arrived and mumbled the words never again. With no fixed plan, I intended to wander through the principal streets, visit a shop selling tourist trinkets, take lunch, and purchase snacks. Curiously, no one ate desserts at the camp, and possessing a sweet tooth, I suffered.

Walking along, I could have been a 19th-century pioneer. My eyes admittedly sought out the unusual sights, but the street life portrayed a time warp experience. Several women, rather than wear skirts, trousers, or dresses, swathed themselves in cuts of colorful printed cloth as if wearing a bath towel in public. I marveled watching ladies balance clay urns of water precariously upon their heads. Others strapped bundles of firewood onto their bodies that I might struggle to lift. I noticed one man with elongated earlobes had tied his stretched and sagging lobe-skin into knots, and he accompanied a lady with a small wooden plate inserted in her lower lip. She exposed a generous amount of body flesh and displayed skin lacerations over her chest worthy of an art exhibition.

Donkeys and citizens alike pulled cranky wobbly-wheeled carts carrying all manner of items. The traffic stood as a horrendous jam of sooty disorder, and from what I perceived, the pedestrians possessed no rights at the crossings. Although I searched, I did not spy a solitary foreigner—I guess the *matatu* had not placed me in the tourist zone.

Strolling along River Road entranced by the sightings, a hive of activity hooked my eye. A boisterous crowd of fifty-odd people yelled at the top of their lungs, huddled tightly in a circle. Moving closer, I queried the nearest man,

"What is going on?" As I peered, I thought I identified a dusty limp body on the ground. The youth, lassoed by two car tires, lay soaking in blood beneath a sea of kicking legs. A body beat so severely it no longer cared to move.

"He is a thief. After they conduct the beating, he will burn up in those tires," replied the fellow by my side. What? How could these two places co-exist? A few miles separated the tranquil undulating hills of N'gong from this scene and its medieval form of street justice. Instinctively I strode briskly towards the crowd—I must save the boy.

"No," the man gripped my arm till the muscle hurt, "Do not interfere, or else they shall flog you too as a collaborator—it is our justice."

I had to act, do something, "Let us call the police then!"

"It is already too late, the boy is with the lord, and besides, this signals a stern message to the boys treading in his footsteps."

Once on a dare to steal a smurf in England, my friend and I were caught red-handed. But the irate shopkeeper did not scream for mob violence. Alternatively, he reported us to a corrections officer. The sergeant issued a lecture I already knew—you must not steal—then to shame me, he rung my dad. The dead boy looked the same age as me when I stole that toy. Had these kids received similar values and lessons? He without sin cast the first stone, and no way could I believe I stood alongside a band of angels on River Road.

Horror-struck and sick to the stomach, I ambled on wondering what exactly his heinous crime had been—dressed in rags, I surmised a hustling pickpocket. Another sad encounter happened when I stumbled upon a footless disabled man. Chatting over a soda, he admitted his family dissected those body parts, "Being birthed a cripple and unable to work, my parents deduced that begging would be best." But because panhandlers were aplenty, he must attract attention and soften hearts, and this is how he ended up owning eye-popping stumps.

Repeatedly, I saw dire circumstances and blessed the lucky stars that I escaped from a life born into destitution.

Clusters of children, looking as young as five years, hobbled along the streets in rags and torn tatters. They paused only to gather discarded food scraps, chucking the edibles into their mouths. Glue sniffing bottles, like a tusk to a walrus, stuck to the lips of others—kids too young to comprehend the concept of a stolen childhood. Wow, the people preaching how humans are created equally should take a ramble along the Nairobi avenues. After a couple of hours, I had had enough and headed to creep back to my sanctuary in N'gong and risk stepping inside another dreaded *matatu*.

Aboard a battered vehicle—caught in the moment—I barely noticed the suicidal driving habits of our chauffeur. I am not so naïve and still recollect the Amsterdam days and scrounging for a plate of food. However, what looked like a continuous cycle of poverty and its byproducts, left me emotionally shattered in Nairobi. What would happen if I lived in this city where petty theft claimed a life? Poverty had been a picture I could step near then retreat from, but today, the deprivation shook and rattled my body for the first time as if I sat locked inside its cage. Only when N'gong's nature replaced the harsh mechanics of the streets did I relax as if I had slipped out of a straitjacket.

I hoped I could forget the scenes. Yet, it is ironic—the more we crave to forget, the deeper we remember. I feared the image of that poor child would haunt me forever. Staring at the passengers in the overcrowded *matatu*, beads of sweat trickling down anxious faces, I knew I was living in a reality out of all but the wildest of imaginations. Still, a routine life that nurtured the swiftest runners in the world.

Noel had not included this gem in his travel guide. I arrived in Kenya to acquire running tips, never guessing I might associate with civil disorder. I had witnessed many reasons why the Kenyan runners are the best, but traveling back to N'gong, I recognized I sought the superficial wishy-washy answers.

Beyond the measures applied by sports scientists when deliberating upon which attributes constitute the make-up of a champion lay an abundance of grit to navigate through the quest for basic daily survival. Without exceptions, the elite runners I encountered all originated from families of acute poverty. Hunger, desperation, and a lack of viable options fuel ambition, and the question was not how they ran but why they ran.

CHAPTER 6. 1995

KIBERA, KOITALEL, AND CROCODILES

Mistakes are the portals of discovery. – James Joyce

Have I won the jackpot? Darting through Zambia two days later, a district of N'gong, I completed a rewarding ten-mile (16 km) tempo with the world cross-country champion, Paul Tergat. This sweaty vacation was brilliant; the Berk was correct, and Kenya played out to be a runner's nirvana. Besides famous athletes for training partners, I formed friendships in the administration and the coaching fraternity. Today I could overfill a book regarding subjective experiences. But instead, I will whittle down the holiday to three incidents. Episodes that altered my perspectives and chartered a future. Neither of the three took place at the camp, and the initial incident occurred at a location that has today become the charity center of East Africa.

Following an afternoon run, the easiest session of the day—if a third run classifies as easy—an athlete pulled me aside. Would I visit his family? To enjoy a cup of tea was his friendly request. Why not and I eagerly accepted the invitation. The next day Michael sought confirmation.
"You are coming, right?"
"*YES*, as yesterday and I am looking forward to it," I answered, slightly irritated he doubted my word. Yet Michael explained that

he had met another *m'zungu* in town, welcoming him home, "Mom invited the neighbors and purchased biscuits (cookies)," he explained, pronouncing the word bis-kwets. Disappointment washed each letter of his speech as he resumed the story, "We brewed a big pot of tea, waiting all day long, but he never arrived." He spaced the words all day and long, with such emotion, I could imagine myself lingering beside the family members.

A national holiday approached, and the athletes scheduled a short break to visit family members. Ready to atone for the tourists who dropped the flag, I volunteered for a homestay—besides, I wanted to explore Kenya. Sightseeing sounded like fun. The name of his town, Kibera, indicated nothing, but I guessed we would be traveling all morning. Wrong, boarding the *matatu*, Michael surprised me by saying his home sat inside the heart of Nairobi.

Until now, he had failed to mention the location is the largest slum in East Africa. What? Had I willingly agreed to camp inside a slum? Now I understood why the visitor remained a no-show.

Traveling over five continents, I have witnessed poverty, but what I encountered in Kibera shook my senses. Walking into a sprawling mound of makeshift mud and iron sheet shacks, stacked closer than rusty-colored dominoes, I wondered how on earth did this jumbled mess even function? Later I discovered that Kibera constituted 700 acres of land, but on this day, the labyrinth of squalor appeared to lead to the moon. I became fascinated with my surroundings in a way only a man who was able to enter and exit, at his own will, could be. What happened after pouring rains? I dreaded to imagine the devastation of even the feeblest of mudslides. These living quarters promoted a building like The Shade to The Ritz Carlton.

We forded a stream of clogged sewage—I squirmed, ogling trickles of water separating a sludge line of exposed feces. Each clearing along the rows of huts stored piles of stagnant trash, blocking any obvious path. Looking closer, I realized I stared at the garbage of the poorest of the poor. Litter combed through so thoroughly not a single shred could be of use in any situation. Shivers tingled down my backbone, watching an elderly crooked man coated in dirt and charcoal scraping through the muck. He foraged out a blackened cabbage leaf from the mire and stuffed the food into his mouth.

Inside the maze, I saw no clear roads or streets to direct our route; the further we progressed, the more the footing worsened. Although Michael hopped from stone to stone as an expert might, I slipped and slid like a drunkard, and in what was the question. I kept treading in the wrong puddles. The watery silt, often ankle-deep, produced a nauseating odor of human waste. My sports socks became tinged in a chestnut slime.

Tramping along, I ticked with ideas concerning resettlement, drainage, and biogas opportunities. I thought of the untapped human potential of people who survived here and longed to hear their solutions for change. Rather than seeking an immediate exit plan, I bubbled with questions ready for Michael *if* I became confident of the footing. What systems could mitigate the risks of diseases, improve health conditions, and reduce the chances of escaping from a full-blown epidemic that might wipe out thousands in a day? What parasites thrived and wriggled in the mud below, and what harm did they cause? How could I help?

Born in Kibera, Michael narrated his parents traveled into Nairobi seeking jobs but discovered unemployment and could not afford the city's exorbitant rents. Hearing of a zone where others from their region sheltered, they migrated as a temporary measure. Although a minority of residents retained regular work, Michael claimed the majority here were day-to-day survivors, "And most of us do not survive long. The average life of a Kiberian ends before thirty years."

Now I instantly recognized why he threw every ounce of his energy into running from this reality. But what truth did I run from? Middle-class blues? Each step evoked a deeper and more profound understanding of the psychology and the hurdles of abject poverty, which traps and hinders too many lives. Hustlers selling a single tomato, lumps of charcoal, an item of clothing, or what looked like scraps of a fried fish could never hope to climb the greasy ladder out of Kibera. Stories here are not working towards the upcoming holidays or saving for a smart outfit, but instead of outlasting the week.

We arrived at the place Michael's parents called home. The welcome was genuine, enthusiastic, and extremely loud. Inside the shelter, the putrid smell of the paraffin lamp fumes burning those oil-soaked wicks was, for once, appreciated. They partially blocked the nauseous stench of the rotting garbage and pools of sewage. Although the hut carried the dimensions of a decent-sized British living room, around fifteen of us managed to cram and settle by the central cooking space. Neighbors elbowed in as others darted out. A foreigner symbolized a novel attraction.

Doubtful of our arrival, Michael's mother, dressed in a colorful *kitenge* (dress), scurried to simmer a pan of water. But, concerned about the risks, I offered to order a crate of sodas. I feared the task of stoking the fire would roast us alive, and I dreaded to imagine what form of liquid sat inside the pot. I learned a common reason for hospital visits from Kibera residents, an area that serviced no medical clinic, legal electricity, or running water, was due to cooking burns. The stove, fueled by charcoal, was a handmade perforated cylinder the size of a three-gallon can of paint. A larger aluminum pan balanced precariously over the flames presented a time bomb. I could see how kids, shoving siblings in play, might easily knock and spill the containers filled with scorching oil or scalding water.

The cramped earthen room functioned as a sleeping, living, and kitchen quarters. Only the front-facing wall included a window, and there a three-foot square hole, chiseled out of the mud, sufficed. No pane of glass filled the skylight, but a couple of ill-fitting wooden shutters served to restrain the numerous passers-by from peering within. Clever recycling ideas inside the house, like plastering newspapers as a wall covering, ensured no discarded items went to waste.

Later, consuming dinner, we enjoyed the foodstuff eaten at the camp: Ground maize boiled in water for a good twenty minutes to form a stiff carbohydrate, slightly resembling mashed potatoes called *ugali,* and *Sukuma wiki,* a finely chopped kale flavored by adding shredded onion, tomato, and salt, to complement the starch.

At nightfall, the women prepared a bed of sorts on the packed mud floor, and due to my presence, departed to lodge with neighbors. Three men and I shared two mattresses jammed together to function as a double bed.

A torrential downpour thumped throughout the night. I woke early, requiring the toilet but did not want to disturb the hosts, and even so, where should I go? Raindrops hammering on the tin roof like sticks on a snare drum did not help bladder matters. I chuckled, not believing I lay here on a holiday excursion.

By daybreak, I felt recharged with a venturesome spirit. What tourists would gain an insider's view like this? Little wonder, I did not meet a single foreigner in Kibera. Surprising myself at breakfast, I announced I looked forward to spending the next few days here. Had I sighted the pit latrine—a miserable wooden hut with a concrete slabbed floor, caked with dried feces around a dark hole the size of a cup saucer—I may have expressed a conflicting decision.

The shantytown served as my home for the week. Like a sponge, I tried to soak up and comprehend how this society functioned without income and support. In an unexpected fashion, my unscripted visit revealed a desire for my involvement in community work. The resilient souls of Kibera did not allow birthright to drag them down. Nobody I met felt pity or crooned about an unfair life. At the crack of dawn, slum dwellers awoke, making the best of a grim situation. They squashed the undercurrent of the social critique that often accuses these folks of being lazy idlers as this collective burst into a beehive of activity. People determined to conquer the overwhelming odds against them, not wistfully praying for a transformation—hands clamped on a bible—but acting to improve their circumstances. Poverty in life did not lead to poverty of the soul.

But how could an ordinary guy like me galvanize support to help these folks? A decade ago, as Sir Geldof implored the world to pay attention to a raging famine in Ethiopia, I thought only of myself. My teenage anxiety wondered if I purchased enough snacks for the sixteen-hour music marathon viewing party at a friend's house. Clearly, I missed the boat aligning with world poverty. So, what would Bob do? He had dialed influential friends, like David Bowie, famous people. This issue swallowed an ordinary person like me, but if I bumped into any ABBA or Roxette members, or Mr. IKEA, Kibera would be a conversation starter. What an experience I had—and never could I have guessed I would have volunteered to scrub those communal toilets.

ತಾನ

Back at N'gong, friends offered a variety of options for Christmas. Being the lone foreigner sparked some advantages. A runner I nicknamed Hez suggested we travel to his village near the Masai Mara, home of the Maasai. Before leaving Sweden, I purchased an SLR 35mm camera—now came the chance to frame the exotic wildlife. Unlike a fashion photographer who employed make-up artists, wardrobe designers, hairstylists, and scene composers, the jungle cameraperson had it easy, point and shoot. Watch out, Mr. Attenborough, because the competition is here.

When traveling to this rural site, after enduring a torturous five-hour *matatu* ride over tarmac and dirt roads, followed by a bony bicycle taxi through rutted fields, we tramped the last few miles on foot. To pass the time, I questioned Hez what role models inspired the Kenyan runners—any childhood idols? Had he heard of Kit Carson? Chortling, Hez explained the tales he remembered were fables of animals from his mother or aunts.

"But actually, I did have a hero, probably the reason I started running now I think about it. A man called Koitalel Arap Samoei." He then related a story of the first-ever known Kenyan runner. "We have around forty-two tribes. Koitalel was of my father's tribe, a Nandi. Most runners, the familiar names everyone knows—are Nandi. Inside the tribes are clans, and Koitalel represented the leader of the Talai. We call this chief an *Orkoiyot*—a man who foretells the future, speaks of destiny and predicts the outcomes of battles."

He continued, "One day, Koitalel prepared his followers for the worst because he had beheld a vision of violence. The ruler saw a black iron fire-spitting snake crawling through Kenya and causing disruption. Prophesying, he foretold his own death would come about after wrestling this wretched snake. He explained that two fig trees would sprout at the spot where he fell, and only when the full-grown branches intertwined would peace return. As the plant grows gradually, he warned people, 'We are in for a long grind.'"

Hez paused for breath, "Koitalel's dream materialized—the British invaders ventured to East Africa, grabbed our lands, and began laying railway tracks dividing the Nandi pastures. The *Orkoiyot* gathered his troops and, in the black of the night, uprooted those irons. To escape from the Britons' sophisticated weaponry, the Nandi, armed with primitive tools, ran like the clappers covering vast distances. For a decade, the British could not fathom this vanishing tactic." Hez glanced across to check he still held my attention.

"Bamboozled, a British Colonel named Meinertzhagen requested armistice talks with the night runners. But it was a trap, and the fat cats shot the *Orkoiyot* at close range. Koitalel fled, but a second bullet proved fatal." Hez explained two trees did grow where Koitalel fell, and I could not help but blurt out, no pun intended, "Maybe planted?"

"Who knows, this story is ancient—ninety years old. But decades later, in 1963, finally the branches intertwined, and as they did, the British conceded, and we gained independence. Coincidence? No, destiny came true."

Hez and his age mates worshiped Koitalel, "When dashing to school, we wore the legs of the old freedom fighters."

I longed to hear more, but unlike Kit Carson and his numerous comic book adventures, the story ended here. Nevertheless, I hoped to hunt out those knotty fig trees, see the spot since the location stood a scant thirty-six miles (60 km) from Eldoret.

Initially, this Christmas vacation had been unadventurous, a little dull after Kibera's vibrant swing. The size of Hez's community did not warrant a marking on any map. He dwelt inside an enclave of thirty-odd mud and thatch huts structured upon a canvas-flat scorched sepia-colored soil. This cluster, far from the closest town, projected the energy of a sluggish, slow drip. Thistles and thorns wavered in a slight breeze, yet little else moved. With bounteous land available, each home, nicely spaced, enjoyed surrounds of unkempt scrub and barren nature reaching out as far as the eye could see. If I searched for washed-out cowboy homes, I had discovered an African hut version of the Little House on the Prairie.

Approaching Hez's abode, his bride waddled out to greet us, and I struggled to conceal my surprise. Out plodded an adolescent girl with the face of a thirteen-year-old. I learned she schooled for four years before her dad had unambiguously cast her future by accepting eight cows in return for her hand in marriage. Several men, Hez's age, had wed young wives. He described fathers became eager to offload daughters for two reasons. A cow generated an immediate income, and as years passed, the chances of unintended pregnancy, family scandal, or odd behavior could slash a girl's worth.

"Pauline was reasonably priced. Had she been further educated, her father might demand twenty cows," he explained with a wistful grin. I could barely imagine the frowns if I presented a preteen as a bride and then the glares when proclaiming, "The gal's a bargain, and she only cost me eight cows!"

Enjoying visitor status and being excused from all chores, this holiday promoted running, resting, and little else. Each morning, we explored never-ending dirt trails, dashing across breathtaking savannas before returning for breakfast. Following our exercise, we slouched in the sun and chin wagged with the neighbors, drinking endless cups of tea. As they spoke no English and I crucified basic Swahili, these talks led nowhere. After two days, going off my rocker, I sorely missed the camp chitter-chatter. Christmas approached, and I hoped for a memorable occasion beyond saturating myself in tea to celebrate. What could I do to defeat the boredom, hiking? Any option would be better than repeating yesterday's small talk. Therefore, on the 24th of December, I bid goodnight to Hez, having no intention of sharing greetings at daybreak. My second experience was hours away.

I rose just before dawn on Christmas Day, left my little hut, and crept through the fields aiming to capture stunning landscape shots with my camera. After ninety minutes of jogging, I spied a Maasai vaulted upon a pile of grayish rocks. Straight as a spear, an ochre tinge coloring his braided hair, he looked magnificent. Like an ebony mirror, his skin gleamed, and I presumed in Vaseline. As I stepped closer, an aroma rekindled childhood memories of farm visits, and I would discover Maasai often slather their skin in sheep fat. He wore the traditional crimson *shuka* (robe), just like the Eldoret Maasai pictures I observed as a child.

An idea popped, and I rapidly removed the camera. This pose could herald my breakthrough as a famous photographer. I had spotted Maasai's in Nairobi hawking herbal remedies. But here, with the backdrop of his vantage point, cerulean skies, and the dawn's ripple of pink cumulus clouds clashing against his traditional attire, it portrayed the perfect shot.

Exchanging greetings, and thankfully not the customary spit-in-the-hand salutation the runners at the camp had forewarned was the Maasai tradition, he voiced a question. What the heck was I doing in these outlying parts?

"You never see the white man alone, and you are on foot too," he chuckled. He stated Caucasians inevitably traveled in groups inside comfortable jeeps. I explained as a poor vehicle-less tourist that I searched for a unique experience to commemorate Christmas, nothing more. After pausing, he asked, had I seen crocodiles? No. Would reptiles suffice? Yes. He knew a river where foreigners gathered, for unknown reasons, to stare at these pests. Great, now I owned the Nat Geo cover picture; the croc-

shots could embellish the middle pages. Life as a photographer was easy—in 1/1,000th of a second, I created a sellable masterpiece. Riches were coming!

As they say in Kenya, we footed it, moving by a combination of jogging and walking. Half an hour later, crouching on top of a high riverbank, I spied hippos wallowing in muddied, brown water. Engrossed in perfecting my camera skills, I failed to identify the crocodiles until the Maasai pointed them out. Those prehistoric reptiles slunk farther up the river. The crocs looked docile, inept, and depressingly, like unphotogenic sleeping logs. Was it possible these guys shifted as fast as I had observed on nature programs? Should I fling a stick to induce an underbelly action picture?

My impromptu tour guide grinned, "You are enjoying. Do you like seeing elephants too? I know Elephant place." Maasai habitually live nearby, and inside the game reserves, I could be in for a treat—what a terrific way to view the wildlife, in grace with the landscape. The irony is back in Europe, people peer at wild animals behind bars in zoos, yet here in exotic Africa, animals glare at humans caught inside movable metal cages.

To discover the giant mammals meant traversing the river—the same waters with savage crocodiles? Are you kidding? Back-peddling, I wanted no part of this stupid scheme. The Maasai slanted his eye, "I cross many days. I safe. Walk careful and not stopping. Not making splashes, and be slow because splashes making changes, and he will come fast for you."

Well, if the method worked for him, as his bare legs bore no scars or teeth marks, I thought in for a pound, in for a penny. Why not. We hiked upriver to the narrowest crossing point, far from where I spotted the crocs but nevertheless, my nerves danced in flames.

Gingerly, I inched into the murky river after removing my shoes, but there must have been a chemical reaction because as soon as the water touched flesh, I dashed forward. Sprinting like Usain Bolt, the world's speediest man, I reached the far side in a flash. Yet, I lacked Bolt's silky stride. Instead, I leaped like a flea in a circus ring. Using a finger and nail, I clawed myself to safety, clambering up the riverbank—thank goodness I survived. Glancing behind with a panting heart, I saw the Maasai, looking surprised or angered at my antics, now splashed and stirred up the sediment in the waters behind. He was none too pleased,

"You waking the waters," he cried, "causing risk. Now they watch you, move from the river edge." Although a little ashamed, my reflex action resembled that of a sensible man—he would do well to take a lesson from me. But the Maasai harbored no grudge. He shrugged off the cowardice and directly began rummaging in the bushes, "Look for long stick," he called out.

"What? Why?" I cried out. To my shock, the branch functioned as an insurance measure against lions. Lions?

"When walking," he explained as if discussing the price of green tea, "if seeing lion, stand tall. Wave this stick high. You see, in sunshine, lion not seeing sharp, but seeing tallness. Now, we giraffes. Giraffes strong kick."

Undoubtedly, I needed to escape from this lunatic. But as the croc-infested muddied waters offered the sole option for retreat, I remained stuck.

Maasai's, I read years ago, unlike me, did not fear the king of the jungle. At one time, the custom stood for junior Maasai to slay a Simba to demonstrate their bravery. But, acting in self-preservation, I hunted for an intimidating length of wood. Although cumbersome to carry, maybe his theory worked? Should I include sound effects too? Mooing for a cow, but what noise for a giraffe? I asked and received disappointing news.

"This giraffe, he is silent," responded my friend.

My luck, the first wild animal I chose to mimic, was mute. Thinking on my feet, I conceived a clever scheme—I figured if he desired to portray Tarzan, fighting the beast mano a mano, I should be willing and able to harness my talent for running in the opposite direction. Looking at his clumpy sandals versus the fine Nike's, I could guess who would fare better. But as I hesitated to think, didn't lions hunt as a pride? Oh, Lord.

The Maasai now explained how to track elephants. The job

involved scouting for a trail of poops or a path of destruction. What an outlandish Christmas—I played Indiana Jones, except my jewel represented a pile of elephant dung.

We traipsed for miles before spotting a modest herd. As the Maasai indicated, those trunked giants performed an excellent job in destroying and uprooting the shrubs. The wind blew in our favor allowing us to creep close and trail the Heffalumps for a pleasant half-hour. I knew editors would clamor for these authentic shots, and I might commandeer the entire magazine.

Time flew by, and I needed to head back to the tea village. I had my fill of elephants and promised to visit in the future. Besides, hunger cramped my stomach. The Maasai, who refused to stop walking, wished to safari further. He placed his hand inside his weathered *shuka*, "No, walk more, I have the food." Underneath the grubby shawl, he pulled out a cloth folded into an improvised pouch. Inside the material—moist from his sweat—lay one large chapatti, and he graciously tore the bread in half, offering me the more generous portion.

Strange how an appetite can suddenly vanish. But at this moment, he hunkered down, and his eyes widened like saucers. I peeked, dreading the worst. I recognized nothing of alarm, but far off, up a shrub-less tree, I would glimpse what had captured his attention. Only after I utilized the telephoto lens of my camera could I identify that blob as a beast.

"Lucky, lucky seeing leopard," wailed the man owning the outstanding eyes. He spoke as if we were birdwatchers, spying a rare woodpecker. It did not sound like fortunate news to me. Thank goodness, leopards are solitary creatures and nocturnal hunters. But in any case—Nikes do not fail me now. Should the Felid as much as blink in our direction, I would dash a hasty retreat. Nervously I captured the brute on film, but more than ever, I longed to return to the uneventful life in the village and pubescent Pauline's scintillating gossip. Consuming tea offered a better option than wrangling a leopard.

"Time to go as my hosts will be worried." I reasoned, fearing the current treacherous situation, "They don't know where I am. I could not leave a note. There were no pencils in the hut,"

The Maasai, hypnotized by the leopard, continued his gaze whilst the animal slithered down the trunk and slunk into the camouflage of the foliage. Seconds later, I heard the rumble of a car engine. Hallelujah, what luck to see a safari vehicle approaching 300 meters (328 yards) ahead. They must be tracking this big cat.

I yelped, screamed, and leaped high to engage the passengers' attention. The Maasai possess innate jumping skills, but I assure you, in these desperate times, I gained the legs of a Kangaroo. The tourists' vehicle quickly spotted us. The cavalry had arrived, and the driver cut the diesel engine. I hollered, yelling like a crazy man, "Help, please help!" And I threw in a Happy Christmas in case the white travelers held a grain of spirit and charity in their souls. A couple of the sightseers poked their heads out the car windows, pointing their long lenses in our direction. But to my amazement, when we dashed to within one hundred meters (109 yards), the trekkers sped off, leaving us stranded.

In disbelief, trapped under the burning sun, I muttered, "On a day like Christmas?"

Later a reflection struck, I dropped the menacing stick, but I wondered, did he brandish his? My troubles continued as although the Maasai are notable trackers, I selected the one directionally challenged warrior. Aimlessly wandering, the hours flew by before we eventually relocated that Crocodile River. This time, as the copper sun slid into the earth's crust, I calmly navigated the waters. Tired and starved, I cared little for crocodiles' teeth. The Maasai nodded his head, smiling in approval as if at least I had learned one lesson this day.

Parting ways, I took a shortcut over the hillside, which had become familiar from my daily runs. In rural Africa, when darkness arrives, the moon and the galaxy of stars emit ample light. I jogged with haste, eyes to the bushes, cautious for any nocturnal creatures. I still had a couple of miles footing when the amber flicker of a paraffin lantern broke out of the navy-blue veil. A shrill child's voice, hidden from view, cried aloud, "Jesus, Jesus is coming, and on Christ-mas night, *He* has arrived!" I should add my dirty-blonde hair, flopping to the shoulders, dangled in messy straggles. My shirt, torn from catching thorns and prickles, revealed patches of flesh. Even in the remote bush, Christians had imposed their impression of a thin pale, emaciated Jesus. Now it appeared to the child that *He* had arrived upon Christmas Day.

Half dragged, semi-escorted, by a score of squealing kids, I entered into a community clearing. Chants and whoops announced, Jesus is here—the cries alerted the elders who hurried out to see what the ruckus was. The adults too approached with open arms—Africa again taught me humility, empathy, and above all, a sense of belonging. Each location offered novel sights, but the rich hospitality remained the common thread. Naturally, the grown-ups grasped I was far from a godly figure, but since no other foreigner had stepped inside the commune, my arrival caused avid interest. One elder voiced a simple request, would I agree to greet each household of the few huts? Of course, no problem, and I made sure to mention if anyone had brewed a pot of the sugary beverage, please spare me a cup.

Walking around, I did not see a hint of a Western Christmas. No tinseled trees or sparkling lights shone for this community. No colorful wrapping paper lay disguising gifts, no feasting with friends, or family shows played on a TV. No TVs in any of the huts. No electricity. The absence of the commercial fluff somehow amplified the honesty of the salutations, and the sincerity, of these villagers.

Consuming tea like the Queen of England, I clasped hands with every person as we wished each other a Happy Christmas. The huts were forlorn and empty, and the possessions of the people less than at Hez's commune. In the last home, a meager heap of fusty clothes, shabby bedding, and three items of furnishings lay soiled in the brownish dirt. No mementos sat on the mantlepiece—there was no mantlepiece—and not even a solitary framed memory hung on any wall. Gosh, these folks had it rough. A shallow hole, chiseled from the soil, the width of a double kitchen sink, and lined in cloth, functioned as a cot for the family's child.

As I stood in a daze, my hosts bubbled with glee, "We are not owning a goat, as it would be fitting, but have one hen to welcome you. Please be patient. We will cook the food fast."
Shoot, this should not happen. I explained I carried no cash, or indeed taste, for the meat. Nor did I wish for the poor bird to die. The man extended both his palms before answering,
 "No money is required. Please eat as you are famished. It is a gift to us that we are able to help you."
  That they would willingly relinquish their last hen to a stranger portrayed the spirit of people far beyond my imagination. How ironic those wealthy European brothers—no doubt residing in luxurious lodges—had refused my pitiful cries. Yet these Kenyans, probably never in a lifetime able to afford a single dinner at the lodge, had straight-up volunteered to aid an unknown *m'zungu*. Their own Christmas supper, I observed, was a fist-sized plate of kale and maizemeal, and their sacrifice has touched my heart to this day.

  Biding goodbyes, I felt utterly humbled—I genuinely did not believe such individuals existed. Although appreciative of the hospitality, I experienced a tidal wave of profound sadness. Tears welled and flowed over my eyes. Would I ever open up to an unknown visitor and hand them my last possessions? Never. Even now, my notion of charity operated around helping this village *only* because of their kindness to me. What was I doing in Kenya, running, or pretending to be a photographer? Why were holiday experiences twisting into heart-wrenching lessons? I came to Kenya looking for the A B C's of running fast, not the X Y Z of humanity.

Chapter 7. 1996

SHOES to AFRICA, An *AÉROPORT* EXPERIENCE, & A SWEDISH ANGEL

No one has ever become poor by giving. – Anne Frank

How would I fare, racing with the champions? A couple of days later, back in N'gong, the team traveled for a competition. The event took place in Machakos Town, a brief drive of forty miles (64 km) east. Here was a chance for me to evaluate my form. I needed to refocus and concentrate on myself. Daily I listened to the never-ending personal problems of the runners. Could I offer a solution, support their family, or did I want to secure land? How about marrying a relative or investing in joint property? No, now presented the moment to push issues to the side and concentrate on running. I planned to run faster, not become involved in domestic trifles. Else, this training camp would constitute a waste of time.

We climbed aboard an ancient Bedford open-backed army truck, a relic imported in the colonial days, to drive to Machakos. Squatting on the unforgiving wood benches in the rear with around thirty athletes, I gazed at the countryside, hoping to formulate a race strategy. But mental preparation was impossible upon such a scorching sweltering day. Unable to settle, I chatted to Christopher Kelong and Joshua Che'langa. Both men had the same question,

'Why do you run?' The identical query I had asked myself in Kibera. I knew my answers would be confusing and pathetically weak. To feel good, or because I can travel and meet interesting people—so I can be here. Embarrassed to word a reply, I bounced the question to Chris. He replied with conviction,

"Money, all of us in Kenya are running for money. And because we have no other (options). Look around the camp; no one owns skills apart from running. None of us can establish a business; our parents are subsistence farmers, not even owning bank accounts. Villages will support you to run because if you make it, you become the bank manager. We run as it is the road out of poverty. There is no luxury to run for health or medals. Look at the last Olympic Games trials. One man holds the world record in the steeplechase; another is the World Champion, and the reigning Olympic Champion is there. Even the defending silver medalist is there—yet not one of those men wins a ticket to the new squad. That new team sweeps the Olympic podium, one, two, and three! In your country, if you are at the top, you go directly to the Olympics. In Kenya, even if you win the trials or are the best in the world, you can be omitted from the team. So, we train to win money, to place food on the table. If a medal comes our way, fine, but you cannot stuff a medal in the stomach. In Europe, you enjoy social security, food stamps, and assistance. Here there is nothing, nothing. We run to improve our life. To run for fun, as people do in your country, is not our luxury. Did you see a single fun runner on the streets in Nairobi?" Of course, I had not.

Chris cobbled his winnings from the British road running circuit to capitalize on farming opportunities near Nakuru, and his success motivated the young bucks like Joshua. When the truck lurched, double-clutching as the driver fought with engaging a gear, others complained at the jolt, but Joshua laughed. He usually had to run miles to reach a starting line. The race entry fee—of a dollar or two—always caused a problem. But today, the armed forces footed the bill. The leading results this morning would be reported overseas. Like Chris, he would then pray that a European manager invites him to events where cash, not medals, was the reward. An action in turn that magically procures a gold dust passport and fixes an impossible-to-get visa.

Phew, thank goodness I kept silent with my ambitions. My race presented nothing more than a personal challenge. Competitions reap solid feedback—was the endurance enough, or did the hills need pounding? Yet, instead of a race result, a third experience was moments away, providing the bridge to my destiny.

Despite arriving early, delay followed delay. I jogged a thirty-minute warm-up, stood on the line at ten a.m. to hear, 'Soon, starting soon.' Being unsuspecting, I completed two further warm-ups—I bore the legs of a flogged carthorse before even starting the race. Worse yet, the flaming sun, which now flowered directly overhead like a mean-eyed vulture, blistered both my scalp and shoulders. Embarrassingly, only I was bothered by the heat and the continuous delays. As a passing tourist, I should have been the least perturbed. Why did the fluff affect me? I knew this behavior would irritate every Swedish teammate with such inadequate planning, but why weren't the real runners ruffled? I mean, ten minutes late, okay, but two hours and no outcry?

A TV crew had caused the delay—now, their cameras swept the line of runners as we awaited our final instructions. The reporter paused, focusing on my legs, and I guessed my skin color to be the reason. Wrong, he filmed our attire. The lens panned from my feet to those of the fellow runners. When I glanced at the footwear of others, I recalled the Michael J. Fox *Back to the Future* Nike moment. The classy shoes stacked in rows underneath my kitchen table, along with the stockpiles of tracksuits in my wardrobe, could furnish a substantial number of the front row of runners. Suddenly, a fabulous idea popped into my mind. Perhaps these bizarre experiences of late provided backdrops to prompt a bigger action? Why not raid my Swedish apartment then donate the surplus gear to needy athletes? When the gun boomed, I grinned, imagining how I could help boost the lives of these hard-working souls. Struggling in the pack, at least I managed to keep pace with Christopher. But Joshua? Well, he won the event and soon became world-famous.

The following day, I telephoned a friend Lasse Jonsson. Could he please exercise his ingenuity to enter my building, collect the countless pairs of shoes and piles of running gear strewn around my apartment, and airmail the boxes to Kenya? I provided him with the address of the central post office in Eldoret because—*drumrolls*—that morning, I would travel to visit the fabled town. And topping it all, William Tanui, the reigning 800 meters Olympic champion, would act as the chauffeur.

Driving to Eldoret in 1995, I never guessed how the city would transform my life. Here, William and I stand close to the Equator line and, in Eldoret, greet each other twenty-six years later. The Equator, and indeed William, returns to the story in this book's epilogue.

The journey along the Great Rift Valley was spectacular, and, after a four-hour drive—glancing to the right—I noticed a circular weather-beaten red signpost announcing *Welcome to Eldoret Town*. The strangest emotion swept over me, perchance the mind played tricks, or did Eldoret promise to be more than a checklist destination? Gosh, I sounded like my parents.

Named after Eldare, a Maasai word for a place of hard rocks, Eldoret today stood as a municipality of a couple of hundred thousand people and the capital of Uasin Gishu County. The name, proposed in 1911 by Sir Percy Girourd—the Governor of British East Africa—marked a Boers' settlement, originally compromising of a bank, a drinking bar, and little else. Nowadays, the center consisted of rows of dilapidated low-rise buildings— shops selling agricultural wares filled both sides of the streets.

After waving goodbye to William, I grabbed lunch at Sizzler's café on Kenyatta Street. A random customer stepped forward to introduce himself; it was Kip Keino, the 1960s athletics star. As he ordered food, he pointed to a store close by that he owned. If I wished, I could visit his farm—*Kaza Mingi*—during the New Year, "Just find me at the shop," he generously offered. Kip's likeness adorned the country's twenty-shilling banknote (20 cents), so I yanked one from my pocket for him to sign as an '*arrival in Eldoret*' souvenir.

Although runners in N'gong had provided direction to local homes where I could reside and join training camps, I had different plans. I fancied the idea, since today was New Year's

Eve, to track down Brother Colm. I hoped Noel's friend, the priest, might be hosting a western tea-less celebration. Purchasing a bottle or two of Merlot, I decided to pay a visit to Iten town.

Twenty miles (32 km) from Eldoret, snuggled in the clouds at 2,225 meters (7,300 feet) above sea level, Iten is today a popular destination in the athletics fraternity. The excellent facilities offered by The High Altitude Training Centre (HATC), established in 2000, attract global stars like Mo Farah and Paula Radcliffe. Visitors, predominantly runners, flock from around the world to train The Kenyan Way. In the last twenty years, the village mushroomed to a town, but in the mid-nineties, beyond Colm's training group, little took place in this lost location.

At the crowded Eldoret bus station, I hailed a jam-packed Iten-bound *matatu* and paid the forty-cents fare. Once clear of the sprawling city limits, the journey traveled along a single-lane meandering road. Distance and time do not relate when driving on Kenyan soil, and the direct route took longer than expected. Sizable chunks of tarmac had crumbled away, and the road quality was terrible.

The rural scenery reminded me of motoring around Devon, in Southern England, with pastures of grazing Friesians, Merino sheep, and fertile cornfields. Fortunately, I scored a seat alongside the driver, and he provided a colorful local history of each site. A solitary hill burst like a barnacle from the landscape, and he explained the Kruger's—relatives of the original Boers settlers—maintained a 5,000-acre farm here. He stated, in the olden days, the area stood as the stronghold of the Maasai. Was this plateau the one I spied when first searching for the African Eldorado?

Arriving in Iten, which is all of a mile and a half long, we parked by a central grass field. The *matatu* driver pointed out St. Patrick's school and Colm's residence, just behind this green. Few people, cars, or buildings gave me a reason to guess a population of only a couple of thousand must dwell in this small village.

The school, however, looked to be sizable and impressive, well-maintained, and spacious. On the left, as directed, I spotted Colm's white-walled bungalow. Built by the Irish missionaries, the structures inside the compound captured a European styling. The Irishman's house sported a well-kept rose garden and tidy flower beds. I noted iron bars secured each of his windows—a measure typical in Kenya, but one that always presented a sense of both alarm and safety. Rapping at his door, I found Colm away for the day, but his staff welcomed me to sleep that night at his house.

As the sun set, the wine flowed freely, and the story of how a priest became a world-leading coach unraveled. Nineteen years ago, Colm, a geography tutor and a brother of the Catholic Church, stepped off the plane for a three-year stint of overseas teaching.

Upon arrival, he learned he would also be the school's games instructor. With zero experience, nobody expected miracles from the priest. Yet on his first overseas trip, journeying to the inaugural world juniors, Colm collected an outstanding eight medals—stunning the organizers who had not even considered bringing a recording of the Kenyan national anthem to play at the medal ceremony. No problem, as Colm conducted, the youths sang the anthem a cappella through the microphones over the loudspeakers for one each of the four gold medals his athletes earned. Yes, more than your ordinary man, Colm played the architect who made the improbabilities happen.

January 1st, the five-foot six-inch (167 cm) ruddy-cheeked Irishman arrived as his staff promised, with his thick Irish brogue still intact. Wearing a grin, he matched Noel's description perfectly.
"When José Abascal came visiting, he ran from Eldoret. Did you?" He quizzed with a sly smile, referring to a Spanish Olympian's endurance feat. Admitting I did not but sensing a challenge, I suggested he drop me tomorrow, back in Eldoret. Then, I could create a grander entrance on foot, like Abascal. Colm, with a twinkling eye, chuckled. I think I had broken the ice.

His athletes lodged on the grounds in a variety of rundown

outhouses. If I wanted, I should roam around and identify a spot myself. Was it this easy? I discovered a condemned, crumbling red brick house where Colm and the Irish Brothers inhabited until 1993. Once more, I gained the ultimate insider's view. My neighbors were world champions, record holders, and runners on the fringe of a breakthrough. How could I be so fortunate, and if anyone held the answers to why the Kenyan distance runners remained almost unbeatable, it would be the resident Irishman.

The next day, slogging those twenty-one miles (33 km) back to Colm's house practically wiped me out. We departed from Iten at six a.m., yet as the priest knew every person we passed, our journey became riddled with impromptu stops. Incessant cups of tea and a full breakfast later, it was eleven a.m. when I prized myself out of Colm's white sedan at the Eldoret post office. Imagining I would be tramping before the sun rose, when the air is invigorating, I brought no drinks or cash—this replicated the method we completed early morning long runs in N'gong. Additionally, I discovered the route was an arduous uphill grind. My Iten re-entry—two and a half hours later—portrayed a ragged performance under a belting sun that had slapped my fair skin without any mercy. However, the family-sized flask of heavily sugared tea offered as my prize revived me nicely.

The routine in Iten differed from N'gong since we *only* ran twice a day. Following the morning's training, the athletes relaxed, chatted, and performed chores like handwashing clothes or strolling to town to purchase food. Unlike in Sweden, with weekly shopping, this turned into a daily chore. Few citizens of Iten owned fridges but digesting vegetables plucked directly from the earth or drinking fresh unpasteurized milk meant we gained the maximum nutrition.

Frequently, I would eat out, but seldom at a café. Kenya is a country where a stranger can knock upon a random door, join the mealtime, and receive a hearty welcome. The daily diary maintained little fixed direction, and only on Friday did the drill vary with one firm appointment. At seven o'clock, Brother Colm would host a movie night and play a classic from his extensive video collection. The real athletes expressed no interest in Colm's entertainment unless he presented track or cross-country events, again illustrating this iron focus on running. But videos aside, at any opportunity, I just wanted to soak up Colm's wisdom—he proved to be a fountain of information and a landing hub for Rift Valley runners. Hanging around the compound, I encountered numerous running legends who would pass by on a visit, like the Ugandan, John Akii-Bua. John's harrowing story of chasing Olympic gold intertwined with the horrors of escaping from Idi Amin was so striking it was later dramatized into a BBC film.

Before long, I received notification the shoes had arrived from Sweden. Dividing the donations, I dispatched boxes to the camp in N'gong via the *matatu* shuttle and dispersed others to the training group in Iten. Lasse had supplemented with a club whip-round, and I could supply shoes to an Eldoret team. When handing out to the athletes, a man strolled by twirling a large silver Mercedes-Benz keyring. He offered a wink, "Do you have a pair for me?" How nice to see Moses Tanui, whom I met in N'gong. The bliss continued when Tanui welcomed me into his group as he prepared for the upcoming 100th Boston Marathon, a race he would ultimately win. Lessons came from the absolute best, and I could not have scripted a better training camp.

൙൞

Several times, I extended the vacation because I did not wish to step out of this scenery. Breaking promises, delaying dates, did I care I missed obligations? No, I wanted to cling onto the hands of the clock to freeze the hour. Yet after six months, biting bullets, I scheduled my return. Entrenched in Kenya, living like a local might, had been a privilege. Helping in any way possible, I donated what belongings were of use, like the camera or tracksuits, to the individuals who had been generous and kind during my visit.

Now, lugging two empty sports bags, I stuffed the flight

allowance of fifty lbs. (23 kg) of unbleached flour inside the bulkier case to allow me to cook *ugali* back home. Inside the carry-on bag, I broke knotted sticks from an indigenous tree called the *tendweet*. This wood produces charcoal I would grind with a curve-stick into the inner walls of a gourd. The next step is to add unpasteurized milk. The char acts as a preservative for this Kalenjin* specialty called *mursik*. After sitting for a week at room temperature, the liquid ferments like buttermilk inside the gourd. If drunk at bedtime, you woke the next morning wondering how on earth you might have slept so comfortably. *Mursik* is the runners' preferred beverage, and I knew I could wheedle the raw milk from a Swedish farmer, but the *tendweet* caused the hitch. I guess I just longed to take a little taste of Kenya back to Sweden.
  Kalenjin is the generic name for several ethnic groups of Nilotic people based in and around the Rift Valley.

 A rickety *matatu* transported me to Nairobi. The seven-hour trip covering around 200 miles (320 km) cost five dollars. The flat tire pulled no surprise, the vehicle swap after the engine blew like a steam train at Molo played out seamlessly, and at eight p.m., we parked at the crowded central bus station near Haile Selassie Avenue. From here, I boarded a beat-up taxi to the Jomo Kenyatta Airport named after the former President. When driving, as I rode shotgun, the chauffeur kept eyeing my shoes.
  "Those are nice Nike's!" He pronounced the word in a single syllable, unlike the Americans. "They could make changes. I will become a runner, earn money to help the family, like the neighbors. You see, I am a Kalenjin." His head nodded as if each shake convinced himself of the possibility—*if* he received the shoes.
  "They are nice," I replied, "named after a mythological winged horse—but they are my last pair. Else, you could have them." When answering, I cringed as I was unable to help. Back home, a quick phone call would deliver a pair to me within the day. What if this used pair could transform his life as he proposed? Since the Icelandic race five years ago, running for nothing more than a frivolous beer, I gratefully accepted an abundance of sponsors'

free running gear. Abruptly, an idea flashed to mind—alighting from the taxi at the airport, I handed the Nike's to the man bound by hope. How could I be so rude and not help in such a simple situation? Purchasing a pair of Maasai sandals from the souvenir kiosks inside the airport I saw upon arrival would be easy.

No one even batted an eye as I padded barefoot into the terminal. Yet, slightly uncomfortable, I scuttled like a cockroach. Clearing immigration took a little longer than expected, and when I rushed up the escalator to the departure gates, the memento shops had closed for the night. Shoot, I rapidly devised plan B—to purchase shoes at the Paris Airport. Not a fan of sandals, a pair of French duty-free ankle boots would be perfect.

I must admit entering the plane did feel peculiar, but the flight attendants failed to glance downwards and utter any awkward remarks. The hour closed in on midnight, and I dragged my jacket obscuring those bare toes, eager to jump into my seat and catch some shut eye.

At the Charles de Gaulle Airport, I switched airlines for the Stockholm flight. Suddenly feet became a hot topic. Collecting my checked luggage from the carousel, travelers giggled, and eyeballs confronted me along with snide comments. Embarrassingly, the bag zipper split and *tendweet* sticks poked out of the hand luggage like red flags over a stone castle wall. Now, using an arm to cradle the snapped branches, I unclipped one end of the heavier baggage and dragged that carrier behind like a sleigh. As fast as I could, I strode to the shopping zone to purchase the shoes. Welcome to Europe, meters from the carousel, the shoeless tramp encountered problems.

Two obstreperous *Gendarmerie des Transports Aériens* stepped forward to apprehend then escort me to a cubicle where a third officer addressed *Le vagabond*. I understood the word, but the rest of the mumbled speech might as well have been gibberish—I only grasped schoolboy French. Because I recognized the word vagabond, I placed a wad of greenbacks on the table. Counting out twelve one-hundred-dollar notes, I questioned, tongue in cheek, *"Ca fait combine un vagabond s'il vous plait?"* (How much money does a vagabond require?) Meantime, the police now mistook the flour for contraband. I spring-boarded from a scruffy vagrant to an international drug smuggler—two sniffer dogs bounced into the room. Fortunately, though not surprisingly, the hounds did not take a liking to the Kenyan flour.

The officer who confiscated my passport reappeared. After a crossfire walkie-talkie exchange, I received an escort to the Swedish plane, arriving fifteen minutes past the departure hour. Unlike on the Nairobi flight, plenty of passengers noticed those bare feet. For your information, if you want to make friends on an aircraft, do not arrive with shoddy timing, shoeless, and accompanied by the armed police. If looks could kill, I would be a corpse. Mothers with octopuses' arms shielded their tykes and jabbed a wagging finger in my direction.

Hence, much like how I departed from Kenya and landed in France, I flew into Stockholm—shoeless. Worse luck followed; a ghostly white had washed over Sweden. Engulfed in a blanket of an April blizzard, you could hardly recognize Arlanda as an airport. The saggy and colorless clouds struck a stark contrast against the magnificent vibrant sapphire skies of Africa.

After clearing the customs and hiking up the trouser legs, I exited to the arrival's platform—my mood slid from annoyed to exasperated. Tramping gingerly and shivering like a man expecting his execution, I darted to the taxi stand, ignoring the gawping onlookers. As I hopped from one foot to the other, a car stopped right where I stood. What is this stupid woman doing? I waved her away as she had parked in the taxi zone. Rolling down her window, she started yelling,

"Vad i hela världen gör du?" (What on earth are you doing).

"Oiy... Det är en lång historia," (It is a long story) I replied.

"Story? Come with me, if you are going to Stockholm. Are you not freezing?"

What a stroke of luck. Well, the majority of the traffic gravitated towards the Swedish capital. But after half a year of chowing down a ninety percent carbohydrate fat-free diet, I must have embraced the frame of a paroled prisoner from a Mogadishu war camp. Colm's scales had docked my weight at sixty-two kgs (136 lbs.), and this shabby, gaunt appearance explained why the cops detained me in Paris. Regardless, I gladly accepted the ride.

Stockholm is a picturesque capital, and I resided in Lidingö, an affluent wooded island inside the city's limits. The lady graciously offered to drop me at my door, promising it would not be much of a detour. Whilst motoring, she absorbed my adventurous stories in awe. Her impressions of Africa mirrored mine six months ago, underlying St. Augustine's truth that, *'The world is a book and those who do not travel read only the first page.'*

My apartment stood one hundred meters (109 yards) from the car park, and the snowdrifts lay as high as the car's headlights, smothering the walkway leading to the porch. I might have managed, but the kind woman insisted on carrying the hand luggage. Due to the lenient days of the nineties or the police suffering remorse, I had retained the sticks and, of course, the flour.

Unlocking the front latch, I dashed in and placed the bag on the white laminated tabletop in the kitchen. The lady did likewise as I grabbed a towel to warm my feet. As she turned to leave, she hesitated. "Here," she said, pulling off her shoes, "I want you to take these to Africa and give them to a person who needs them more than I do." With no further words, she tiptoed to the car park in her woolen socks. Standing in the doorway, staring at her tracks in the snow, as clichéd as it sounds, I thought, this is crazy—she is showing me a path.

Returning to Sweden, I now regarded the world as if wearing a chip on my shoulder. Witnessing diners wasting food churned my stomach. The stolid gardener who ignored the overflowing hosepipe as freshwater trickled down the driveway riled my blood. People in Kenya trudged up to six miles (9.6 km) at dawn for contaminated water, and he just let the tap run? And a friend whined his new Audi rolled on steel wheels, whereas his wife's model sported alloys. 'Luckily,' he snagged a new set. For me, each hubcap bloomed as the cheeky face of a Nairobi orphan he could have assisted. I had sunk into a culture-shock funk and transgressed to a yappy judgmental idiot. Naturally, with the myopic vision of a worm, I conveniently overlooked my pre-Kenya trip behavior.

Last year, I purchased a Triumph Bonneville motorcycle in England, bought for any exceedingly rare visits I might enjoy. Yet now, friends must return hubcaps? Come on, Toby, be serious. For the last three years, I had traveled extensively, visiting over twenty countries, often witnessing inspirational lands—but this trip caught me like a fishhook. Even before leaving Kenya, I longed to return to the Great Rift Valley.

Ironically, now a faster, stronger, and better runner, my energies flowed away from desiring a future as an athlete. Before leaving Kenya, I had sat with one of the world champions in his N'gong apartment. Leaning back in his armchair, cradling a cup of chai, he exhaled, "Too many chefs crowd the kitchen. Unless you prepare to give everything to this sport, then you will never succeed as a champion." And listening to the well-qualified Paul Tergat, I knew my priorities had shifted, and it was time to scat from the kitchen.

The thought of uplifting the less fortunate people of Kenya, instead of furthering myself, became an obsession. My competitive nature asked how I could make a worthy philanthropic dent in this world, and like that, the goal to be a helper became a superior dream to pursue. Witnessing the flow and pulse of life during the last six months had punctured any athletic ambitions—I ceased attending our team sessions, enjoyed a month's vacation in America purposely without my running shoes, and all but quit running. My accidental sporting career, I came to understand, played as the flintstone to discover my destiny.

Today, like years before, I always grab any opportunity to catch up with the illustrious Brother Colm O'Connell.

In Paul Tergat's apartment, the moment when he explained the 'too many chefs' concept.

CHAPTER 8. 1996-99

WORDSMITH, WIND RUNNING, & A WAY FORWARD

The price of anything is the amount of life you exchange for it. – Henry Thoreau

Smitten and seduced, Kenya grabbed me—the land, but particularly the people left a thud of an impression. Time and again, I recognize moments when individuals influenced or altered my way of thinking immeasurably, yet now Kenya, a nation, had birthed a wave of inexplicable emotions. My small act of gifting shoes was definitely the highlight of this trip. Helping out always gave me a good buzz, especially if I aided others by partaking in a basic and inexpensive act. What did the Salvation Army, or other do-gooders, say? Yes, unshackle yourself in the service of others.

In my teens, I joined the Sheffield Car Hire company and helped to hand-push an eight-ton truck from the city to the Silverstone racecourse. Gathering donations in buckets along a 130-mile (209-km) route to support the deaf community, we celebrated by completing a flying lap of the track to enter the Guinness Book of Records. Had it not been for picking up a murderer on the run and food poising for the meat-eaters, the trip proved to be a resounding success. With little cost—nothing to me—we partied along the journey, and the charity benefited. Everyone won. When the Swedish lady handed me her footwear, it was as if she stood as a reminder, 'Don't you get it, Toby? Continue what you started.' Donating shoes would be a wonderful way to assist the people in Kenya and, in turn, help myself to feel I made a small difference in the lives of others.

※

Upon my return, hounded like a national lottery winner, athletes in Sweden begged to hear the secrets of how the Kenyans trained. At probably the twentieth time of reciting identical stories, an idea sprouted. Kenyan runners are world record sleepers—a typical day includes hours of rest time. Searching distraction over tranquility, pen at hand, I filled three textbooks of observations as the real athletes slept. Everyone had unique tales, and realizing the limits of a human's memory, I wrote with zeal. Friends browsing over the scribblings promised me this was a veritable goldmine of information—why not assemble a book? Fully expecting a rejection, I mailed a sample chapter to a publisher. Could I become an author? Highly doubtful.

Shockingly, the editors enjoyed the works. Whipping out a typewriter, 'Train Hard, Win Easy. The Kenyan Way' developed into a readable volume. The slogan spelled out the ethic I first learned on the stage and observed in Kenya—practice repeatedly, and the performance will become the easy part. The title's first two words simplified the supposed Kenyan secret to success.

Barely a month after the release, the agents went to press for a reprint—the title launched as their fastest-seller. Speaking requests arose to lecture at marathons, universities, schools, and clubs. Somehow, I morphed into an expert. I even received invitations to unexpected places like Disney World for author engagements. Most thrilling was the endorsements from friends I admired. Plenty of world-class runners told me the paperback became mandatory reading. Bruce Tulloh*, an author, coach (trained

Kenyans in the early 70s), and distinguished athlete, sent an email, 'I've recently read your book on the Kenyans—really good, the best thing I've read, because it is so direct and factual.' Britain's Athletics Weekly noted, "The most complete look at the Kenyan Running phenomenon" and listed the works in the top twenty running books of all time. The prestigious Running Times magazine labeled the work 'A cult classic.' A few years later, Nike released a stylish T-shirt printed 'Train Hard, Win Easy.' Imagine my glee, out running in Los Angeles and meeting a team of young students parading the streets and wearing that shirt!

In 2010, Bruce kindly ran the original Athens Marathon, aged seventy-five, to raise funds for the Shoe4Africa hospital.

※

Although discarding Ms. Olrog's advice to develop into a focused athlete, I never stopped running. After quitting training alongside the team and attending workouts, I exercised more out of habit. I continued competing because the sport provided a convenient vessel to earn money, with the bonus of allowing me to explore and fly for free when invited to events. However, the passion of competition had vanished, and my underlining wish fell upon bolstering the support for Kenyan athletes and sending equipment overseas—everything else sunk into a distant second place.

When the weather in Scandinavia turned disagreeable, I relocated to milder climates. At the start of 1997, I drifted to Albuquerque, as I planned before meeting Noel. Arriving stateside, entering two half marathons on consecutive Sundays, I surprised myself by clocking a credible 63-minutes in each.

In the second event, running with a training partner Benoit Zwierzchiewski, we sprinted off, hollering a complete verse of 'I believe I can fly' during the first mile. Benoit practically did—after dropping me at the five km marker (3.1 miles), he raced on to miss Moses Tanui's world record by a wispy ten seconds!

Colleagues again urged I lodged in one place, relinquish

partying, and give athletics a realistic chance. You possess talent but cut the vagabond lifestyle. There is a limited time for an athlete—use it or lose it. Try philanthropy later in life *if* you achieve security and ambition first. Logically, had I listened to wiser heads, I might have accomplished both goals, but as an aimless drifter, I attained neither.

For the following twenty-four months, I sashayed right and left, back and forth, lacking a scheme or schedule, rarely staying in one location longer than a month or two. Bogota, Colombia, Heraklion, Crete, San Francisco, California, and Huancayo, Peru. This itinerary illustrates one three-month block of my life; living out of a suitcase, I had become a stranger to my home.

I extended the tradition of chasing unique Christmases and spent the recent celebrations on a Native American reservation in New Mexico, learning the Buffalo Dance and gaining an Indian name. Hey, no chance to be a top athlete, but if these travel invitations arose, let me experience life as I dreamed about discovering myself and fathomed how I might make a mark in philanthropy. These days, airports, hotels, and road maps blocked out my calendar.

During this period, I continued the boxing up and sending of shoes to Africa. Moses Kiptanui, the star who first smashed the eight-minute steeplechase barrier, volunteered to assist. As a coach to young runners, he distributed shoes to the neediest people of his region. Several supported athletes began claiming championship medals—our plan worked with remarkable results. Other coaches followed suit. On its own, the project expanded. Giving shoes to non-runners because they, like me, aspired to uplift their lives also brought great satisfaction. A transition started as I shifted more emphasis to health issues and less on performance. I never forgot the putrefied infested bogs of Kibera and the sight of barefooted youth wading in the mire. Researching, I read hookworms, which infected hundreds of thousands of Africans, attack the immune system after crawling under the toenails, causing anemia and worse rot. By advising the use of toe-covered shoes, showing graphic visuals, and warning of the risks, we could make a dent in this disease wherever we distributed the footwear.

My next issue to target? Africa's firestorm. One UN report predicted half the teenagers on the continent would perish from the human immunodeficiency virus (HIV). With scant testing, the 25 million positive cases must be low-balled numbers. Nine out of the ten countries with the highest infection rates sat in the sub-Sahara: Kenya crouched at number five. The disease, due to misinformation in the areas where we operated, aligned with people of ill morals. Victims became social outcasts—shunned from society, seen as offenders instead of casualties. Stunned, I had listened to a speech by a former African President, promising males enjoyed immunity from this virus. "Sow your seed, as it will not affect you," boomed the worrying message cast out to the crowd. Another influencer suggested sleeping with three virgins to cleanse your body if promiscuity, as he promoted, was your habit.

Combating hookworm was achieved with shoes and education, but HIV? I researched and found little preventative information in the circles where I operated, with scant advice of what you should do if contracting the disease. With 0.2 physicians listed per 1000 people, I searched for solutions that addressed the masses.

After visiting charities, clinics, and hospitals, I was shocked to find only one organization even possessed leaflets—tattered paper sellotaped to a tabletop. No printed material was available for handouts. Waiting for individuals to drop by, expecting they read the pamphlets, was not the ideal solution. Nor did it attack the stigma. How could I get involved?

The white-jackets profession in Kenya, for many, raised a red flag. Hospitals are a location you discover devastating news, contract contagious diseases, and accrue enormous expenses. Typically, no medicines are in stock, there will be zero vacant beds, and accessing treatment, no matter how long you wait, is never guaranteed. Requesting for an HIV test might unearth a vortex of problems. I realized I must reverse the process and bring the 'medical' into the communities.

I sketched out a plan. I could support established running races by adding a health package. My edge could be offering an abundance of shoes for prizes and convincing one of my famous crowd-pulling athlete friends to deliver a brief instructive message before gifting the footwear. Yes, and print *Promoting Aids Awareness* on all the race day T-shirts to help reduce the stigma by introducing the phrase into the daily dialogue. Also, I would draft leaflets in English, Swahili, and the local dialect, with facts to distribute to medical officers who would mingle with the gathered crowds providing advice and counseling. Lastly, direct people to where affordable antiretroviral treatment was obtainable.

Perfect timing for an exciting project—now approaching the millennium, I could introduce the AIDS awareness angle in the New Year. But why not also launch the new me? Had I made good on the pledge when I returned from Kenya in 1996? Nope. Of late, I duplicated the parallel pattern of lifestyle I abandoned a decade ago.

First, let me prepare for Y2K. What could be the most sensational way to celebrate the arrival of the year 2000—a scheme that would outdo not only all my friends but any person's plan? Finally, after weeks of dreary ideas, I scored a winner.

My publishers suggested I authored the second edition of Train Hard, Win Easy. Why not jet to Kenya, scribble away, and then scramble up Mount Kilimanjaro on New Year's Eve to party on the peak at midnight? The creativity of running the world's highest free-standing mountain, timing myself to crest on the dot of midnight and cracking open a snow-chilled Heineken, was surely unbeatable. Who could top that? I quizzed a fellow athlete, Simon Robert Naali's brother, "Do you think the run is feasible?"

"My friend, of course, that land is ours. We are officers of the Moshi Police, the ones protecting this mountain." He spoke with boundless confidence and promised his assistance.

Past that landmark thirtieth year, no more coasting through life—version 2.0 of Toby for 2000 would soon appear. I longed for a transformation, and boy was I about to get one—little did I know how drastically my life was going to alter.

Chapter 9. 1999

CRACKING THE CRANIUM & THE MESSAGE OF THE MILLENNIUM

If there is a meaning in life, there must be a meaning in suffering.
Viktor E. Frankl.

During the last quarter of 1999, the Big Apple appeared on my travel agenda as, after some alcohol-induced behavior, I hooked up with a lady dwelling in Manhattan. Learning of my unique vacation, she decided to tag along. Explaining the workload of running and documenting stories at the training camp, I strongly warned against her participation—this would not be a holiday. However, to my dismay, she insisted on following me to Africa.

◈

With the car gearbox locked in first, Peter Nzimbi, the driver, apologized and warned of the bone-rattling vibrations. We drove painfully slowly from the Nairobi Airport as the engine squealed and screamed. But I did not care; I rejoiced to be back on African soil. The New Yorker instantly regretted her decision. Not understanding a car is a luxury in Kenya, she complained bitterly, shaking her head and mumbling under her breath. In truth, this should be the ultimate adventure *if* you were a running buff. I kept silent—wait till she saw the accommodations. The initial intention scheduled a fortnight of research in N'gong, then bussing to Tanzania for a week. There, run up the mountain before returning to a month of writing in Eldoret. However, sharing the summiting plan with my companion, she expressed no interest in stepping one foot on Kilimanjaro. She depicted a woman who demanded to be within the arm's reach of a hairdryer at all times. She reasoned, since she would 'tough it out' in N'gong, I should concede to her wish of a beach holiday for the millennium. Seriously, what was extraordinary about a beach? Beaches satisfy the people who wish to relax with a paperback, slobber under the sun, and sip sickly cocktails—everything about a beach holiday bored me stiff.

Moreover, compromising was never my style, but, against my better judgment, I somehow agreed to a vacation on an island called Zanzibar, fifteen miles (24 km) off the Tanzanian coast.

Thus, four days before Christmas, after one of us enjoyed a superb experience training with the world's best athletes as the other person sulked and soured in bed suffering from twenty-four-hour headaches, we boarded the Dar es Salaam bound jitney. Upon arrival in Tanzania, the bus scheduled an overnight stop in Arusha. With an old telephone number, I tried unsuccessfully contacting the parents of my deceased friend, Simon Robert Naali. Tragically, in 1994, Simon died of a head injury when struck by a car. I wanted to pay my respects and relate how the cigarette-day story had dramatically changed my life. Sadly, no one answered the telephone—I felt empty at not connecting, and an overwhelming urge to turn back to Nairobi rushed through my mind.

At daybreak, the coach motored us to the coastal African tourist resort of Dar. Although the vehicle limped along—decrepit, cramped, and musty—gazing out of the windows, viewing this jewel of a country proved to be most enjoyable.

In Dar, we went straight to an affordable hostel, eager to ferry to Zanzibar the following morning.

On the tropical island, our accommodations underwent a dynamic upgrade. Stunning describes the location of The Coconut

Beach in Jambiani—built just a hop and a skip from the brilliantly blue Indian Ocean. Yet for a man who longed to run in a lesser humidity, socialize with vibrant souls eager to uplift their lives through sport, and delve into the writing project, this laid-back sanctuary bored me senseless. The upgrade did little to reduce the grumbles and dissension in the relationship; that partnership had drizzled to a complete dead-end. It was bad luck she spoiled the millennium dream, and I blamed myself for allowing her to manipulate my plans. After the New Year, I would insist she fly to New York rather than accompany me back to Kenya.

On December 27th, we relocated to Stone Town for the anticipated festivities. Lodging at the Dhow Palace, a quaint, smart boutique hotel formerly owned by the Omani royal family, we settled in the center of town. I succumbed to the reality of no Kilimanjaro, but although I would never admit it, Zanzibar appeared a suitable runner-up prize.

Stone Town, steeped in history, arched as the ancient entrance to East Africa where explorers gathered supplies in the nineteenth century before embarking upon treks to navigate and map out the continent. The pioneers David Livingstone, H.M. Stanley, and Joseph Thomson all docked here. The town's architecture is elaborate, and the sculpted masonry reflects the influence of the Arabs, Persians, Indians, Europeans, and Africans, who have all resided in the heritage settlement. Breathing in the exotic smells of coconut, a wind tinged with sea salt, and whiffs of cloves and cardamom spices from the local market, I recognized how fortunate I was to holiday in such a dwelling. Yes, location-wise, ending the century here could be described as an incontestable privilege.

☙❧

December 29th, 1999. The day's plan: Tourist meanderings in the morning, followed by a light lunch, and then conclude the afternoon with a fast-paced tempo run. Running brings serenity, fitness, and balance to my body, and a completed session acts as a stamp of validity to the day. My system operates like a dynamo, and if I do not expend energy, I explode. I have never regretted the time I spent running, and even by the conclusion of this chapter, I am sticking by that statement.

Around three p.m., I was ready to run, and after waiting in the lobby for thirty minutes, my travel companion stomped down the wooden staircase—only today did I notice how heavily she trod with her splayed feet. Honestly, I could hardly wait to return to Kenya alone and dive into the writing project.

Steering our rented motorbike, I drove, searching for a recreational field away from the congested town center. Full of tumbling handcarts, bell-ringing bikes, arm-grabbing aggressive traders, who cluttered the spiderweb streets, jogging close to the Dhow was impossible.

Speeding through town, navigating the perplexing traffic, I scouted for a park. Presently I spied a field with people out exercising. Perfect, I positioned the bike next to a lofty building because it would be a landmark for orientation on the run. The week before in Dar, my cohort insisted on joining me for a pre-breakfast jog. Disregard the irritation that I could not train at a reasonable pace, she complained from the first step to the last. The heat, the pollution, people, and the smell of the city *all* annoyed her. Listening to the prattle today would drive me insane—I advised she mingled with the joggers circling the green. To the left, I caught sight of what looked like the opening of a secluded beachfront. "See you in forty minutes," I announced, sprinting away before she could answer.

After a quarter-mile along the beach, the urban noise dissolved as the roar of the waves drew me into a hidden paradise. On the right, the immense turquoise-teal Indian Ocean glistened under the rays of the dipping golden sun, and on the left lay a thickset emerald wallpapering of flowering palm trees. The bleached sands, perfectly leveled by the waters pounding, made for a heaven-sent footing. The tempo increased effortlessly as my feet danced off the beach—every sinew inside this body synchronized to propel me forward. Two dolphins, thirty meters away, soared from the surf heading north like aqua stallions for my chariot, inspiring me to run farther and faster. After training in Kenya with the athletes who conquer the world's premier marathons, I felt I could charge through brick walls. Nothing in sport beats the sensation of racing at top speed, the glorious adrenaline surge when your legs spin as smoothly as a greased bicycle wheel.

For the last fifteen minutes, there had not been a soul in sight, yet glancing ahead, I noticed two men moving briskly from the shade towards me. Due to the excessive heat, I would have relaxed near the leafy palm trees. Surprisingly, the slighter man donned a jacket in the scalding weather. His companion bore a blazer slung over an arm. Although loathing to break the momentum, I cantered to a jog before grinding to a halt.

Taking the initiative, I smiled, "Hello. How may I help you?" Hearing nothing, I shifted to Swahili, *"Habari, unataka nini?"* The next couple of seconds occurred in a lightning flash. Exposing an ugly machete concealed under his jacket, the slender of the two crooks sprang into action. Unleashing hatred and targeting the dead center of my skull with an iron blade—both broader and lengthier than his forearm—I was under attack! Instinctively, acting in self-defense, my right hand flew up to shield my face. The blade struck with force and easily carved through the flesh on my wrist, cutting into the bone. Concurrently, the taller man, wielding a baseball bat masked by his jacket, swung as if attempting a home run. Spotting his actions, a fraction too late, his club cracked against the side of my skull bone, and I blacked out, collapsing to the sands.

I could not have been unconscious for long, but when I came to, my lips lay pressed against the salty sand. The perpetrators, squatting behind, struggled to untie the triple-knotted lace of the one remaining shoe. Engrossed in their activities, the villains were oblivious I had roused. They chuckled, referring to me as 'dead meat.' Should I lay still, wait till they departed? But what if the man took another swing?

I knew I must fight to defend my life. Rapidly scrambling up caused Mr. Machete to rise. Thrashing the blade, he again focused on my head, but this time I was alert. Eyeing the threatening metal, I frantically brandished a bloodied arm, foisting the limb like I might a sword. With the uninjured hand, I strived to snatch his wrist. Meantime, the pain of all the pains merged and swirled like one vengeful demon prancing inside of my skull.

The lanky man must have clambered up too—his club smacked my flesh. Diving and darting, by luck, the blow missed my head and fell upon the mid-back. Flinching, the strikes were a minor distraction, and I knew I needed to concentrate on seizing the machete. When the lunging blade next thrust forward, I threw my body weight against the skinny villain, knocking him sideways, and managed to grasp hold of his arm. Some frantic gripping and twisting caused him to drop the blade. Quickly I plunged and grabbed the deadly weapon. The game changed.

Each time my mother dragged me as a child to any youth activity, she noted that one day, these skills would become of value. Only now did I appreciate the fencing classes I attended as a preteen at the YMCA. Emboldened and lurching like a swashbuckling pirate, I yelled,
"Okay, fairer odds, huh?" The fight ended, but not to the satisfaction of the robbers. The baseball man castigated his colleague for releasing the blade, *"Mujinga,"* he screamed, labeling the man a useless fool, *"Fanya kitu,"* do something! Defeated, Mr. Machete spat out words in English, "Give me that shoe. That shoe is not doing you good."

Fleetingly, I thought of the irony of donating footwear, yet here I stood, life on the line, arguing over one solitary shoe. Had I been asked, I would have gladly provided the gear to the men when leaving Zanzibar. But that Nike symbolized the victory of this fight. The shoe became a friend—my partner—giving the item up meant to throw in the towel and accept defeat.
"The shoe is mine. Do you want to steal it? Well, walk forward and try." I responded, raising the blade, making all intentions clear. After conferring in garbled Swahili, the svelte man retaliated with astonishing absurdity, "Alright. But I want
that *panga* (machete) as that *panga* has a belonging to me."

Hardly believing his words, I wondered, were they serious? I countered, "No way, do you think I am stupid? NO WAY!" Cursing loudly, the men slowly began a retreat towards the palm trees. They carried the treasures of my left shoe, a wristwatch, and a pair of plastic sunglasses. With muscles quivering and the machete still raised high, I waited till the outlaws passed from sight before I relaxed my stance.

Standing in solitude, I assessed the injuries. Gore dripped like red treacle from the head and seeped out of the gash on the wrist. Splatters of blood dyed my singlet and shorts. A five-inch opening ran along the front of my hand to near the little finger, exposing white bone. How can a life-changing episode like this take less than ten minutes? An acute sickening ache pulsated through my brain. Using the left hand and a fair amount of trepidation, I touched the right cheek and brought my fingers higher up the face. Realizing the head, of all places, was fractured freaked me out. Nausea, to the pit of the stomach, provoked my knees to buckle. Incongruously I assumed I should lay on the sand and rest for a while.

Sinking to my knees and extending the left arm to support the weight, I lowered the non-injured side to the beach. With rest, I reasoned, I might recover some strength. Drowsiness, with a magnetic force, pulled me to the sands. Sleep must help, a brief nap, not long.

When my head reached within inches of the sand, a voice vaporized every thought. As if a bullet had fired, the words rang with urgency. *Get up, Toby. Do not dare to lie down—your purpose is not complete. Get the heck up.*

Whoa, what is that? Despite being alone, my head jerked to the right. But, looking for what? I have never undergone an out-of-body experience, seen visions, or incurred hallucinations, yet the words sounded like someone else's voice.

Quickly, I scrambled up. Who spoke, or did I talk to myself? Nevertheless, those words presented the bitter truth; time slipped away. Immediately a deluge of depressing thoughts brought shivers. What if I did go to sleep? Would those men creep back for the shoe and drag a knife across my throat? Did the felons hunker behind the coconut trees? Why did I contemplate sleeping? After running at full pelt and entangled in a violent brawl, my pulse should be racing instead of slowing down to restful beats. And if I did go to sleep, was that the end? Is this it, and have I lost too much blood already and would not wake up? Seeing the scarlet dribble from my body is under no circumstances a pleasant sight. A clammy sense of urgency overcame me, cold sweat in a burning heat—I desperately needed help.

Fear flooded my veins, crying for me to act, do something. I removed the stained Irish team singlet, and yes, it was a gift from The Berk. I tightly fastened the material around my wrist above the gash, hoping to lessen the bleeding. Scared, I had no idea how to halt the globs of blood oozing from the skull. What to do? Should I walk the approximate distance of three miles (4.8 km) back to the bike? But I might collapse if I did not receive assistance soon. On the other hand, if I ran, although significantly slicing time, the blood would pump faster from the wounds as the heart rate will increase. In a split second, I knew if I wished to survive, I must run to save my life.

I set off on the toughest task I had ever undertaken, wading forward through relentless and agonizing hurt. Shuffling my feet, the notion of whispering yoga Oms, with the mad hope of keeping the pulse at its minimum, came to mind. Never practicing yoga, I had only read about this method, but let me try any ploy. The excruciating pain drove me forward, and as I ran, I battled the mind. *I cannot run, but I can run. Om. I will not run, but I must run. Om. I cannot run, but please run. Om.*

It was both the worst, and I later understood, the most significant run of my life. Each footfall hit like a sledgehammer striking the bone of the skull, and I begged to know how many more steps before I crumbled woefully to the beach? A blurring smudged my right eye's vision, and tiny colored stars, like cartwheeling crystals, confused the view in both eyes. Despite slogging along the shoreline to hug the most direct route, I barely heard the roars of the breathing ocean as a clamorous droning hum ricocheted off the hardened bone inside my head. Moping in misery, I limped with the understanding I had one option if I were to survive; keep on running.

At last, I recognized the vague shapes of people. I must be close to the green exercise field. When I staggered in their direction, wailing for help like a drowning sailor, the two sunbathers stood and scampered. Looking back, I understood why. Should a skinny foreigner—drenched in blood—come hobbling along and waving a machete calling Om-Om, I bet I would bolt too. Dejected, I pressed on, relieved that I now recognized the imposing building where I began the run.

Cutting from the sands, I slipped through a patch of prickly grass higher than my knees, stumbling as the footing presented a challenge. Why me? Feeling utterly sorry for myself, I craved to slump down and cry. But with the destination close, I inched onward. Half-blind I slammed into a barbed-wire fence positioned between the beach and the building's parking lot. Straddling the obstacle with my right leg, in desperation, I forgot to lift the other leg; what a sorry state.

Reaching the bike brought a gush of relief, and only now did I feel safe. I discarded the blade that had both wounded and saved my life. Given the circumstances, I scored a lucky escape. Thankfully, the bike's ignition keys had remained wedged in my hand, as when running, I always hook those items on the index finger. This way, if approaching anyone from behind, I rattle the metal to avoid unnecessary alarm if people do not hear the footsteps. That little trick helped today; otherwise, I would have lost the keys.

Looking towards the green field, I yelled with urgency to gain the attention of my companion. She saw me, walked forward slowly, then expressed the words to the effect of, 'God! What happened?' Having little energy for details, I burbled an explanation, handing her the ignition key, and implored, "Rush me to hospital. I must stop the bleeding." As I vocalized this, she exclaimed she could not drive the bike. When would the troubles end? The parking lot, barren and deserted, offered no options. I must escort myself. Fortunately, the thieves had pinched the left shoe because I could not have kick-started the bike without my right. I know from painful experience how impossible firing up the engine is without footwear.

Unable to operate the injured hand properly, I loosened the bloody singlet from my wrist and bound my palm to the handlebar rubber grip. This way, I would be able to rotate the accelerator. We then set off on a most precarious ride. The blurs and stars continued marring my vision, and I feared I might collapse. Utilizing the white lines painted in the center of the road, I navigated the route guiding us straight into Stone Town. At any opportunity, I forced my thumb to sound the horn.

Whilst driving, I grasped onto the vain hopes to spy a medical center to halt the bleeding, but seeing none, I decided to aim for the hotel. The staff must understand what to do and whom to contact. My mind became fixated on the plush bed and the notion of sleep. Yes, head for the Dhow Palace.

My thoughts were interrupted by a man on a bicycle hollering out. The Samaritan sped up to pedal by my side, offering to guide me to a clinic. I must have been a sight to behold; no wonder I caught his attention.

Presently, he directed us down a street and, when approaching a row of houses at the bottom of the hill, signaled with his arm and yelled, "You can receive help there. Good luck."

But now, on the slope and lacking a footbrake, I did not possess enough strength to engage the front wheel's brake lever with the injured hand. Never mind, I could slow the bike by grating through the gears—fourth directly to first.

When almost stopping, I urged the woman to jump from the bike moments before I crashed into the stone building. Unable to balance the machine upright, I tumbled to the ground. But I did not care—this dreadful journey had ended. Pulling myself up, I limped towards the clinic like I might approach the finishing line of a grueling desert ultramarathon. Thank goodness I made it.

But opening the building door brought pure shock. Gray walls, yet to see a lick of paint, smoothed concrete covering the floor, and a spacious, virtually empty room, induced a near heart attack. Where the heck are the IV stands and flashing monitors, and the beds or even one bed? What of the usual fluorescent lights and the eye-watering odor of antiseptic?

Glancing to the far end of the long room, I noticed a lady stepping forward. Tall and erect, the woman held the facial structure of a Somali friend, Sahra. Clutching my good hand, she guided me to a wooden bench, the type befitting an old English country school. The nurse stated the doctor had scurried off to break his Ramadan fast, but not to worry, he should be returning shortly. Then, after asking me to recline, she examined the wounds. Fetching a tin milking bucket, she scooped a cupful of chilled water to trickle over the lacerations.

"Oh my God, oh my God." She spoke in English and pronounced Oh like an R.

"How bad is it? I am going to be OK, aren't I?" I nervously asked, dreading yet longing for her reply. She looked at the floor as if the answer lay there.

"Aren't I?" I repeated now with an apprehensive tone. Then, as I forced her to speak, she muttered two words.

"Very bad." She sighed and squeezed my hand tighter.

"But I will be OK, right?" I pressed, anxious for at least one optimistic word. She repeated in clipped English,

"You are…Very. Bad. Very. Bad." Her eyes could not maintain contact with mine. I stopped asking for reassurance. Still rational, I grasped it only a matter of time until I might pass out. I presumed I required a blood transfusion, given the amount I detected outside of my body. Yet, months before, I read horror stories of infected transfusions in Africa being a principal cause for the widespread transmission of HIV. Although I experienced a deep urge to sleep, I stayed conscious—if only to instruct the doctor, I would not accept plasma. Instead, I must leave Zanzibar and fly to Sweden. Yes, leave this was not medical care—a clinic possessing no machines? Getting home to Sweden became the focus. I knew of tourists who, when injured, received airlifts to

Europe on medical planes. The concern was I lacked any insurance plan, but I could address that issue later.

Before long, a cheerful Asian middle-aged doctor entered the clinic, delighted to discover a client. Unlike the nurse, who tilted on the verge of tears with wetness hanging like cobwebs in the corner of her brown eyes, he chatted away cheerily as he doused more water on the wounds.

"How did this happen? Have you enjoyed your stay in Zanzibar? Have you seen our colobus monkeys? Could you please lie down on the tarpaulin stretched on the floor? Have you visited Africa House?" All the words were sandwiched into one short sentence as I lowered myself to the floor. Meantime, the sister now lit a lamp, allowing the doctor to inspect the head wound as darkness fell. Suddenly, I recalled my request, "Please, no blood transfusion."

"You should be so fortunate," he laughed, inviting a view of his resources with a sweep of his arm. He added, "I certainly do not maintain a blood bank here, but I will cleanse these wounds, cease the bleeding, stitch and bandage you up. OK?"

I made the correct decision to get up and fight. Scraping away the dried blood, the doctor surmised that a stone had also damaged the skull. Who knows what happened after I blacked out? Today, if I trace my fingers, it feels like a tennis ball smacked furiously against the head but did not rebound and consequently indented the bone. Cleansing the wounds, the physician shook his head whilst wiping crumbs from his mustache,
"Sorry, no anesthetics or antibiotics. We don't even have antiseptic cream. We are on short stock." What? What kind of medical center is this?

Following the treatment, both medics advised I recuperated upstairs. Presuming the nurse to be on call, I willingly accepted. The brief walk of ten-odd steps felt like a mile, and climbing each stair took an immense amount of effort. The recovery area—it could have been a budget youth hostel with nothing but junior beds—stood dark and gloomy. My companion, wringing her hands, lurked uneasily in a space between the bunks and the entrance. Addressing the awkward silence, I suggested she return to the hotel, and she nodded. Since we constantly bickered, the thought of her lingering gave me nothing but prickly palpitations.

As the woman departed, the doctor drew the drapes, offering words of comfort, "Don't worry, in the morning, you will wake up smiling." His assistant approached and placed her hand gently upon my forehead. In Arabic, she muttered what I deemed to be a prayer before she also vacated the room.

Leaning back on the unforgiving mattress, I longed to fall asleep to escape from the incessant chamber of pain. Yet, I fell into a roller coaster of temperature change. Initially, I shivered as if submerged in an ice bath, then, after dragging the cotton sheets above my chin, I roasted in a bed of hot coals. Throwing off the sheets, I again plunged into soaking chills. Nothing made sense. Although utterly exhausted, both eyes stared wide open. The 29th turned out to be the most everlasting night I can remember. Minutes bulged into hours, and seconds swelled to minutes. With the watch stolen, I had no idea of the time and waited impatiently for daybreak. No sound slit through the silence of the night, except the deep throbs of pain beating like a bass drum inside the bruised cavern of my brain. You idiot, why did you stop for the thieves? The one talent you possess, you failed to use.

My first bodily fractures, aged eleven, occurred with a foolish accident at the theater. Having relinquished the long jump competition, which entailed diving over the stage's open trap door from an ever-lengthening take-off spot, I was determined to win the high jump contest. I decided to bluff Liam by climbing to the highest rung of a towering ladder and pretending I was willing to leap from that lofty height. I scampered up the metal steps affixed firmly to the wall leading to the theater-roof fly gallery. With scuffed shins after falling into the trap door, I must reclaim the honor of the high jump gold. The plan backfired, "Jump, three, four…" yelled Liam, who sneakily implemented a five-second time limit. In desperation, scrunching my eyes, I thrust backward.

Unfortunately, the flare of the shoe heel caught on the rung, and

I upended and plunged headfirst to the concrete floor. Several bones from my shoulder down to the wrist broke as my right arm withstood the worst of the fall. The head hit a nanosecond later, knocking me out—Liam immediately raced to fetch our parents.

My dad, after using a theater props stretcher, lay me flat on the camper van bed before motoring to a public children's hospital. Meantime, after stirring from a fog of concussion, I proclaimed a high jump victory to anyone who would listen.

My recollections today forgot the agonizing pain but recalled the superb healthcare offered. Because the fractures damaged my elbow, I heard the arm would be set permanently at a right angle. The doctors diagnosed with the mangle of breaks I sustained, that full mobility would be out of the question. But by luck, a visiting Canadian specialist, who happened to be lecturing on a modern form of traction therapy, asked my parents, would I volunteer to be a case study? Yes, what extraordinary timing. For ten weeks, I lay in a ward with a long metal rod inserted inside my elbow. Suspended weights kept the limb hoisted up in the air and forced the hinge of my arm into a healing angle.

The treatment was brilliant, and I enjoyed kid-friendly hospital fast food, the greasy fried fats that my mother forbade me to eat. A team of attractive nurses entertained me each day with get-well cards and candy arriving in a constant stream from school and theater friends, but the best news was a personal TV sat at the foot of the bed. What fun; I had never wanted to leave, whereas this African medical experience reflected the exact opposite.

At long last, a solitary cockerel cracked the tranquility announcing a bustling morning. One by one, like an orchestra practicing for a concert, the day broke open. The trundling sounds of hauled carts, the varying pitches of car horns, and a jumble of cheerful and not so cheerful greetings. The yelp of a scolded dog and the scream of a school-bound child all promised that a new dawning day had begun, oblivious to my dire condition.

Parched, I hollered, gasping for a glass of water, but no one answered. Was I alone? Using abnormal effort, I slid out of bed and gradually descended the stairs. Yes, completely alone, so I unlatched the front door to face a searing humidity and a burst of fierce white sunshine. The motorcycle lay tipped over by the wall, and the idea flashed to try lifting the engine, but I dismissed the notion, recounting how fatiguing the walk *down* the stairs had been. I hobbled off in the direction of what I believed was the fastest route to the hotel. Completely disorientated, I stopped each person, pleading, "Is this the quickest way to the Dhow?"

Alarmingly, when they instructed a turn, I could not distinguish left from right. Although startled with this queer confusion, severe dehydration caused by exercising in the boiling heat was certainly to blame. I had lost copious amounts of blood, so the problems seemed understandable. Yes, I had not drunk a sip since yesterday's lunch hour.

After questioning at least six people, I recognized our hotel. Relieved, I shuffled across the lobby. Sadly, the building lacked elevators, and I doubted the ability to ascend the staircase without stumbling backward. Consequently, using my hands and knees, I began crawling to the third floor. A couple of the hotel guests, descending the stairway, side-stepped, devoid of any sympathy, and none inquired of my condition or offered to help. Likely they presumed here comes another drunken tourist involved in a midnight bar-brawl.

The woman roused from sleep as I pushed open the door. She inquired if I slept well and suggested we make the most of the holiday. 'Buck up Toby,' she grinned before fading back into her dreams. In the past, after an accident, I knew healing aligns with patience, having suffered multiple injuries over the years. But this attack halfway across the world, lacking support, troubled me. Why could I not differentiate left from right? Sharing the uncertainties of this condition with my companion was useless— she held no sympathy for my welfare. Resting and hydration would restore my health, not her whining words. The thought of conversing, even attempting to explain, gave me pins and needles. Instead, fighting a thumping headache, I strategized on how to exit Zanzibar. Phoning the local airlines brought no relief because the answering machine stated the offices had closed for the millennium celebrations. Try calling back on Monday, January the third, a recorded message suggested.

   Later, as the daylight waned, after laying for hours on the bed watching a paddle fan turn and turn, my partner desired to purchase holiday gifts. Stating I was sick, I hinted she shop alone. Tutting, huffing and scoffing, she asked, did I not know of a man's escorting responsibilities, "Or is it your wish that I should be attacked out there too?"
   Avoiding a quarrel, I mustered the strength to traipse behind her steps like an orphaned shadow as she sought-after shops selling African print cloth. At nightfall, she wished to drop in on a tourist restaurant in town. Once seated and with no appetite, I proposed she ate—I could keep her company. But, to force her to eat alone in public was such an insolent request. Had I indeed considered her feelings? Countering, I suggested the waiter wraps the food, or we order room service at the hotel? But she insisted we lingered at this particular restaurant, else what remained the point of embarking on a vacation? Consequently, to appease her, I ingested a plate of basmati rice and sipped a glass of water. What an evening.

   In the morning, after a fitful night of chronic headaches and sharp unexplainable shooting pains, I noticed the wounds discharged an ugly pale puss. Glancing in the bathroom mirror, I recoiled at how awful I looked.
   Every day at The Coconut Beach, I had enjoyed a mango brunch with the Finnish proprietor, Antii Yliverronen. We bonded, and I had saved his contacts. I called, questioning if he knew of a medic on the island who could inspect my injuries.
   "Gaurang Mehta," he replied, "is your man, more than a doctor." Those words, more than a doctor, sounded like the helpline I needed. Straight away, I dialed Dr. Mehta, and he approved that I come directly. Fortuitously, his clinic stood on Pipawaldi Street, 150 meters (164 yards) away from our hotel. Therefore, after a breakfast of rye bread, I hurried to the office that doubled as the medic's office space and residential home.

Dr. Mehta at once examined the skull, "It looks horribly nasty. A head wound like this is dangerous and will become infected." He administered the much-needed antibiotics, cleansed the wounds with antiseptic cream, and changed the dressings advising me to fly home to Sweden for further treatment straight away.

It was the concluding day of the century and two days after the attack. Deep down, I knew both my physical and mental conditions worsened rather than recovered. I am a runner—trained to monitor bodily improvements. Years ago, before I started exercising, if I woke with a stiff leg, that might indicate I slept in an awkward position. As a runner, any ache that may impede a training run sparks an immediate health evaluation. Athletes learn to read bodily signs.

Earlier, as I tumbled out of bed, I had dressed by placing both the shirt and trousers back to front. To dispel what I feared, I re-arranged the clothes and started afresh, annoyingly to repeat the bungle. My cognitive skills matched the wounds. Yet, at the doctor's office, I kept silent about the weird mental confusion and allowed Dr. Mehta to deal with the external injuries. Back in Europe, I would address those brain issues. Besides, they could be just heat and humidity problems caused by my current location.

Before leaving the clinic, the doctor asked for our evening plans. Hearing nothing better than a meal at the hotel, he insisted we spent New Year's Eve alongside his family. Ha, I had dreamed of this momentous night for months, never guessing a doctor's office to be the chosen destination.

❧

The flavors and unique tastes of Indian cuisine have long been a favorite of mine since childhood. My mother offered free English conversation classes to Indian, Pakistani, and Bangladeshi immigrants. When she refused to accept a payment, each week, plates of colorful cookery arrived as tokens of appreciation. My body grew by devouring eastern delights, yet tonight at the millennium dinner party, my sensory organs failed. Celebrating on the doctor's roof deck, trays of cooking lay displayed for our consumption. But the spiciest of foods possessed no tang—I could have been nibbling recycled cardboard.

I might not crack open an altitude-chilled Heineken on the mountain's apex, but the starry night sky vaulted over Stone Town did offer spectacular views. An ocean breeze had swept away the day's humidity, and the moon painted the buildings in a charming silvery-blue beauty. Yet, the grinding pain was ruining what should have been a festive celebration. I remained silent, hoping not to be the party pooper and praying for an early night. Meantime, Dr. Mehta, a born narrator, amused our table with vibrant tales of Stone Town. He related how his most famous neighbor, Freddy Mercury—raised just 200 meters further up the road—always entertained the community with a flamboyant flair. "Seeing him prancing in a dress gave me suspicions about that little chap. Quite a character."

The family were faultless hosts, but by ten-thirty, I flagged, desperate for solitude and sleep. Given the auspicious occasion, I fought to be sociable and, at least, outlast the midnight hour. However, I could not—after thirty minutes, I excused myself as engaging with the trivial task of making small talk hurt. Every hour my eyelids propped open, the deeper the headaches reached. I could not concentrate on completing a single sentence. Again, I questioned why me? Assaulted for one pair of running shoes sounded like a pathetic joke.

Excusing myself from the table under the guise of a bathroom visit, I shuffled to the staircase to retreat to the living quarters. I craved a private space to be alone. Upon entering a darkened living room, I hid on the hard-wooden floor behind the sofa. As the pounding in my head intensified, I thought if I could grab forty winks, I might perk up before twelve. Let me wallow in my own misery and suffer in silence. Whether I lived or died felt inconsequential; I longed to escape from this intense torture.

Twenty minutes later, Dr. Mehta, wondering where I was, ventured down the stairs. Entering the living room, he sauntered past me as if it were a routine occurrence to discover visitors hidden on his floor tucked behind the furniture. Who knows?

Coming to a stop at the far end of the room, he gazed at a portrait of an Indian God hanging on the wall.

"There is a meaning for this. Baba has delivered you to my care on your journey," he said with his eyes locked on the canvas. Gaining the strength to stand, I hobbled over to the doctor. He clasped my shoulder and repeated those peculiar words, "There is a meaning for this—events in life happen for purposes." His warm eyes focused and now pierced mine. Sensing my skepticism, he added, "You will learn why you came to Africa—there *is* a meaning, trust me, Baba knows."

Crimson seeped through the white gauze wrapping over my wounds, the new millennium fell on the cusp of dawning, and this Zanzibaris doctor quoted a riddle? I expected a blank question, 'What the heck are you doing stashed behind the sofa? A meaning? The hacking, and my skull fracture, occurred for one reason, those desirable Nike Pegasus running shoes. How there could be any meaning in senseless violence was incomprehensible—I merely ran in the wrong place at the wrong time.

Returning to the roof deck, I patiently waited for the bewitching hour. The clock ticked too slowly. At this rate, I might die here in Stone Town.

At midnight, church bells clattered and chimed in cheerful chorus to inaugurate the once-in-a-thousand-year occasion. Flaming fireworks and screeching rockets exploded, shooting rainbows of dissolving flares falling into the ink-black ocean. I was alive, barely, and I proposed a toast to our kind hosts. Now came the moment I pledged to add purpose, but instead, I must try to cling to the threads of a faltering life.

Hours later, undressing for bed, after passing by a beachside pub—the Zanzi-Bar where I did little but gaze at the ocean and pray the tide would drag me to foreign shores—I ruminated upon Dr. Mehta's words. Did he possess such an unshakable belief, and how long would it be till I discovered this specific meaning? And if it were true, which I doubted, would I survive to witness this mysterious meaning?

Waking up on January 1st, 2000, disturbingly, the headaches spread down to the uninjured arm with a series of pulsating shooting pains. Touching the upper shoulder against any object, even the mattress, felt like a torturer was yanking my fingernail from its fleshy base. Confused, I presumed the hurt should rest upon my wounded arm. In a shiver of cold sweat and with a flurried heart rate, I dialed the operator. Copying down the digits of the British and Swedish embassies, I decided to escalate matters. The receptionist at the British consulate in Dar answered straight away. She stated the following day that a staff member would visit; perfect, encouraging news. They must follow an emergency protocol for sick citizens. Meantime, the hotel TV screens aired festivals and celebrations from around the world. The globe—minus me—savored a fantastic millennium night. Highlights from the capital cities beamed joyous faces and extreme cheer. The replays of hearing 'Happy New Year' only magnified my mournful predicament.

On the second, waking with the sensation three of my six pistons fired, I alerted the hotel staff to expect important visitors. I dialed the ferry ticket office, wondering how much time I should allow for the helpers to rush half a mile from the docks up to the hotel? Carefully, I balanced the telephone on the pillow, just in case I dozed off. The entire day I stuck like iron filings to a magnet onto the mattress, desperately anticipating a knock on the hotel door.

Phoning the embassy at five p.m., I asked why nobody had even bothered calling to cancel. The receptionist replied several citizens required assistance,
"Sir, relax, wait until your flight date. We have other business to attend to, apart from you."
"Please do not think I am trying to be dramatic," I responded, "but I am unsure I can survive till then. My flight reservation is for the end of January and from Nairobi."

Earlier, dialing up the international airlines, I pleaded to exchange my ticket, but all flights until the 15th were over-booked. Even the waiting lists bore waiting lists. The post-millennium migration home had begun. I asked if the embassy might contact these airlines, reasoning they held greater clout than me. A pause followed before she retorted, "Under such circumstances, it would not be right for us to ask." Disappointed, I found myself speechless. In that brief silence, the receiver went dead. The consulate did act—days later, they tracked my brother in England. Yet, by then, I had left the Dhow without a forwarding address.

Browsing my contacts, I recalled Alfred Shemweta, a Tanzanian athlete residing in Sweden, was vacationing in Dar. So, on the third, I telephoned Alfred, whose mother worked at an embassy, and he provided an answer—easy, request a police report. A document, he promised, should force an airline into exchanging the ticket. Receiving an established plan brought hope—I might yet make it home. Since this pain in my head worsened, evacuating the island became critical. Slouching at the hotel, going nowhere, drove me insane. Meantime my companion, having browsed the excursion brochures, now recommended snorkeling classes. Marvelous, a chance to become shark bait.

On the morning of the fourth, we journeyed to the police station as Ms. America also desired to leave Zanzibar because this holiday was her 'worst e-ver.' In silence, feeling like a spineless skeleton, I hailed a taxi as the intense outdoor heat throbbed unbearably. Trying to maneuver to protect the hurting left arm, I clobbered my head climbing inside the cab. Nothing went right. This morning I limped on the left leg as the bodily deterioration continued. My brain was losing command of the limbs as if a shadow of death followed, getting ready to consume me. No longer was it left or right decisions, or dressing, as now, even my hands failed to obey straightforward commands. I must board a plane and fly out of Zanzibar.

The ordeal at the police station was nothing short of bizarre. After waiting for a couple of hours squished on a low bench, I noted nobody received attention—what caused the holdup? Impatiently I began stalking the building. Through a cracked door, I spied a man looking like the station commander, and I must have looked desperate because he beckoned me in. As I narrated the story, the chief took down handwritten notes, berating me for not retaliating, "Had you slashed the criminals, then I might unearth these rogues. You are fortunate they allowed you to live in such a desolate place. To avoid identification, they can finish the job. Dead folks do not talk." He grimly sealed this sentence by trailing a podgy middle finger across his flabby throat.

The chief explained my stretch of runner's paradise played as Stone Town's most notorious spot—a hideout for lawbreakers and drug addicts. His idea of maiming the robbers for detection had not even entered my mind, and I cared not for retribution or prosecution. Plain and simple, I merely yearned to fly home, but frustratingly, now he could not find any official letterheaded paper on which to transfer his notes. Or feasibly, lacking a secretary, he did not fancy the effort of transcribing the records. Either way, I departed without a letter but clutching a useless piece of notepad paper with a hand-scribbled report.

Again, I felt the blood draining from my head, another failure. However, I should not lose hope—there must be a means to leave the island. But how? Taxiing home, the idea to hitchhike to Kenya occurred as I gazed at the gridlocked traffic. How many times had hitching opened doors in my youth? Why not try? Excitedly, back at the hotel, I dialed Dr. Mehta, "Kindly keep an eye on my companion as her flight booking is on the 16th. Tomorrow I am off to Kenya." How rich I felt relaying that sentence.

January 5th, 57 years ago, my dad popped into the world in Tunbridge Wells, England. Reflecting, I realized I never thanked him for his fatherhood—those endearing workings of the heart conversations speaking of deeper emotions or appreciation. Not once had I muttered that homely phrase to either parent; I love you. Only now, vulnerable, broken, and fragile, did I uncover the words that an ungrateful youth had buried. Intimate family conversations were alien in my childhood—we sported stiff upper lips to shield our hearts. Since slipping off to Amsterdam, I doubt we had spent more than sixteen days together. One day, for each of the sixteen years that had fluttered by in a flash. My parents traveled for the holidays as they habitually did, and God knows where. Like me, they did not retain a cellphone. Tears trickled from my eyes, maybe for my dad but probably for myself. Cheer up—today marked the departure day.

I hobbled to the dining room and braced for another argument. After eating, I would break the news and leave, but right now, my stomach growled. On the buffet table, I handpicked some sweetened bread that I enjoyed for both breakfast and a packed lunch. To my astonishment, after placing the cake on the plate, it rolled horizontally and then plunged to the floor. Wow, how could this happen? Intrigued, I selected a second piece and watched a repeat performance in bewilderment.

With a hand upon my heart, I believed I had contravened Newton's laws of gravity. The scientific revelation received a rude interruption as the American screamed as if the house caught fire, "What are you doing, are you stupid?" This folly, to her, was the last straw. Having lived together for weeks prior to the accident, how could she not recognize the fault? Unbeknownst, I balanced the plate at a severely skewed angle. She continued flinging her voice to all corners of the mellow breakfast room—as if the words were balls in a sling, "This is like living alongside a handicapped person!"

Nobody talked but her, and the guests wriggled uncomfortably, observing the woman fly off the handle. I, too, reached my limit, and that final sentence caused the crack. As an adolescent, I spent several easter and autumn weeks playing as my parents helped at the special needs centers called Camphill Villages. As volunteers, they taught independent living and work skills to adults with disabilities. Those folks, suffering from misfortune, became family. Her words, hurled with an intent of an insult, cemented the break-up.

Squandering no time, I staggered like a discombobulated rag doll back to our room to stuff possessions into a rucksack. I would hitchhike first to Arusha, stay overnight, then travel on to Nairobi. In any condition, hitching 500 miles (813 km) may have been irrational, but it was doable and surely, done before. Eight days had dragged by since the attack, eight days of proceeding nowhere. Time was running out, and rather than stew in Stone Town, I hankered for action. What is the motto? Yes, Just Do It.

As I gathered clothes, the lady entered the room and shrieked about the consequences of leaving. Did I understand what would happen to my belongings in Manhattan if I departed? Did I realize the depth of the East River and that possessions do not float? I cared little for her blather and continued packing. Her shrill ranting—like a train whistle inside a metallic tunnel—increased. Then, with no warning, I blacked out and collapsed. Considering my collarbone snapped, I must have struck the floor forcefully.

My companion, shocked, now grasped the gravity of my illness. Dashing down the stairs, sprinting along the flagstones, she yanked Dr. Mehta from his appointment. He rushed at once, and only when examining me did I regain consciousness. The doctor then arranged a passage out of Zanzibar. He deduced this signaled the beginning of a series of seizures—the house of Toby's body began closing its doors.

Half dazed and carted to the nearby harbor, I sat, balancing upon a raised highchair. All the color and description disappeared—but I focused on a boat, water, and a glorious escape. When the men hoisting me approached the ferryboat's gangplank, the leader at the front left slipped, losing his footing. Falling forward, with a decrepit body now sporting a split collar bone, I dreaded an agonizing landing. The pain, like pincers, spread in all directions. I should be grateful, as the wooden walkway only bruised and dislocated my nose; at least I did not roll into the choppy waves slapping the dockside. Pitifully I wondered what else could conceivably happen. Confused and wounded, I managed to stumble onto the ferryboat.

It was a far from a smooth sea ride to Dar es Salaam, and each lurch or tidal rush brought further discomfort. After embarking, a taxi shuttled us to the Shree Mandal Hospital, a charity-run institution serving the poor. Dr. Mehta knew this establishment could not heal my ailments and that I must fly home, but he planned to leave me here to rest as he organized a flight. But even if I skipped the extended waiting lists, there would be no airline willing to accept a severely injured person aboard a jumbo airliner. The risk of a mid-flight forced landing might spark lawsuits if they knowingly transported a sickly person. If I could not procure a medical plane, I required an inside connection at the airline to turn a blind eye to my health issues. The chances of flying appeared bleak, but the doctor remained strangely upbeat.

Miserable, no other word suffices for my initial evening at the hospital. With the beds packed like tinned sardines, the stinking breath of the patients—either side—wafted, smelling of ammonia, into my nostrils. The gentleman to the right, with a phlegmy ceaseless cough, and his neck cranked my way, like me, suffered a sleepless night. If I extended an arm in either direction, I could stroke the neighbor's coarse gray blankets. Surprisingly, neither patient returned my conversation, making me feel even more of an abnormality than I was.

Although a trolley's squeaky wheels gave hope of breakfast in bed, it was not to be. Seeing a client hauled clumsily out of his cot onto the stretcher, I deduced an inmate perished during the night. Did he die of a contagious airborne disease? Who came next, and how come no doctor monitored my condition? I felt like a doomed character in an Africanized plot of an Agatha Christie murder, death in Dar. Today I could barely muster the strength to sit upright in bed, and now, sporting the snapped collar bone, even scratching an ear proved impossible. Optimism failed me; I counted down the hours to my demise. At the current rate of decline, I recognized I might not outlast the week.

Of course, I had no idea the tenacious faith of Dr. Mehta was soon to save my life. This is not the outrageous claim of a pouting grateful survivor but the professional diagnosis of a couple of British neurosurgeons.

※

Bright and cheerful, his life devoted to healing, Dr. Mehta wandered door to door of all the travel agencies in Dar, believing he would prevail. "Baba says we shall find the way. Your journey is not ending. I told you, you have a purpose. There is a meaning *why* you came to Africa." His encouraging words gave me less than a little hope, but Dr. Mehta retained steely beliefs, and true conviction enjoys mysterious powers.

As I lay demoralized, a miracle occurred. At a random travel agent's office, one of many he had visited, Dr. Mehta recognized a woman. After glancing at her name badge, he spoke up,

"My dear. I delivered you into this world. Was it twenty-seven-years ago? I am a friend to your father. Today, I request a favor." What were the chances? There are over four million people in Dar. What an astonishing turnaround. Pulling strings, the lady transferred the ticket, "Though he must board as an able-body passenger, so maybe cover his head wounds with a hat?" She suggested after embracing the doctor. Against the odds, I now held a passage to England. Expressing the good news, Dr. Mehta stated with a nine-hour flight to Amsterdam—before shuttling to Stanstead—even in a pressurized cabin, there might be dangerous cranial pressure. He warned of an increased possibility of a blood clot and a higher chance of the following seizure, but these risks washed over my head in a millisecond.

The embassy, unaware of my location after I checked out of the Dhow hotel, now received a computer alert of this booking upon a British-bound plane. The staff, having tracked my brother, immediately relayed the flight details. Liam, in turn, located our parents, and as a family, they aimed to be at the airport.

☙❧

Upon landing in England, an ambulance whisked me to the nearby hospital. My mother stepped forward, expecting to greet me, but an attending doctor stated in no uncertain terms, she must stand back. 'Ma'am, this is a matter of life and death. Let us carry out our job,' she remembers hearing.

After a brief examination, the doctors deemed they were ill-equipped to manage the extent of my injuries. I now found myself, sirens blaring and blue lights flashing, back inside the ambulance racing across London to the Charing Cross Hospital. There the admission report recorded that I arrived, *'Confused, disorientated, and inarticulate. Sluggish and not conscious of place or time.'*

Despite believing myself compos mentis, I could not name either the American President or the British Prime Minister. I had reached my absolute limit but perfectly synchronized because as my body clock slowed to a single tick, I now lay inside a state-of-the-art hospital. Immediately, I underwent an MRI examination, but lying still for the scan triggered further agony. Leave alone the pains wrapping my skull, but the collarbone cried as I received instructions not to move inside the machine for a solid twenty minutes. Yes, at this stage, I was feeling very sorry for myself.

The scan revealed an enormous blood clot pushing and squashing the brain. I heard it measured a blockage of record proportions. This build-up of fluid explained why I experienced problems on the left side of the body. One doctor presented a brief on the associated risks of surgery, "The procedure is critical, but it is not without considerable danger. There is a grave concern that" I interrupted the doctor. Words wasted time—no matter what—I implored the surgeons to operate. I needed the experts to halt this incessant hurt that over the last few days ached as if a rusty corkscrew was grinding into the core of my brain.

The operation on the night of the eighth—or the wee hours into the ninth—of January 2000 returned a resounding success. Waking from surgery, the first words out of my mouth today sound corny and scripted, "Is this heaven?" I swear to God I believed I lay in a place I questioned had ever existed. Yet, gaining consciousness, to lie in a sanitized spaceship of clean cotton sheets and modern medical technology monitoring my recovery *was* heaven on earth. Over those past eleven days, as I crept closer to death, the four-lettered word life became gigantic. Nothing better than surgeons chopping your skull open for you to grasp your mortality.

What a moment to cherish, a sense of relief as if the last days had been a roguish nightmare. Titanium plates had repaired the skull, and a transparent plastic tube stretched up my nostril, down the throat, and into the stomach. A second pipe ran from the top of the head to drain away fluids. Needles looking like giant darts were stuck in my arm, and wired patches covered my body—all attached to screens and monitors that constantly beeped or flashed. Yesterday, it had been too exhausting to live, but now I embarked on a new chapter emboldened with hope and rekindled dreams. Even the gash on the wrist was a heart-stopper. Had the wound cut two inches to the left, the laceration could have severed the Ulnar artery, spelling lights out.

Doctors and nurses nipped into my room to assess the progress and boasted smiles instead of frowns. Dr. Grice, the attending anesthetist, surmised I should have endured four days, not eleven; another miracle, he concluded.

How did I survive, and how could I not draw a parallel alongside Simon Robert Naali? A passing car wing mirror had smashed against Simon's head as he ran on the streets of Moshi, close to Kilimanjaro, and like me, he had suffered severe disorientation. Then, after four days, he dropped dead. With four days being the projected number, somehow, I lived upon borrowed time for an additional week. I wondered how I managed to survive. Or, if I believed Dr. Mehta, then why had I survived?

Recently, when drafting this story, I discovered I dodged another flying bullet. Questioning Liam about this incident, below is his shocking text message reply.

The embassy telephoned, saying you left the Dhow Palace and went on a ferryboat to the mainland. The next day I received a call—terrible news that pirates attacked your boat, people were hurt and possibly killed. Since you were missing, I should prepare for the worst. Some hours later, they informed me you had just skipped that ill-fated ferry and caught the earlier one, which arrived safely. But they had no idea where you were after that.

CHAPTER 10. 2000

NYC—VENI, VIDI, VELCRO. I CAME, I SAW, I STUCK AROUND

Life is not about finding yourself. Life is about creating yourself. – George Bernard Shaw

Discharging myself early on January the 14th, the doctors warned I must take it easy, and certainly no flights for a month. Charing Cross offered in-house therapy, but I had other plans. The powers of running would rebuild my health. The sport had proven to be an escape ladder out of any situation, and logically, a fitter body recovers faster during rehabilitation; I must regain maximum strength. I identified the ideal location for a fortnight boot camp with a royal twist.

Queen Victoria adored her privacy. She and her husband Albert purchased a remote hideaway in Balmoral, northeast Scotland. A diary revealed she had discovered a place *'to make one forget the world and its sad turmoil.'* Lucky for me, my parents presently lived thirty miles (48 km) from Balmoral Castle. I caught the sleeper train to Aberdeen, and then my mother motored me to Dungeith House, Banchory. The next day, training began with a brief hike. Walks around the block grew to lengthier treks, and I progressively added distance and hills to the routine. I pushed myself, bit by bit. When I read in a book that Victoria enjoyed four-hour treks, I immediately doubled the exercise program.

Traumatic Brain Injuries can force the body to relearn balance and the bodily basics. Like a drunk donkey on skates, I acted with awkward and clumsy movements. My left bodyside continued to lug along a microsecond after its counterpart. Along with the physical exercise, I practiced the guitar each night, figuring that forcing the hands to harmonize might speed the recovery. Both my parents were supportive, offering time and space, and beautiful conversations occurred daily. Surprisingly, I discovered their relationship originated from a wager for a pint of beer and a run. Attending college, the fat dad ran a two-mile loop each morning, and my mother, a non-runner, boasted she could crush this distance. Fellow students held little faith, and pops should be the officiator. A pint at the Black Bull dangled as the prize if she succeeded. Completing the distance without stopping, she downed the beer and won my father's heart.

✼

Agreeing to be grounded for a month, I almost complied. On February the 5th, I flew to New York. Over the phone, the woman who had returned to America and I repaired our relationship, and regardless, I wanted to try living in the States. I thought if I should begin this century with a resolve for purpose, then the Big Apple, the city famed for launching thousands of careers, presented the obvious destination.

The Charing Cross doctors recommended I visit a hospital for a check-up after one month as a precautionary measure. Yet no longer under the wings of Great Britain and its gratis national health service, I feared the costs. Housing the world's most expensive medical system, the USA is not the land of the free. I wondered, did any of my new American friends possess medical contacts? Sure enough, one guy—Michele Tagliati—held the title, Professor of Neurology. Perfect, I zipped to Beth Israel Hospital, presenting my scans for a free check-up.

After the examination, Dr. Michele deduced I could count the lucky stars that I survived the incident. "But can I start running?" I begged. Getting permission to push harder than a jog was what I needed to hear, again it came with a disclaimer—okay but take it easy, you almost lost your life.

Although folks like Michele repeated how terrible the accident had been, I knew I matured from this experience. I developed an increased appreciation for the life I almost lost, and a sense of empathy, both emotional and cognitive, had drastically risen inside of me. During those dark Zanzibar days, part of my character I was not so proud of withered away, and I emerged a better man.

෴

On February 26th, 8:58 a.m., seven weeks after the surgery, the butterflies hatched. Running, the God-given talent, came naturally; simply heading out and putting the legs into motion had been an ability that seeped into my bones. But since the accident, my heart felt weak, my legs wearied, and my spirit breakable. Nerves rarely affected me, but lining up for a four-miler (6.4 km) in Central Park, I quivered on tenterhooks for the starter's horn. This therapy plan of running for recuperation had reached its examination time.

Although I introduced jogging to hasten the recovery, I struggled to increase the pace of the runs. Impatiently, I presumed placing myself in the rigors of competition might propel the body to notch up a gear. Like if a ferocious dog vaults the fence, somehow you can miraculously sprint faster than you imagined possible. My stiff shuffle, the limping leg, needed to transition into a steadier stride.

As the race began, a former Ethiopian street boy and now a professional runner snatched the lead. Tesfaye Bekele, adopted by the Norwegian government as a political refugee after competing in the Stavanger World Championships, was a familiar athlete, and I had beaten him at our previous encounter in November, so naturally, I locked into his slipstream. Immediately I experienced the free-flying feeling I enjoyed last when racing along the Zanzibar beach *before* the attack. Passing one mile in 4:40, I danced on cloud nine. Running, my healer and life director, assured me I would be okay. Although slipping back in placings, I finished in a solid twenty minutes. My gait altered, knocked out of sync, but hey, I celebrated like Neil Armstrong.

The recovery produced three steps forward, one back—the difficulties were not over. The effort at reconciling a cracked relationship with the woman was like picking up the pieces of a shattered mirror and expecting that a tube of glue could restore a perfect picture. Each day sparked arguments, and I invented every excuse to avoid her presence, and life at home turned to torment. Dragging my feet along the pavement, concocting any pretext to delay, I knew it was a bitter mistake attempting to re-ignite an expired relationship. So, carrying an overnight bag, I walked away one evening without hindsight or heaviness to begin a fresh start.

Gosh, I felt fantastic that night, but little did I realize the possessions innocently left behind would be grabbed from my reach. Money, clothes, papers, books, and medical records; all gone. Ditto the laptop, shoes, camera. Even my underwear! Ironically, she had forewarned me of that sucker punch, but losing objects like the first printed book I wrote, which had been inscribed with intimate messages on most pages, hurt.

Chris Kelong, one of my close friends from the 1995 trip, had recently perished in a road accident. His parents begged for any photos as they owned few memories. With the pictures stuck inside the apartment, I felt awful informing Chris's parents I could, but could not, help.

Losing, lock, stock, and barrel caused me to re-evaluate life. My priority must be to recover from a near-fatal head injury with no insurance and now without possessions. I did not even manage to retain the CAT scans I required for further medical check-ups. Should I fly to Sweden, where superb healthcare was available free of charge? The easiest option suggested to leave, regroup, strengthen, and later return—my former apartment stood vacant. But my entire life, I try not to go backward—I like to believe I will always go forward. When you prune a tree, trim off the rot, and the roots strengthen. Time always tells who rotted and who represented the root. I opted to blot out the experience and start anew in Manhattan A favorite quote of mine is Virgil's *Audentis Fortuna iuvat* – Fortune favors the bold, and fortunately for me, staying put opened up an alphabetic rainbow of introductions. New York City holds buckets of opportunity, and I fell headfirst for the American dream.

    Years later, I bumped into both our building superintendent, Kevin, and Alan Bautista, her next partner, who both related stories assuring me stepping out of that murky shadow proved an excellent judgment.

    Déjà vu, back to how I survived in Amsterdam; for a week, I street walked, strolling around wearing the same clothes—rain or shine. I rented an apartment on the Upper East Side from a trusted friend and fellow athlete, Mike Guastella. Having witnessed the relationship's demise, he endorsed my plan to leave the woman. Now I must fathom out how to climb back on my feet financially. Of course, running became my fallback. Dialing up Fred Tressler, a sports agent, he offered sponsorship. Within two days, a box the size of a seaman's chest arrived bursting with clothing and shoes—running placed me back in business. Not ready to travel and hardly in the best of shape, I picked local road racing events and began competing like a crazy man.

    Frequently, I raced twice in one weekend and once twice in one morning. For the first month, I had to pull up the bootstraps and economize. But a bonus to entering competitions is the abundance of free nourishment. I befriended a worker at Central Park who always set aside a sack of forty-eight post-race bagels. Then, for the entire week, three meals a day, I survived on bread. By Wednesday, the dough was less tasty, and on Thursdays, I resorted to toasting. Come Friday, and I loathed bagels. Yet a fresh batch on the weekend reset the taste buds.

    Clouds in Manhattan contain unexpected silver linings—this deep submersion in local competitions made a name for me opening up a corridor chock-full of prospects. In today's Internet world, many athletes promote their own articles, but in 2000, with fewer outlets, the overall winners captured the amplified story.

Checking on the emails to Fred, I notched forty-two victories over the next fourteen months and placed on the podium in all but a few of the seventy-five races I entered, so I earned fair recognition in the New York City running community.

Roaming the streets, I invariably bumped into a new connection who had attended the events. Straightaway requests arose from individuals for coaching lessons, businesses requiring lectures/talks, and the media for a wide variety of work, both national and international. Before long, I began jogging three hours each morning with private clients, leaving me physically drained but boosting my finances considerably.

Individual runners naturally led to coaching clubs and teams. During days of the week, as relationships developed, I received invites to fancy restaurants and parties where I encountered influential people. The social calendar in New York is spectacular. My Rolodex flourished, and potential avenues opened up for an array of varied work. Be it photoshoots modeling sports clothes or impersonating an athlete in a TV commercial—I said yes to any opportunity that sounded interesting.

Five days after arriving in Manhattan, the New York Road Runner's CEO's executive assistant contacted me. Right away, I began assisting the club in a medley of roles, like speaking at their marathon lectures, aiding the international athletes invited to their events, or writing for the club's monthly magazine. The 'NYRR's' portfolio was impressive; they coordinated the famous New York City Marathon, weekly competitions, and fitness clinics. Realizing the organization commandeered the roads of all-things-running, I ran for the election to serve on their board of directors and won a seat. What did the directors do? I would soon discover.

In the balloting, I became the first individual in their storied forty-four-year history to knock off an incumbent director and claim a seat—and I would be the last. The NYRR lawyers promptly amended the by-laws to veto membership voting, permitting the committee to self-govern.

This team constantly reminded me running changes the lives for the better of every person who laced up a pair of sports shoes.

Sitting on the board was illuminating and nominated as the Chairman of the Race Quality Committee, I learned to understand how the events operated. I poured over the financials with the eye of an investigative reporter. Unknowingly, I prepared myself for an upcoming job of a lifetime.

When I did not run or talk, I scribbled articles or columns for newspapers, magazines, or websites. Since the *Train Hard, Win Easy* books sold, I planned to author another title and secured a contract with Penguin. I blush to admit *The Essential Guide to Running the New York City Marathon* was thrown together like a bowl of cornflakes in less than three rushed weeks.

Manhattan's electric energy always ignites & excites. Photo Mike Kobal.

One morning during the summer, I wondered why the Americans place the month before the day and end on the year, but for the Independence Day celebrations then switch over to an English format? It was a topical thought when jogging to the start line of the Tommy Hilfiger Independence Day 4-miler. The Fourth of July boasted a stifling, sticky, humid day, and heat advisory warnings leaned against outdoor activities—but a monetary prize and a decent number of Tommy products for the winner provided my incentive to participate.

The event went as planned, and after starting a cool-down jog, Richard Finn, the head of the media for the NYRR, flagged me down, "Toby, will you be the New York City Marathon's Elite Comeback Runner award winner this fall?"
"Me… Are you kidding?" But, as I launched into a spiel of excusing myself, citing the A-Z of the medical book, Major Ramachandra's voice piped up, 'Why not?' Why not indeed.

Henry Stern, right, the NYC Park's Commissioner, holds the tape. This road race introduced me to the concept of charity running shortly after my first brain surgery.

Although flattered at Richard's gracious offer, I hardly fitted the title of elite *or* marathoner. But Richard explained a healthcare company would grant a sizable donation to the Fred's Team foundation if I laced up on their behalf. The idea of running for a charity instead of myself intrigued me.

Fred's Team raised money for cancer initiatives; the organization took its name from a co-founder of the city's marathon. I doubt Fred would have remembered me had he been alive, but I greeted the Romanian seven years before in Lisbon, Portugal, at a competition. He wished to hear my race result and then remarked I would need to speed up if I wanted to attend *his* event. Fred was the world's most prolific road race director, but I expressed no interest in participating in any marathon.

Slightly offended at his words, I am sure I sounded brusque when indicating I preferred five k's (3.1 miles). The half marathon today measured the longest distance I had covered in my three years of running. Well, in that case, he retorted, the performance proved to be excellent. So much, I must fly to his race merely to gain experience, "Just talk to Anne," he advised.

Fred likely said this statement to any athlete he met, and I thought little of it. But that evening, at the lavish banquet held inside a castle, I was seated next to Anne Roberts, known as Fred's right hand. Now, years later, the opportunity was offered again.

"Yes," I told Richard, "Why not, and I'm grateful for the honor."

P.H.S. healthcare financed the $10,000 comeback award, and over the next few months, Karen Coughlin, the company C.E.O., became a mentor. Sharing bi-weekly check-ins, she always queried my health, asked if the training was rigorous, and inquired about the African projects. Whenever we met, she focused on being fully present despite leading an entity involving over a million people.

Once lunching at the Tavern on the Green, her phone rang off the proverbial hook. For three hours, she never even glanced to check who called, let alone answer—a lady who was generous with her time and constantly offered me her undivided attention.

The months flew by, and the grand day arrived. The event is the largest marathon on the globe, a 26.2-mile (42.2 km) street party. If you plan one day to explore New York's five diverse boroughs, spend it running the marathon, you will enjoy the ultimate tour.

November 5th brought winter chills, and at five-thirty a.m. I traveled on the bus to the start line for a seven a.m. television interview. The station requested I dress as if ready to compete, as the footage would air three hours later in conjunction with the main start. Unfortunately, I lost sight of the person holding my warm-up tracksuit—meaning, for 180 long minutes, I withstood blustery biting winds, underdressed in skimpy shorts and a singlet designed to keep you cool. The Verrazano-Narrows Bridge catches the worst of the weather, and with a slim frame—teeth chattering uncontrollably—I almost froze. Making matters worse, the escort allowing a fast-track to the front line of the 30,000 runners for a preferred starting position failed to materialize. Yet, for once and unlike in Machakos, mishaps bothered me not. Nobody looked more ebullient than me this morning.

The purpose of cause-running spurred me on as I bounded with a beaming smile through the scenic course. Linking the beauty of marathoning, which can be a selfish and time-consuming passion, to produce better health outcomes for sick people was a winner. I had run hundreds of races, but today's experience was unique and priceless. If I should ever organize a marathon, I would deduct a cut from the entry fee to ensure all runners enjoy the inspiring feeling of running to help a cause. Why not make the world a better place by lacing up your shoes?

During the final miles, memories of steps along the sandy beach to survival merged with strides on the city streets. The last ten months had passed as an emotional blur. That I could run, let alone complete the most arduous event on the Olympic calendar, remained a blessing. Running 26.2 miles (42.2 km) is no easy task for anybody. Years later, I led Lance Armstrong to the podium for a press conference following his debut marathon. Waiting for our call-up, amidst a flurry of colorful words, he declared the marathon race to be the toughest sporting endeavor of his life.

On the finishing line, Karen stood smiling, waiting for my arrival. "The announcer said you won a cash bonus of a few thousand dollars for being the first Manhattan finisher!" She held a garland of blue flowers for me, and as we waltzed over to the V.I.P. tent, she explained, "I know your family lives in Europe, so I wanted to be here for you." As she talked, she cried with water streaming from her eyes. She added witnessing my miraculous recovery gave her heartfelt satisfaction and repeated how much she had enjoyed our last few months together sharing this journey. Handing Karen my finisher's medal as a souvenir, I do not remember much of our chat, but I am certain it centered around my welfare.

Although we bonded, she had never once mentioned she fought a losing battle against cancer. I cannot imagine the immense personal discomfort she suffered during these moments. I wish I had the chance to bid Karen goodbye. Just three weeks later, she succumbed to a painful death—a colleague wrote, describing the devastating news. He stated, for her burial, Karen had conveyed written instructions that she must wear my medal to the grave. Her death flattened me. Racking my brain, I cannot even recall a time when I questioned Karen about her health. No, I recognized the same self-absorbed Toby leaving an African hut near the Crocodile River. When would I wake up and act instead of merely feeling empathy? The intent is pathetically weak if not saddled to execution—the roar of the lion does not capture the kill. What was wrong? The millennium had approached with a pledge to practice purpose, and then the beach experience occurred. Zanzibar should have heightened the vows, but no, and now hearing of Karen's death hit me like a stinging slap in the face.

As Karen had expressed avid interest in the shoe programs, I decided upon my subsequent journey to Kenya in January 2001, I should include a modest project in her memory. When friends learned of this trip, they flipped. "Are you insane? You practically died and want to return? Luck played on your side, but next time there will be another outcome." A colleague advised me to purchase a gun, "Go back, but for revenge." Funny, until these individuals voiced concerns, risks had not even entered my mind. Dr. Mehta, whose opinion I valued, declared my mission—my purpose—was in Africa. Nothing, warnings, or machetes would keep me from returning.

⋧⋦

Urban legend states if you reside in Manhattan for a decade, then consider yourself a New Yorker. After settling for a year and a half, I had practically become a fixture in the city and felt right at home. September 11th, 2001, started like many other mornings. Linda Hallinan and I exercised in Tribeca, trundling along the West Side Highway. We passed a vaulted building with a red umbrella sign lit up. "Isn't that bad luck?" she quipped. I missed the logo but, instead, I admired how brilliant the sky projected over the buildings that morning. Linda, who worked as Martha's Stewart assistant, and I parted ways around 8:15 a.m. Then I nipped south, cutting directly through the World Trade Center to work out with my following client, Lieng-Seng Wee, a risk-management CEO.

Lieng-Seng and I scooted along the East Side of Lower Manhattan when a muffled boom sounded, but we thought little of it. The first plane—American Airlines Flight 11—had slammed into the Northern of the twin towers. Immediately a constant screeching of sirens, not one or two, but a steady buzz of beeps, blares, and bells polluted the air. The noise did not cease for the next few hours as an army of emergency vehicles crowded the streets. Plumes of gray smoke began rising from Southern Manhattan—curious and concerned, we at once started jogging towards the trouble. What on earth had happened? When asking passersby, the replies were contradictory. Lieng-Seng, the convergent thinker, darted inside a 7/11 to purchase a pocket radio to glean facts. Meantime, billows of smog, instead of lessening, spread, curling into the sky, cloaking the clouds, and covering the World Trade Center.

As we pressed south, the United Airlines Flight 175 must have shattered into the second tower. More balloons of haze appeared, looking like a Saharan-style sandstorm, and then a string of cars sullied with a coating of dust began advancing the wrong way up the streets heading north. Lieng-Seng recalled, "How could I ever forget that day? We were the only ones running south. Everyone else headed north fast!" But for a valid reason, he maintained an office on Rector Place, one hundred meters south of the WTC. Judy, his partner, would be at her desk. Meantime, I house-sat an apartment at 84 West Broadway, 200 meters north of the towers.

Arriving at the site of destruction, the two of us parted ways. Bodies splattered in debris, dirt, and blood stumbled towards me. A man shrieked, "We are under attack. Get out of here. It is war." The two planes had decimated the Twin Towers. Clouds of dust swarmed over the sky to confuse the day's bearings, and ash lay over the ground like a fresh snowfall. The smell could be described as a burnt mixture of fires, fuels, plastics, and worse. Coughing and wiping muck from my eyes, I walked onward, aiming for the apartment in a state of disbelief. The police did their utmost to communicate a sense of control in the madness, blocking streets and dispersing crowds, and I kept overhearing the words, 'Are you OK?' Not to myself but to those who froze in a state of shock and seemed incapable of moving. Time passed with a blur, and yet time stood still.

In the fallen rubble, over 2,700 beings lost their lives, and around 6,000 people suffered injuries. The intense bold colors from the morning skies had vanished, smudged into a dirty canvas. 9/11 stands as the most destructive terrorist assault in history and the deadliest foreign attack on American soil.

My connection to this community, beyond the apartment, pertained to coaching the team of Urban Athletics, based in the adjoining World Financial Center. Jerry Macari, an amiable chap and the outstanding master's runner of New York, owned the store, and the previous year he suggested I trained his team. Most members lodged nearby, and several worked at the Twin Towers. Miraculously and to my relief, due to various coincidences, none stood inside the towers at 8:46 a.m. The closest being Claudia Aquino, a Brazilian/British friend employed by American Express. She walked forward to enter the North Tower as the first plane exploded into the ninety-third to the ninety-ninth floors.

The value of life became the fixed topic of conversations. I am always astonished by how random acts play out. Had I not run along the shore in Zanzibar, had the taxi not been late for morning commutes. Had Claudia departed three minutes earlier. Living by the grace of God, I, for one, needed a reminder not to take days for granted, no matter how mundane the hour may seem. 9/11 screamed as a constant reminder of our fragility, and the city cried in mourning whilst dreading further attacks. People slunk like silhouettes into the subways in silence, fearful that the vicious masterminds, still on the loose, might strike anew. Vulnerability forced vitality into our lives, and America's most populated borough morphed into a village of sadness shedding endless tears. Firm handshakes transferred to hearty hugs, feuds were promptly forgotten, and the vocalized terms I love you, let us spend more time together, and so glad you are safe, strengthened our beliefs. The heroic stories of firefighters, and the police, who, instead of fleeing, climbed high to help those trapped in the towers lit indomitable flames. These valiant heroes once again demonstrated that the timeless undercurrent of love will always triumph over hatred.

Again, I reflected on how I failed at my half-baked hopes to tackle matters of purpose. I kept on promising I would step up as if I began a running race but never finished. Then ironically, stopping is how the action started.

A month later, during a competition, I ground to a halt and wandered off the course. Despite relaxing in the pack, cruising and confident, the elements suddenly slotted into place. Why the 9/11 disaster anchored my actions, I am not sure. I could have obtained these notions crossing the finish line, but that is not me—the belief was overpowering that I must quit at that moment, enforcing the commitment. An inner dialogue began; *'Stop racing every single week because that's the distraction.* Sure, after this race. *No, do it now, as you always procrastinate.* Okay, later, let me concentrate on this race. *Look, see what I mean? Do it now if you mean it.'*

Pablo Picasso stated, *'The meaning of life is to find your gift.'* Running represented the gift. He had added, *'The purpose of life is to give it away.'* What had I given away? What if I perished on the Tanzanian beach; was that it? What had I done with my talent apart from furthering my own direction and interest?

Dr. Gaurang Mehta, above, not only saved my life, patching me up and securing a flight just in time, but he convinced me there was a meaning to why I came to Africa. How I wish he had lived long enough to hear of this story. I will never forget his kindness.

As a competitor at the New York City Marathon, people marveled at my speedy recovery. Both the articles above include the word luck. "He was very lucky. If I hadn't seen the (CAT) scan, I would never have believed it," stated Neurologist Dr. Michele Tagliati. And 'His luck didn't run out' wrote the journalist Wayne Coffey. Was *luck* the correct word?

141

Chapter 11. 2001-05

A SMELLY SHOES CHARITY

It's the possibility of having a dream come true that makes life interesting. – Paulo Coelho©

The shoes recycling had dribbled along throughout my economic recovery in a slipshod fashion, and although I slacked, the program never stopped. Possessing little money, I mailed pairs rather than the cartons to Africa. Yet now, in October 2001, I resumed lugging larger shipments to the post office and committed to sending a monthly minimum. Due to the beach assault, I labeled the project 'SHOE4AFRICA,' referring to the single Nike Pegasus aiding the escape. The shoe that had defeated death and symbolized the run to trigger the next leg of my journey. Naturally, people presumed I suffered from dyslexia, and the title must mean sending shoes to Africa. Their confusion was understandable, as that action was the main element of the project!

Every day I devoted time to the program, and I started to believe the scales shifted from selfish over to—well, not selfless—but, at least, shuffling in the appropriate direction.

Overseas, the success stories flowed like water from a fireman's hose. A fellow retired competitor, Tanzanian Max Iranqhe, maintained a stellar job conducting Shoe4Africa events and sending updates recalling energizing accomplishments from his country. He had an eye for talent and predicted rising stars, like a youth named Fabiano Joseph. Max promised, if given token support, this boy could become a star. We supported Fabiano, and sure enough, he later won the world half-marathon championships. His winning singlet and race bib arrived in my mailbox shortly after with a beautiful thank you card. Inspired, I began a scholarship program to help Max's recruitment of athletes and talented Kenyan juniors we identified. As the number of people that we assisted increased, I needed additional shoes.

Luckily, each person I asked possessed items ready to donate, and I received trunk loads of footwear each week. Needing more floor space for storage, I used a saw blade of a pocketknife to dissect every piece of my house furniture. First the chair, next to the table, then the sofa set; everything went! Becoming overloaded with the product meant the postage costs skyrocketed, but a smellier quandary arose. The accumulation of athletic shoes stunk out every corner of my apartment. To save the shame and embarrassment of explaining about the crusty sweaty stink, I stopped inviting people home.

When my parents flew over to visit, I improvised by purchasing inflatable gym balls for seating. Dwarfed by the boxes, they politely refrained from grousing about the nasty pong. For years, friends wondered why I refused to entertain visitors. Could I have afforded storage costs? Maybe, but the more money I saved, meant the more shoes I could ship.

To further economize, I used a bicycle and looped Manhattan for the shoe collections. Typically, friends left pairs with their building's doormen, and I carted a backpack and overloaded the bike rack. But for the larger quantities, I dragged an additional suitcase-on-wheels making me resemble a mobile homeless man. I must have been crazy, but it worked, and the method matched my budget—I had already shaved any living expense possible to support the rising shipping costs. Hand-washing clothes, not owning a cell phone, and consuming little more than bagels, kale, and rice reaped notable savings. I found numerous ways to economize, and cost-saving became a fun competition. Today I wonder, as friends built up their lives, why was I compelled to throw mine into charity work?

When organizing an event for Mama Fatuma's Orphanage in Eastleigh, Nairobi, I wanted to upgrade to new shoes instead of gently used ones. The kids lived amidst a concrete jungle, with not a green tree to be seen. I planned to hire blinged-out party buses and transport the orphanage to the countryside for a day of fun, nature, and sports. With a minuscule budget, instead of purchasing, I bartered volunteer work for those sixty pairs. Picking up the footwear and forgetting the suitcase, I entered a launderette requesting plastic sacks. After tying the carriers to the handlebars and rack, I peddled home. Unfortunately, a passenger unlocking a car door knocked me sideways—the shoes spilled onto the road. Another bruising indicator that I should brush up on the project's practices. Friends hearing about how poorly the programs functioned suggested I establish a charity and gain support, yet I retained no interest—charities are for teams of people, not individuals.

As a grassroots venture, shoe growth looked infinite. A rock band manager, boasting three sold-out Madison Square Garden shows of 20,000 fans each night, offered to mandate concertgoers to bring shoes before gaining entrance. Sports companies emailed, proposing to offload wagons of 'slight defects.' One day the driver of a stretched limousine pressed my door buzzer. I flew down the stairs expecting royalty, only to receive a shopping bag from Saks Fifth Avenue. The bag contained a pair of running shoes. The delivery service amount surpassed the value of the shoes. But signing the receipt, I noted the donor had expensed the cost to his workplace. The chauffeur explained all contributions in America were tax-deductible, "You are stupid if you don't start a charity—anyone supporting you can receive a tax break. Our company pledges half a million a year, but only for registered charities."

Mm, I wondered, could I develop a tiny charity to offset the escalating shipping costs? I questioned, "Don't charities have to sustain a full staff, with offices and expenses?" The driver shook his head, laughing as he replied, "No, my sister-in-law and her daughter operate a charity between the two of them. They work from their home and compensate themselves nicely too."

I admit my eyes opened, but I resisted. There must be alternative options, and I should exhaust those first. For example, scores of African runners traipsed through the city for competitions—if the athletes carried the shoes on the flight home, I saved one hundred percent of the costs. This idea worked, and I still smile, recalling an endearing incident with the world champion Catherine Ndereba. The day after placing second in the New York Marathon, she humbly dragged a sack of shoes almost taller than her, and probably heavier, across the Hilton lobby to the elevators to distribute in Kenya. If the athletes performed the legwork, then why not me?

Shoe-lugging turned out to be quite a chore: Sweating profusely, I hauled three fifty lbs. (3 x 22 kg) bags to the subway station. Once inside the labyrinth of the underground tunnels, the troubles brewed. Wow, the words of wrath I encountered for obstructing commuters when struggling up and down the long staircases, and switching trains, were plenty. Once, an angry lady spat on my jacket. But why wouldn't I hail a taxi? Did seventy dollars matter that much? Definitely, in Kenya, seventy dollars purchased 175 meals of *ugali* & *sukuma wiki* for the kids. Watching youngsters enjoy a hearty meal warmed my soul beyond any abuse those suburbanites screamed out.

Now, firmly settled in America, I wondered, should I apply for a permanent residence status? And if I did, should I listen to the chauffeur and register a charity? Friends pressed me, 'Take the plunge, and we'll donate.'

I could form the type of charity I like, where nobody would receive payments, and we would rely on volunteerism. Not having an inkling of how to begin, I quizzed the athletes I coached. One lady, Nina Greisman, suggested her family lawyer could submit the paperwork.

By January 2006, the Shoe4Africa project transformed into a legal 501(c)(3) charity. The line-up: Chairperson Toby, Nina, the secretary, and a lady I assisted with a bus ride to the marathon start line, Joy Dushey, became our treasurer. Grossly inexperienced, the board meetings consisted of little more than conversations about running. But accepting public donations transferred us to a position of enormous responsibility; I did not take this burden lightly.

The charity compass, for me, remained the chronicle of Gandhi. Despite his global reputation, he could not sleep at night should he possess coins whilst a person nearby lay starving. As such, Gandhi, whose bones are probably the structure of heaven's gateway, lived a life without wealth yet died spiritually rich. His legacy stood as a testament to the term charity. Wearing a homespun dhoti, dusty sandals, and shawl, he lived inside a makeshift ashram lacking electricity and modern amenities. He never compensated himself and furiously believed in empowering local people.

Meantime, here in NYC, I discovered the opposite. Several 'USA-African' charities maintained plush offices in Manhattan—

the priciest borough of America's most expensive city—and employed almost exclusively American-born personnel to work on African problems. Imagine Gandhi hiring a team of foreigners to sort out Indian issues. Regarding salaries, Gandhi's eyes would have popped out of their sockets. Six-figure sums (not Rupees) spell out as the shocking average. Gandhi's ethics were impossible to match, but I wondered, how much could we achieve without hiring anyone or paying a single salary?

Our cause would center around positivity; to engage our donors into being investor-angels uplifting the lives of the poor. The programs would organically expand but launch with shoes. What about transporting running shoes to Africa when naysayers insisted shipping items ruined the local economy? Numerous Africans, over a decade, had requested, *'Please, please bring footwear.'* Not one African person I had spoken with had stood against the idea. Furthermore, I could not locate a single running shoe manufactured on the continent of Africa. Examining the footwear of professional runners winning the key marathons, you will identify very few brands—everyone desires these authentic models. Running and sports constitute an enormous economic and educational boon to Africa. Millions of dollars, and thousands of scholarships, are generated through this venue. For the non-athletes, quality, long-lasting running shoes promoted a healthier lifestyle.

Charity aid, in various capacities, works, and yet it does not work. Arguments pile up for both sides—I am on both sides. I thought each person should be influenced by their conscience, not by the consensus of what others say. Rather than devote a chapter to this issue, I align with Hon. Kagame's words. The Rwandese President had stated, *'The best way to help is to help people to be able to stand on their own.'* These words summarized our guiding mission. So, for the better, I hope, Shoe4Africa launched as a nonprofit. In that spirit, Joy, and her husband Sammy, kindly offered to host a party to celebrate our *officialis statum.* Grete Waitz, a world champion runner I met aged twelve at an international cross-country meet and had befriended, readily agreed to be our first advisory board member alongside the model Kim Alexis. What an advisory role entailed I could only guess. Though observing that other charities maintained these titled positions, I reasoned that we must as well.

※

Conducting an event, you pray for decent weather, especially in June when you almost expect it. Peering out of my apartment, a torrent of rain slashed its way through a slab of sticky humidity. I did not want to step outside, let alone dash to Joy's fabulous apartment on Park Avenue. Joy had taken up running following a stroke. Running transformed her life like it had mine, and she believed fervently in our work.

Jogging over to the party, I smiled when witnessing the queue of people entering the building—folks wrapped around the block to reach Madison Avenue. The word had gone out to friends, and virtually nobody had RSVP'd, but the attendance blew me away. Joy's living space spanned the entire floor of a spacious building, and our guests crammed into every inch.

Along with a host of businesspeople and notable athletes, a famous designer Narcisco Rodriguez attended that night. I mentioned we promoted an AIDS awareness program in Kenya, and he eagerly stepped up, wishing to endorse us. Narcisco stated, in two hours, he was to dine with the Somali supermodel Iman, an ex-Nairobi resident. He promised to try to rope her into our mission. Perfect, I coached Kim Alexis, another former supermodel, and noticed how the press gravitated towards Kim at events. Personalities, I found, opened doors in America, and another well-known character attended this night, a man who would play a part in the next eight years of this journey. For that, I will be forever grateful to a Goose.

※

When writing for a sports magazine, you can find yourself searching for originality. After exhausting training ideas, running injuries and items, and character profiles, readers recognize the content is often a rehash of old articles. To add spice, developing an alternative perspective can perk an interest. And to enhance the concept, including experts or prominent names boosts the readership. I composed an editorial stating that individuals who chose an early morning run gained more than just fitness over nonrunners. Aerobic exercise defrags the mind and boosts the imagination, but the secret entailed harnessing that energy to jogging's simplicity. Bicycles involve mechanics, gears, and dodging missiles. Gyms remain friction and interaction.

My theory suggested if you rise and head to a green park, you gain the perfect incubator for productivity. The solitude of the sport, the inability to perform other tasks as you run enhance your focus. Art therapy, and traffic lights, imply that greens promote vision and movement. Ugh, the words sounded pathetically weak and needed amplification. Who could add some credibility? Which characters were newsworthy and ran in the city?

The New York Attorney General Eliot Spitzer was a staunch runner, and he produced so many worthy quotes I turned the spiel into a separate Runner's World feature. Next, I chatted with Eli Zabar, a food mogul of Manhattan. The following interview focused on Anthony Edwards. A friend I coached, Denise, related her husband had spoken of my running and philanthropy to a thespian. The actor wished to meet, and he could be another asset for the article. Over email, Anthony suggested a coffee at a restaurant called E.A.T., which I found serendipitous. An hour before his proposed time, I planned to wrap up Eli's interview at this exact location—because Mr. Zabar owned the store.

Anthony, who abbreviates his name to Tony, and I quickly discovered common ground. He is of European descent, interested in theaters, charities, and marathons, and even stands at the same height as I at six foot two (1.87 cm). Both of us shared Rudolf Steiner ties—his kids attending a Steiner school, whereas my parents, apart from years at Tintagel, helped to create a Steiner kindergarten. Philosophizing and swapping life stories, our chat twisted far from a regular interview. Being called Edwards, I presumed he performed on Broadway. Stupid, I know, but it sounded like a theatrical name. ERs and Goose references signified nothing—I remained oblivious of his international film star profile.

Although I complained bitterly about not owning a TV as a kid, now in my thirties, I was yet to procure the first set. Goose in the Top Gun movie—aka Dr. Mark Greene on the TV drama ER—and I cultivated a deep friendship. Running socially three or four times a week, I became a regular at his house. We escorted his kids to school, exercised in the park before doubling back for toast and coffee and long chats to conquer the world's problems. Lunches followed, and we frequently attended events together. Naturally, he became involved with the charity. It was a friendship I cherished and one that helped Shoe4Africa tremendously.

Jeanine Lobell and Anthony Edwards attending a Shoe4Africa event in Kenya, accompanied by Paul Tergat and Robert 'Boston' Cheruiyot.

"We just hit it off. It was like long lost brothers. We are kind of like Frick and Frack. My wife refers to Toby as my boyfriend. Your boyfriend is here, she says. He's come to drink all our coffee."
Anthony Edwards, Runner's World Interview (2009).

Chapter 12. 2007

Women Run Iten, and the Manhattan Marathon

Where there is a will of iron, there is a way of gold. – Toby Tanser (Train Hard, Win Easy).

Giving away shoes was easy, but scrounging money for shipping and holding the events? That is another story. Unfortunately, begging for monetary support was not my forte. But, no problem, I appeared to have discovered a method to finance the charity work and land a dream job to secure my future. First, I ramped up our programs, and less importantly, selected a color for Team Shoe4Africa.

༄

Running competitions in Kenya can be spectacular. One year, a man who finished 75th in the national trials won the world championships two months later—yes, that crazy. Every runner I spoke with desired to journey abroad and win cash, but the problem related to the finances to afford such a dream. When the rare opportunities arose, events drew a capacity crowd and avid excitement. During my visit to Kenya, a sports agent hosted a half marathon with an unbelievable prize—air tickets, passport and visa, and entries for the winners to a prestigious Dutch event. As usual, accepting Pieter Langerhorst and Lornah Kiplagat's generous hospitality, I lodged at The High Altitude Training Centre. Since the race started and finished at their resort, I intended to spectate.

After the starting horn blared, we clambered inside Pieter's truck and trailed the billows of red dust. Hundreds of men dashed over the dirt paths, shoulder locked to shoulder, busting their guts—yet I could not make out a single female. Perusing the results, I read a scant eight women had entered.

The following day, I chided the ladies, "Why? Those presented outstanding odds to claim such a prize."

Several blamed their husbands, stating they were instructed not to run. Various replies piped up, but their absence birthed an idea. Opportunities for females sorely lacked—rather than support races, why not be the one to host and establish the rules? If I built an event exclusively for gender, I could prioritize the ladies. Empowerment is primarily about money, so let us financially award individuals and continue to promote the AIDS awareness angle.

Few races, I bet, offer a T-shirt, prize money, and free running shoes but demand no-cost for registration. To promote the day, I could tie bundles of shoes to a car's roof rack and motor around town with a bullhorn. I was certain women would sign up.

Not wishing to endure the wrath of the countless churches, I confirmed a date for a Saturday. However, herein I struck a problem—Saturday signaled the busy market day. Nevertheless, since the previous race set such a shallow bar, any number over one hundred ladies would constitute a resounding success; secretly, I gunned for 250.

Negotiating an affordable price for the T-shirts meant buying in bulk from 3,000 items down. Figuring I could omit to print a date on the garments, I planned to save the vast surplus for upcoming events and took the number reaping the best discount. When selecting a color, I found the magic answer.

A couple of years ago, following the New York City Marathon, I shopped on Seventh Avenue for a wooly hat with a Kenyan athlete, Joyce Chepchumba. She struck a terrific bargain at one dollar fifty, but it was pea-green, the wrong color. After trekking for three hours, searching for a commensurate price, I implored Joyce, let me offer any amount to prevent us from hiking further. Unlike her, I had not even run the marathon. But she insisted on not paying extra and on the shade of yellow,
"My skin is dark, but I feel bright and cheerful when I wear that color."

Two hours later, at the Hilton Hotel and victoriously grasping a lemon-colored hat, we rode forty-four floors alongside a gentleman whose head almost grazed the elevator roof. He inquired if we competed the previous day. Not one to boast, Joyce nodded but did not let on that she won the entire race. I always encourage everyone to run marathons, so I recommended he should enter the following year. Why not accompany us in the morning for a jog in the park to commence his training? He laughed, excusing himself as a retired basketball player, and when pointing to Joyce's hat, quipped, "Our team, the Lakers, play in yellow." As he stepped out, a fellow guest cried, "You did not recognize him? That is Magic (Johnson)!" Designed with magic, the color to cheer you up became our official shade.

⁜

Imagine, if you can, a town that has never witnessed a mass fun-run competition. Visualize a location where even female professional runners feared entering a public race. Events in rural Kenya were either school matches or exclusive elite contests with a handful of ladies—like the Dutch affair. Ladies trying out for sports were typically discouraged. Take the example of Sally Barsosio, a lithe one hundred pounds (46 kg) world champion in the 1990s. Her build mirrored an E-Type jaguar; created for speed. One day, as I joined her training route, we straddled Iten's town center. Instead of encouraging a national hero, men jeered, yelling at Sally to quit playing children's games and act as a woman should. "This is why I always run pre-dawn," sighed Sally with nonchalance, as a man skimmed a pebble in our direction to heighten his disapproval. Sally described how a schoolteacher had once stripped her and beaten her black and blue when she tried to be a runner.

Dr. Rose Chepyator, a former elite athlete, explained how officials ejected her from the starting line of a local running race—all because she had mothered a child. I heard other stories from ladies who exercised at four a.m. or broke down crying after being ridiculed, often by family members only because they ran. Women in rural Kenya habitually suffered abuse if spotted out exercising. Several ladies, like Sally, crouched in a pack of male athletes wearing beanies, running as strangers in distant neighborhoods to avoid recognition. Following the millennium, views slowly changed, but primarily for the elites. What about the overweight lady who wished to run to improve her health?

The citizens of Iten were first shocked, then stunned, and finally smiling in wonderment on the Shoe4Africa race morning. Why would anyone invest money to host an event for joggers? No entry fees? How are these foolish organizers generating cash? Yet witnessing the post office mistress, seventy pounds (30 kg) overweight, the grandmas, the butcher's wife, all register for free, caused an explosion of excitement. Safety in numbers—every woman or girl desired to participate in the race. Little boys galloped home and returned disguised in a sister's dress, willing to be ridiculed if they could gain the chance to win shoes and a T-shirt. A vegetable seller displayed the toothiest grin, "Since leaving school thirty years ago, I have wanted to run. But how? Collectively, we can do it." The race galvanized the ladies and brought the town to a complete standstill.

From each angle, bursting out of cars, buses, and bushes, the women arrived. They streamed out of the *matatu* station, the roadside, and in droves from the market stalls. Mounds of fruits and vegetables, unguarded, waited in trust as the ladies skipped forward. The grassy field in Iten's center became flooded in yellow T-shirts—like buttercups in a spring meadow. With 2,902 ladies and girls wishing to register, Driver John needed to dash to the storerooms to haul the entire stock of our T-shirts.

A gathering of world champions, including Paul Tergat and Moses Tanui from my N'gong days, spoke eloquently on health matters, commanding the attention of not just the competitors but a teeming crowd of spectators. Two traditional groups, representing the Samburu and the Pokot region, provided song and dance. After the race, we handed out thirty cash prizes, with the least amount being one hundred dollars, a generous sum in Kenya. Then, amid the celebrations, a brave lady called Josephine grasped the microphone and cleared her throat,

"Dropping weight, under forty kgs, surely I would die. With a free routine test you can register for today; I discovered the HIV disease had grabbed me. But do you know," she paused, and you could hear a pin drop, "free medicines, available to us, are here. This day I weighed seventy kgs, healthy, and living strong!"

The gathering, looking like all of Iten, erupted. My methodology was primitive, but it worked as the outstanding 925 ladies signed up for AIDS testing. "Never have we even seen numbers over fifty before, incredible!" Cried Hillary, a local Health Officer from Iten's district hospital.

This Promoting AIDS Awareness Run was unique—even whispering the words had caused bodies to blush. Yet now that scary sentence blasted, with smiles, all across the town. Following the event, the shoe fitting for the entrants took hours. Gently used quality running shoes brought tears of joy—these were not the cheap knockoffs from China, the items usually peddled at the marketplace, but Nike's and Adidas models. A great-grandmother lay on the grass chuckling in sheer disbelief, "Oh lord. I am not forgotten. There is a pair for me?"

In addition to launching other women's Shoe4Africa events in Kenya, I added Tanzanian and Moroccan races in 2006. This plan of hosting competitions rather than supporting them provided much more impact. But if the participants continued escalating, I should seek an effective way of collecting more shoes—and, of course, extra pairs meant more expensive shipping costs.

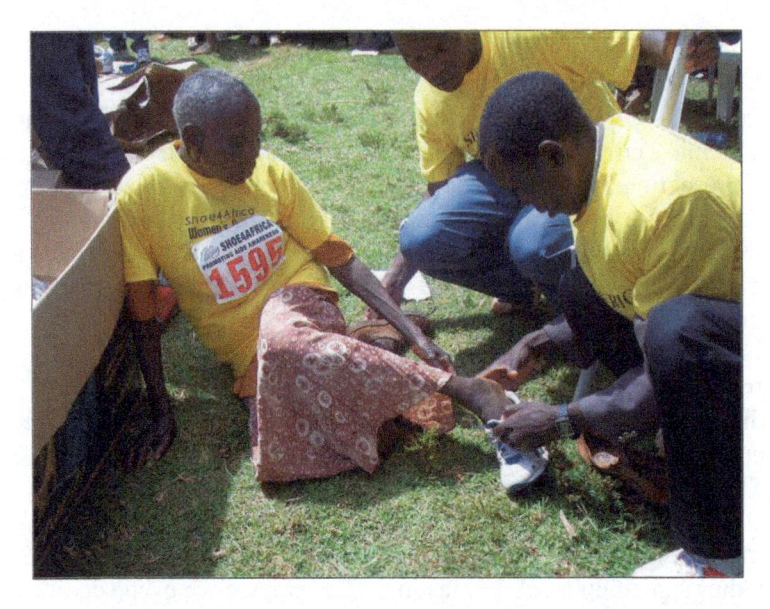

The grandma grins, "There is a pair for me?"

෨෬

A year or two ago, at the New York City Marathon, all four elite Kenyan ladies on the start list were Shoe4Africa alumni. Mary Keitany, four-time NYC marathon winner and the women's marathon world record holder, explained, "Shoe4Africa was my big encouragement. My first senior race. I missed the prize money by one place, but it showed me, if I went home and trained harder, I could make a life by running." It was the first and the last! That Shoe4Africa event remains the single race of Mary's storied senior career where she did not earn money. In 2018, we built and named a school after Mary, who is an ambassador of Shoe4Africa.

෨෬

Following the advent of the Internet, various aid organizations underwent a radical transition. Spending zero on advertising or media, our charity stood out as the vintage peg. Instead of producing the work, as we did by accepting your donation and discharging it at the actual destination, the new charities harped on about an issue, raised funds, then simply penned a check to a 'local partner.' The donor (you) assumed your contribution had been dispatched to work on the problems in the developing world. Hold up, 'local partners' were actually American charities addressing identical issues. It is akin to you donating one hundred dollars to me, but instead of producing a stroke of work, I re-gift *your* donation to another American charity but do so in *my* charity's name. Plus, I lease offices, hire staff, and of course, service my salary to maintain this (arduous?) work. Do not forget the 'local partners' typically now outsourced to a third group over in Africa. Therefore, three teams sort out one problem, tripling the operating costs.

However, as charities receive grades based upon accounting figures over impact, this formula appeared utterly efficient. These new entities win awards, stars, and badges of honor. Their operating expenses are unbelievable because, let us face it, transferring your donation to a 'local partner' and later posting photos of that partner's efforts in Africa makes for light work. Everyone's numbers divided are superior to the overstretched single team performing all the jobs. Could this be why I read over fifty percent of the funds raised in America, earmarked for Africa, shockingly waste away in the USA? Hey, if the new guys trust the 'local partners' with your money, why not advise you to donate directly and save on overheads? Oh no, that would make them redundant. Oops.

With not a penny, forget salaries, channeled to social media, videographers, or advertising, competing for donations against the check-writing charities seemed impossible. These slick units mocked the working organizations who barely afforded to host a website, let alone continually upgrade one because, shock and horror, we were overrun by performing the actual work. If this smoke and mirrors scheme depicted the future, I needed an exit strategy. Or could I bypass and drum up a business method of bringing in funds to stop me dancing in the social-marketing charity circus world? Well, against the odds, I had a brilliant blueprint—The idea of all ideas.

In July 2007, dining in the upscale Italian restaurant Amaranth, I gulped down my second plate of homemade black pasta drenched in a delectable sauce sprinkled with undetectable flavors. Shmuel Harlap listened to my scheme of collecting thousands of shoes, consigning them to Africa in conjunction with a one-day event, and launching a lucrative career for myself. Shmuel, cradling a glass of wine that cost more than my weekly food budget, was an outlier and a successful self-made billionaire. He took me to many of Manhattan's fanciest and fashionable restaurants and, believing I was underweight, would insist I enjoyed double portions.
Shmuel's kindness was exceptional. He had recently flown me, first-class, to enjoy a week basking in absolute luxury, lounging in the best suite at the David Intercontinental in Tel Aviv, Israel. Even today, I can taste the gourmet breakfast platter, smell the spray of the ocean, and feel the kisses of the sunshine as I relive how each morning began, robed in a silk-lined gown, relaxing after a daybreak run along the Mediterranean Sea coast.
But beyond charity, Shmuel savored creativity in business. I explained about a scheme to aid Shoe4Africa and generate a profit. A corporate plan to lighten the time-consuming task of chasing after shoes and securing funds to pay for the escalating shipping costs. What if we created The Manhattan Marathon? The demand to enter the current city event far exceeded the supply of bibs. The idea would be starting small, aiming for a field of 18,000 participants. Believable? Well, the previous month, using bootstrap marketing, I directed a sold-out event in Central Park with over 8,000 runners and walkers; New York's marathon had debuted with a measly 155 contestants. I explained our theme would focus upon World Earth Day, which lacked a global nucleus—we could conduct an annual event to aid the

environment and enrich the NY state. The current marathon boasted a profound economic impact of hundreds of millions of dollars for the city. Yet launching a family event, I might double the digits per entrant. The running race, an earth day expo for the non-running spouse, and a rock concert for the kids promised three or four visitors over one runner. Shmuel embraced the concept and agreed to partner—his lawyers would submit the paperwork to establish our company. Securing the patronage of a billionaire toppled every entrepreneur's fantasy.

Convincing the city officials might be the meaty task, but I concocted a tempting scheme to entice the entities. Besides, what better date than Earth Day to request the city to close the streets and host the No Carbon Footprint Marathon? I knew of the vast profits of the NYC marathon—but for my race, I would share the pie. All the day's entry fees* would channel to the charity funds of the police, fire brigade, and mayor's office. These teams subsequently converted into vested partners, written into contracts, providing a giant volunteer workforce and cost slashing. The multiple sponsors** could efficiently offset the operating costs. My goal of enabling every entrant to run for a cause may come true.

*Entry fees, including the additional amounts that charities & tour groups must pay for bonds, are around thirty million USD. **TCS paid around ten million USD in 2019, a similar figure to New Balance's yearly sponsorship deal.

Business basics suggest launching an idea begins by devising a robust plan, identifying experienced staff, and delivering backers. Tick, tick and tick. Launching in New York a celebrity boost helps tremendously and brings a media scramble for the press to add coverage and credibility. Thanks to Anthony and Jeanine Lobell, Cameron Diaz gifted Shoe4Africa a generous donation. Because the grant slipped under the name of a foundation, I did not twig the contribution originated from the renowned actor. Cameron and Jeanine sat drinking coffee when we met, and she likely thought me ungrateful for not offering a single word of thanks. Anthony advised I forget it, but, at the least, I should email a note of gratitude recognizing her kindness. Mentioning the goof to a friend, he said, "Nice lady, she is a committed environmental campaigner." Ooh really? I thought aloud, "Maybe when giving thanks, I could see if she gravitates towards the Manhattan Marathon concept?" It was the longest shot—but why not ask. A contact working for the city's council of environment rubbed shoulders with Dave Matthews, an ideal star for the planned concert. I saw the pieces slotting together.

Jeanine, married to Anthony, spun into an outstanding resource for Shoe4Africa. She had offered to find a media personality to promote our cause. Being a sought-after celebrity make-up artist who founded Stila Cosmetics, she bore envious connections. Through Jeanine, we landed the luminary Natalie Portman. Unbelievable because several charities finance celebrities for publicity purposes—these are not insignificant amounts either. One nonprofit, where I formerly served on the board, enjoyed a list of notable names attending their gala. Nice, until I heard the celebs each collected stunning six-figure appearance fees. I am honored to say all of the famous folks who have endorsed Shoe4Africa, never received compensation. On the contrary, they *all* donated to our cause. Hugh Jackman even insisted on purchasing our T-shirt.

Natalie's endorsement came with an immediate opportunity—a photoshoot the following day. I raced to purchase a fashion T-shirt and added our graphics. The acclaimed photographers, Inez and Vinoodh, clicked the shutter. Mike Kobal, a talented photographer friend, added the touch-up needed for magazine standard prints. Natalie also unexpectedly gave us a shout-out when she featured on the cover of Instyle magazine. *"I have a friend collecting shoes for Kenya; shoe4africa.org. Each pair that is worn will cut down the spread of disease. It's about doing something constructive."*

After posting the Natty picture on our website, a flood of inquiries filled my inbox. 'Can I buy the Shoe4Africa Natalie shirt?' Gosh, I had not even considered sales. But in short, if Cameron refused, we held options.

Though hold on, the real nugget of my marathon plan did not involve T-shirts or celebrities. The brilliance behind this marque event would be to request the field to recycle their shoes to Africa on the finishing line—placing the worn items directly into shipping containers. Knowing Shmuel's Tel Aviv neighbors owned one of the biggest global cargo companies, I figured they would underwrite the bill if named an ancillary race sponsor. The campaign became, 'How far can your shoes run?' And willing participants would receive handcrafted beaded Maasai sandals, creating sustainable jobs in Africa in exchange for their used footwear. Additionally, not that money played as a motivator, but I could name my own salary beyond receiving the operating costs for the Shoe4Africa projects. "Shmuel, I can elevate from a beggar to a businessman." I beamed, envisioning the swanky downtown offices.

When engaging with the mayor to launch this proposal, his initial question might be, how would the unique shoe concept function? What if I collected 10,000 pairs on the finish line of the planet's largest marathon to demonstrate my model? Perusing the list of entrants for the upcoming New York City Marathon, I predicted Martin Lel of Kenya and England's Paula Radcliffe would be the winners. Both are good friends, and they gladly agreed to smile for the camera before dumping their shoes into the containers to trigger the movement after finishing the race.

Every elite athlete I requested to donate their shoes accepted to join the program. The pied-piper theory suggested that other runners would notice people tossing their footwear and follow suit, especially if I could release an email blast to alert all race entrants to pack alternative footwear inside their finisher's bag.

Now I needed to persuade the NYRR to allow usage of their premier event for the trial. Mary Wittenberg, the CEO, was a close friend and always open to listening to my ideas—however, this request, a month prior to the race, might be a stretch. We often trained together, so fifteen minutes into one run, I revealed the plan. Mary, so surprised, momentarily stopped running. But to her credit, she did not dismiss the viability of a Manhattan 26.2 miler if presented alongside suitable partners—many cities host two marathons. On hearing the immediate scheme of delivering thousands of shoes to women in Kenya, she immediately leaped on board.

The following week, as the lightbulbs turned on, we stumbled upon a problem—36,000 stiff souls stooping to untie laces on a finish line? No way. OK, time for Plan B. Numerous competitors return on Monday for complementary medal engraving and reduced-priced merchandise at a pavilion near the finish area. Why not dump a removal truck by the pavilion entrance on Central Park West and collect the shoes there?

Requiring a coordination kitty, I received a challenge from Todd, a Brooklyn coach, to race the Chicago Marathon. Local runners hedged side bets; whichever man crawled to the finish line first would scoop 7,000 dollars for the charity of their choice. Perfect; this bundle would fund all the costs!

On Marathon Monday, a team of around fifteen outstanding volunteers stood like saints on CPW, gathering a total of 12,800 pairs from eight a.m. until two p.m. Shay Hirsch, the wife of the NYRR's chairperson George, embodied the spirit of the day. Despite recently being diagnosed with cancer, she arrived early carrying countless cookies and carting flasks of creamy hot chocolate. Runner's World helped by holding an office collection, and Warren Greene and Susan Rinkunas kindly transported the load from Pennsylvania. The success of this day was mind-blowing. The thousands of donors reflected the spirit of the woman I met when barefooted at the Arlanda Airport.

The collection produced a win-win scenario because the donors glowed upon hearing stories of how their used footwear would uplift the lives of women and girls in Africa.

Artiste Cara Buono, who I met at the mayor's office (such a gilded resume—Gladiators, Soprano's, Madmen and Stranger Things), and Delilah DiCrescenzo, (*the* Delilah of the US

Billboard #1 hit *Hey There Delilah*) both volunteered to help. Perchance that was the reason why a news channel mentioned the event, which consequently captured the attention of a former US President—you can say the day proved successful.

Packing the shoes into hurriedly arranged Bronx storage units took longer than anticipated, almost four hours, and now I ran late for a party we would host to celebrate the event. Ensuring each shoe matched its pair, cramming sizes to save space, was the less glamorous segment of the day. Paula did ace the marathon, and she and her husband Gary kindly canceled the NYRR requests to attend their events so she could learn more about our programs. Natalie Portman arrived dressed like a movie star but hauling a canvas sack of forty pairs of footwear and a room of beautiful souls gathered for a magical night. Had I found clarity to marry philanthropy to the corporate world? Grinning from ear to ear, I cycled home at midnight, believing so. Step one had proved a resounding success.

Who knows whether the mayor and his administration might embrace the marathon idea? But with the backing of a billionaire, you can bet your bottom dollar he would agree to meet. Additionally, I had met Mayor Bloomberg at functions, and upon each occasion, he had launched straight into business talk. Did I know of this corporation? What about his Icelandic friends who owned a store on the Upper East Side? Trade connections were his lingo.

Another crucial player, Police Commissioner Raymond Kelly, was a gentleman I bumped into a couple of times and always found cordial and open. Then, the race I organized in Central Park maintained robust Fire Department ties. Whenever I had required street-closing for pre-race events, NYFD readily agreed to dump a fire truck to block roads in midtown and make it happen. Permits for any activities? Consider it done. Favors requested became favors granted. Yet now I would return a service. Furthermore, the former NYC parks commissioner was a good friend, and I had recently assisted him for a couple of speaking engagements. The key individuals to initiate the concept stood in my contact circle.

Again, the value of living in Manhattan is opportunities are at your fingertips for innovative ideas.

Weeks later, before leaving for Kenya, I took lunch on Wall St. with an influential gentleman, well-positioned in the Office of the Mayor. My presentation required buckets of work, but I could not say no to the invitation. Over a cheesecake, as I explained the math behind the model, the man listened keenly. Informing me he was sold, he insisted, when ready, I brought him the complete proposal. Better yet, he promised to introduce me to the Commissioner for the Department of Transportation. Biting my lip, I had not revealed my billionaire partner who, naturally mingled with his own billionaire companions, one of which owned the world-famous landmark hotel fifty meters from our proposed starting line. Hey, no hundreds of buses or ferries for our central start; entrants could mosey underground on public transport to complement the World Earth Day theme.

Launching on the globe's best-known borough and shuttling the shoes to Africa boasted a winning combination. A Swiss watch company and a family brand clothing line both responded to sponsorship inquiries. Having supported Shoe4Africa on a smaller scale, they were eager to step up to mid-level supporters. A famous coffee company hinted at an interest in a package. Nobody had replied negatively yet. Being hardened to charity rejection memos, opening the mail where entities jumped up and down to climb on board was refreshing. I set my eyes on Nike for the dream presenting sponsor; this would be a task for January.

Each piece of the scheme fell into place. Landing a salaried dream job, channeling millions of dollars directly to charities, Shoe4Africa receiving ample shoes, shipping, and operating costs generated on a single day—wasn't this a perfect plan? However, a moment in history would soon spin my life upside down.

Anthony Edwards (M. Kobal), Hugh Jackman, Tom Cavanagh, Eliud Kipchoge (A. Sagita). Natalie Portman (Inez+ Vinoodh), Cristiano Ronaldo (Sigurjon Ragnar) & Mary Keitany. Sarah Jones & Tegla, Prince Harry (M. Kobal), & Sammy Wanjiru. Donovan Bailey, Novak Djokovic, & Gloria Gaynor—names wandering into the story.

During the two years of construction for this hospital, I tried to be on site as much as possible. The middle picture shows the gathering of holy men giving words of peace, unity, and love. Dr. Aruasa is on the right side.

CHAPTER 13. 2007

THE KENYAN CLASHES

If you were to sit upon a cloud, you would not see the boundary line between one country and another. - Khalil Gibran.

Cristiano Ronaldo, one of the world's greatest footballers, is a man with a principled philanthropic heart, and I could not have been happier of his association alongside Shoe4Africa. The video featured on our two-bit website revealed the superstar awarding us a phenomenal promotion, "Hello, I'm Ronaldo, I'm with Shoe4Africa."

Back in the nineties, racing in Iceland, I received a generous amount of press. Ivar Josafatsson, an astute businessman, acquired a nutrition company, and short on advertising funds, asked whether I might promote his brand. No problem, I enjoyed seeing my image on the company product labels and joked, 'If you ever make it to the big time, remember me.'
Recently, we caught up, and I requested that Ivar sponsor the Shoe4Africa races. Understanding the synergies, he had launched an entity called Soccerade and wondered, did I want to be involved? Would I like to be a super director alongside the Portuguese star Cristiano Ronaldo, Luis C., who assisted in managing Ronaldo's affairs, and himself? The three received cash dividends, as did the shareholders—and whatever disbursements I

accepted, I would donate to bolster the Shoe4Africa events. Sign me up, and with Cristiano as an ambassador, a sizable bag of his personalized gear arrived. The items could be like Willy Wonka's golden tickets included in the 12,800 pairs of shoes ready for next year's big shoe distribution.

    I liked gifting the celebrity swag to random participants of our events. If possible, I enlarged a picture of the star wearing the donated footwear then said, 'Cristiano delivered this gift because you are an exceptional person.' My wish would be a spark might be kindled in a lost soul. Celebrities like Elijah Wood, Jake Gyllenhaal, Ellen DeGeneres, and Ashley Jensen followed suit donating shoes. Furthermore, Shante Taylor, Mrs. Snoop Dogg, mailed a packed box of Snoop's snazzy blinged-out footwear—I possessed a glitzy collection. But first, I must plan the handout.

    Approaching the end of 2007, I devoted three weeks to visiting Kibera. I had determined this location not only because of how the site molded my future but, I knew I could reach thousands of worthy recipients on any given morning. The slum had altered in twelve years, with more rusty iron sheets, denser crowding, and narrower alleyways. But the same resilience and spirit persisted that I observed in 'ninety-five. Kids now accustomed to foreigners shrieked one word—HOWAREYOU—as I went on walkabouts. The next word? GIVEMEMONEY. Numerous NGOs* had sprung up, and, in awe, I watched tour groups of foreigners roaming the slum ($10 bookings at Adams Arcade). It appeared only I was shocked to see French photographers dressing up fashion models and instructing the ladies to sashay along the oxidized railway lines that dissected the ghetto. Against anything I could have ever imagined, the slums had now adopted tourism.

    Kibera, featuring in a blockbuster movie no less, was dubbed a must-see Nairobi attraction before you boarded a slingshot forty-minute flight to the Masai Mara. The site trended as the hip place to be photographed—both Barack Obama and Chris Rock recently made publicized appearances to be seen in the shantytown. I might be wrong, just a personal view, but I thought the zone had become a victim of presenting the ultimate image of poverty for western aid groups to exhibit. Kenneth Ochieng, a resident, noted, "It is like we are zoo animals. Outsiders snap our photos. Do they capture pictures of the poor in your country?"

Ed Ketta, the Prime Minister's P.A., stated well over 1,000 non-governmental orgs for an area of approx. one square mile.

Before I shipped the shoes, which entailed a ten-week voyage, I wanted to chat to as many residents as possible to ensure the community at large truly embraced our event. An established aid group had attempted building toilets, and the action almost triggered a riot. The Kiberians rebelled, 'We don't have food, and you humiliate us by thinking toilets could be of use? Bring edibles first.' Well-meaning folks had to flee as stones flew.

I decided, if one community spoke out against the event, I would shift to Mathare or Korogosho—slums inside Nairobi with far fewer resources. My method involved listening and listening. Fortunately, I received irreplaceable help from Salim Mohamed. This ever-smiling guy had just starred in a slum documentary alongside the funky rapper K'naan and always welcomed a new project.

For the last couple of years, Salim and I shared countless breakfasts, planning to eradicate poverty by conjuring up hair-brained schemes. I stayed in Kenya's capital regularly during this period—never partying with the ex-pats or hanging around flashy malls that reminded me of an American annex in Africa. No, only now reflecting—and certainly not by design—I did not hang with a single European/American friend in Nairobi. I stuck alongside a different crew, and Salim played a cool sidekick.

The man possessed owl-eye qualities. One evening, strolling along Muringa road, a residential district one mile from Kibera, he sensed that thugs in a car, about fifty meters behind us, planned a robbery. Bolting forward, we skipped inside an apartment complex. CCTV cameras revealed the identical car circled the block and harassed a man at gunpoint fifteen minutes later at the exact spot. When the victim refused to remove his wallet, the thieves put a bullet through the poor man's left hand before fleeing.

In Kibera, Salim knew all the community leaders and, more importantly, they all knew him. Every person we spoke to, bar one, welcomed the plan. The lone voice, always the loudest, belonged to the headmistress of Kibera Primary School.
Helen Otieno cried, "Aid has ruined Kibera—taught us to become beggars, waiting for donations and hindering us from becoming self-reliant. Life was much better before charity arrived."
"Helen, I respect your reasoning," I responded, "but the women earn shoes by completing a tough run—are you sure this is a bad thing? Shoe4Africa is not a handout, but a hand-up, organization."
"Alright, do it, but keep it at a project, so people embrace the day as an opportunity, then leave," she ordered. I promised I would. My friendship with Helen flourished, and I ended up hiring her school as the site venue.

Focusing on shoes and inclusion, and as hookworm stood out as a critical issue, I believed a running race to be the proper vehicle to earn the footwear. The women agreed, but the male community hankered for a soccer match. The ball game is by far the number one sport in Nairobi. One chief requested, "And please add a few cleats to the handout." Hosting an ancillary footie event might be fun. Adding entertainment, I could invite the world's best runners to play a team from the slums. And cleats? I knew the exact person to ask.

Completing all the jobs in Kibera, I channeled my energies to the next mission. Maasai's, their culture and charm, captured not just my attention but countless others. Michael Jordan's mother—Deloris—planned to develop a Nairobi women's health center when we crossed paths. I wondered, guessing she had traveled the world, what enticed her to Kenya? She revealed when her husband James passed and anxious to escape from the media's hounding, she jetted to the Masai Mara. Mrs. Jordan described how the Maasai, and their surroundings, helped her heal.
A magical aura surrounds Kenya's blue-ribbon destination, and with lingering memories of the crocodile Christmas, no surprises, I had uncovered my own Mara project.

Usually, before a day goes by, I will receive at least one email asking for a form of help. For months, certain ladies had been drilling my inbox with a request. Grieving women from a village near Kilgoris by the Mara wrote, "A barbaric act happens to our girls called female genital mutilation. The elders (men) say, our daughters must go to the bush, get cut, else they will be outcasts. Can you build an anti-FGM program because the rite is traumatizing the children? At the last ceremony, yet another of our daughters died. Sepsis is the principal killer for girls in this town."

Initially, I shied away, knowing little about FGM, but the emails, always threading together sorrowful tales, arrived every single Sunday. The ancient ritual had zero health benefits but numerous dire implications. The defenders of cutting up a girl's private parts stated that the procedure played a crucial element in a child's initiation into womanhood. Why a girl required this agonizing removal, typically taking place in the wild bushlands with non-sterilized instruments, using chilly water for an anesthetic, baffled me. If I could inject health information, rally a support group, and pass stories to amplify the message of hygiene, it would be a start. Rather than detracting from culture, could a girl attend the beneficial lessons and lectures of walking into womanhood, then be excused from the ultimate act of the clitoridectomy? Did that make sense?

I met a capable Maasai leader, Caroline Ramet, who campaigned for political office and shared my views. Her voice bore considerable weight, especially as she owned a herd of 4,000 cattle—a measure of success for the Maasai. She could be the trumpet, and I the shadow, assisting in the background.

Frequently in life, opening one door leads to another. Right when I committed to traveling to Kilgoris, Mike Boit, the former Kenyan Commissioner of Sport, requested I bring our programs to the neighboring town of Lolgorien. He related a problem—wasn't there always—five ethnic groups feuded, and arguments escalated with beatings and the occasional murder. The marketplace remained a convergence of constant friction. Mike suggested driving to Lolgorien, gathering ladies from the opposing factions into one busy organizing committee, then bonding by hosting a giant five km (3.1 miles) race. Connecting through a collective mission is a proven winner and offering shoes would ensure a capacity field. Mike's timing fitted admirably; I could research both projects upon the same trip.

The travel day fell on December 18th. With delays at police checkpoints, fatigued by old car seats never designed for comfort, and after six hours of journeying over jarring roads, we arrived in Lolgorien. I discovered a small dirt streets center with churches constructed of iron sheets and ramshackle shops pedaling only the essentials. The largest hotel and I use that word with a smile, served as a general store, bar, and butchers—the community acted as a subsistence-food trading post. Lolgorien stood as the one-horse town without the horse.

Bordering the Mara and a scant fifteen-minute shuffle from the safari lodges, some charging $800 per night, we were offered a room at $2.25. Yet during journeys around Kenya, I resided alongside the locals if initiating a project. When you embark upon charitable work and explore an unknown region, the community embraces you. Hotels are not necessary, no matter how cheap. If you are unwelcome, something is amiss—African hospitality is unmatched. I typically slept at homes upon mud floors wrapped in a woolen blanket, bathed in chilly river water, and squatted over malodorous pit latrines. However, living alongside the people always brought me closer to the heartbeat of the land.

Mike and I camped at a mud-house in the outlands a few miles from Lolgorien. Our Maasai hosts mentioned they settled in this region over ninety years ago, herded south from the Eldoret highlands.

On the first day, we met the individual female leaders and presented our scheme. On the second, I intended to assemble the groups together. Although people became edgy at this idea, they did not want to miss out on what free opportunities I might be offering. Shoe4Africa had received a fair amount of national press, and we had gained a reputation for being changemakers.

The family where I stayed agreed to host the meeting in their compound—we had room for around twenty to thirty people. When the visitors shuffled in, to my dismay, males commandeered all the seats. Annoyed, I questioned, "Where are the female leaders for each group?" One of the men stated the women had gathered to prepare our food whilst others waited outside. "Aha," I improvised, "Yes, I forgot, the kitchens are the meeting spot. Let us go."

Relocating, I at once regretted this decision. Sooty smoke watered the eyes, and I dreaded to imagine what filled my lungs when I entered the low ceiling blackened mud-walls of the cramped cooking quarters. Shuffling my feet for guidance over the compressed dirt in the darkened room, I tripped on a pile of what I guessed to be rugs. My foot had struck a rigid object; an elderly lady huddled on the floor at the edge of the room wrapped in a roll of bedspreads. By chance, I woke the daughter of a celebrated Laibon (an anointed Maasai leader).

A historical story unraveled. The Laibon—Ole Saei—helped negotiate the Maasai migration from Eldoret (of all places) to the Trans Mara during the colonial rule. The Maasai settled on the plateau outside Eldoret, but the foreign farmers desired those tracts. I can only believe the Maasai were duped into exchanging fertile fields for an arid scrubland. Perhaps Ole Saei had been one of the warriors photographed on the Eldoret plateau I discovered years ago? Being a chief made the idea plausible, but even a hint of any likelihood was spooky. Sadly, the grandmother, through her daughter's approximate translation, offered no clues.

That night I dreamt about the Maasai journey to the grounds where I now slept. It was the exact route that Mike and I followed in his old Mitsubishi truck. Did I hope to recreate a link? No, before tonight, I had thought little of the green satchel story. I started wondering if my life traveled on a preordained adventure.

In the morning, destiny again became a talking topic. Mike claimed an Olympic medal in 1972, and an old rival lived a few miles away, so we took a hike to visit Daniel Rudisha. The name sounded familiar as I had presented his son David with an award for being a promising junior at Colm's camp last year. Daniel, in jovial spirits, grinned to hear I had met David and predicted he would be a hero, just like him. "The direct translation of the word Rudisha in Swahili is 'to bring back.' David has the destiny to return the stolen 800 meters world record to Kenya."

What a far-fetched idea, the youth was not even the fastest athlete in the village of Iten, let alone the globe. But the Maasai became enraged that a Kenyan had broken Sebastian Coe's longstanding world 800 meters record yet gifted the glory to Denmark by renouncing his citizenship. His son must return that title for Kenya's honor. Low and behold, a few years later, Dad's vision for David, who today is my next-door neighbor in Eldoret, transpired. The record was brought back, by Rudisha, to Kenya.

The days flew by, and the work progressed favorably, with communications gradually developing between the five groups. Mike was not kidding when he noticed the conflicts. Divisions dug deep, and I predicted a substantial task lay ahead. Yet considering what we achieved in six days, at the least, we had spurred exciting progress—adversaries now bonded in willing conversations. Planning for further action in January, I began supporting the anti-FGM group. If I searched for meaningful projects, I had discovered them. But today, I appreciate we trod with angels perched on our shoulders. Just three weeks later, Wesley Ngetich, the Grandma's marathon champion, forfeited his life attempting the same task. As he promoted peace nearby, a poisonous arrow aimed squarely at the center of his back claimed a young and promising life.

Christmas approached, and I accepted an invitation to celebrate at the home of Martin Lel, the marathon champion. Mike—also traveling to Nandi—proposed we resume our programs after the New Year. During the car journey, knowing of my destination, Mike repeated the legend of Koitalel. I had not believed him, owning a Ph.D., to be superstitious, yet he narrated, "That area is the heartland of the Talai. The British shifted the warriors to this spot following Koitalel's murder. Not all, but some of the descendants possess special powers and will influence a person's life." Mike's eyes oozed with conviction as if I traveled to an enchanted land.

Driving to Sironoi, the closest village near Lel's home, orange balloons and banners adorned every rural center. The general elections were a couple of days away, and citizens gathered to voice their support of the Orange Democratic Movement (ODM). The party leader, Raila Odinga, or his father Oginga Odinga, had chased after the country's principal seat since the 1960s. Daily, the newspapers crammed the most recent polls and predictions, and as in America, the contest focused on two factions. The Rift Valley, where I stayed, would be, in large, voting for the ODM and opposing the current President Mwai Kibaki from the Party of National Unity (PNU). Tittle-tattle gossip hinted at hostilities following these elections, but trusting in democracy, I dismissed the notion.

After enjoying a beautiful day-long Christmas celebration, the champion runner drove me over the winding tarmac back to the HATC camp in Iten. Listening to jovial banter on the local radio, the host reported we should look out for certain minivans armed with troublemakers. Rebels, he jeered, attempted to rig the elections in favor of the PNU party. I wondered, how could a general election be unrailed by a few vans? The concept sounded ludicrous. Martin, however, advised caution, "Keep a low profile. Best you stick at home during the voting as there could be issues."

Staying put presented no problem, especially hearing Douglas Wakiihuri lodged at the camp. Douglas, the very man who battled Simon Robert Naali and Carl, on the day I stopped smoking and began running! Aside, I welcomed some downtime because the Manhattan Marathon business plan demanded attention.

The voting process passed peacefully on the 27th. The following day sparked questions and queries. Delayed results, inevitable as the votes traveled from remote counties, caused both jubilation and jumbles. As districts generally voted en masse, each splurge of ballots could cause a suspiciously large swing from one party over to the other. One report granted Raila, a Luo, a favorable position, yet the next prompted President Kibaki, a Kikuyu, the likely victor. Kibaki's PNU dislodged the KANU party at the last elections in 2002, a huge shock—KANU had ruled Kenya since independence in 1963. Tribalism, rampant over sub-Saharan Africa, finds each ethnic group fiercely loyal to locally born leaders. Living in the Rift Valley, an area holding an impressive forty-four of the 188 parliamentary seats, appointed you an ODM supporter because the Honorable William Ruto, an Eldoret-born political giant, backed the ODM party.

By the 29th, still, there was no declaration. People camped on street corners, arms akimbo, angered and exasperated. Slowly like the advent of a storm when the air cradles a scent of change, I sensed terrible troubles were brewing.

On the 30th, it became evident there would not be a candid resolution. Immediately, Kikuyus, remembering the violent ethnic clashes that occurred in 1992's voting, wished to exit the Luo and Kalenjin strongholds—I am surmising it to be vice-versa for Kalenjin living in the central (Kikuyu) provinces. John Mutai, our camp driver, received instruction to escort Douglas, a Kikuyu, and his guests Diane and Gerard Hartmann directly to the Eldoret Airport. I decided to accompany John, deeming it unwise that he traveled back alone because navigating the congested streets of Eldoret is a hazard at the best of times.

The five of us piled into the Land Rover and set out on the seventy-five-minute journey. To our surprise, the roads lay deserted. On the way, we passed roadblock after roadblock, with freshly painted ODM signs displaying crudely written slogans. Bonfires burned by, or on, the road where rebel stations sprouted up. Cumbersome rocks and boulders, a couple that must have required a group of men to shift or delivered by a tractor, blistered the tarmac to hinder the traffic. The unguarded barricades were no deterrent to us, and I joked, glancing at my watch, "Lunchtime, and the rebels are off duty." Even then, none of us guessed at the extent of the eruption landing on our doorstep.

Eldoret resembled a ghost town. The chaotic and bustling agricultural center, the fastest-growing urban zone in Kenya, with 300,000 inhabitants, was spookily quiet. We glided down the principal street, barely observing a solitary civilian. Only the highly trained General Service Unit (GSU) soldiers, outfitted in fortified riot gear, stalked the streets. Cradling an AK-47 in his arms, one soldier shifted his eyes on us when we passed. I held my breath because although there was no instruction not to drive, zero traffic on the road indicated otherwise, and as they say, *ignorantia juris non excusat.*

The former Olympic steeplechase champion, Matthew Birir, had called warning us that the town had been impassable for him. Birir tried navigating through Eldoret to visit me that morning though the army obstructed his progress. Maybe luck stayed with us? Likely, Pieter's royal blue Land Rover—painted the shade of police vehicles—snuck a case of mistaken identity. Used to dodging the hectic and fender bender driving scene in Eldoret, it felt surreal drifting along the vacant streets. Cautiously we departed the town center via the Kisumu Road. A gradual climb took us to the outskirts of the city and past Kapsaret towards the airfield. With no traffic, we made it there in record time.

The airport, awash under military guard, waited for the day's last plane departure before shutdown. The staff informed us after the thirty-odd seater shuttled back to Nairobi, the terminal was closing down. Thankfully, Douglas, Gerard, and Diane had secured seats, and immediately following the plane's take-off, we spun the car and scooted back to Iten.

Now, around three p.m., the situation began looking dicey. Leaving Eldoret, drunken rioters controlled the roadblocks. Agitators brandished machetes, clubs, and arrowed bows like war flags in the battle trenches. When you have little else, you will always remain with excuses—suddenly, every idler acted as a soldier of fortune.

We trailed a large white SUV, hoping for safety in numbers.

Coming closer, I recognized the car belonged to the world steeplechase champion, Shaheen, a former Kenyan who now represented an Arabian state. His driver performed admirably navigating the bulkier rocks placed randomly in the middle of the tarmac. The scenes, particularly the yelling citizens flanking the roads, evoked memories from the Hotel Rwanda movie. A machete, gun, or poison arrow is never a pleasant sight when held in the hands of drunken looters. I crossed my fingers that I would get home safe.

Ahead, as Shaheen's vehicle crawled towards the next barricade, his driver received orders to stop. A burning tire set upright in the center of the road screamed trouble. My heart started beating faster, things were thick, and God knows what things were, but the energy edged off the road.

Under instruction, the driver cut the engine. Men, armed with an array of weaponry, immediately rolled rocks behind the vehicle to stop the SUV from reversing and fleeing. One yobbo stood with a soccer ball-sized stone balanced in both hands at head height, eager to smash the windscreen. Hard to tell, but I presume money passed from one party to the other before they received instruction to proceed.

Presently, a man bearing a bow and arrow beckoned us forward. But as we approached, an unseen mob surged from behind several roadside structures and shacks. Out of nowhere, boisterous hooligans swamped the Land Rover—delighted cries of '*M'zungu, m'zungu*' brought new excitement to the day. Surely a stranded white man would be an easy pushover for a bribe?

The roadway now bristled with armed human traffic, and worryingly, the rocks before us became invisible under a sea of swarming sweaty bodies. The thugs clambering to yank open my door screeched like tortured geese, "*Pesa* (money) for the ODM, or you do not pass. No peace till Raila (is President). We will die for him." The chances that one of these troublemakers could scribble five lines on the policies of Odinga were slim yet, they repeated, 'We will die for Odinga Raila.'

Other drunkards demanded the men upfront drag me out of the

vehicle, "Pull him out," they chanted, and "*Choma, choma,*" which translates as burn in Swahili. Did they refer to the popular roast meat (*nyama choma*) and suggest I fund their lunch, or did they mean roast Toby? Heavens, images of the murdered boy on River Road resurfaced.

My door was open—I had been caught off-guard. Pulling harder on the handle, I tried to prevent it from opening further as grabbing arms lurched to tug me out of the passenger seat. Pungent smells and slurs hinted that alcohol constituted the main course at lunch. John's door was also open a crack, and he pleaded with the rebels in the local dialect.

"Toby, he is one of us. Leave him. Don't you know Chebaibai* and how he has helped this area? Do not harm him."

My Keiyo nickname, denoting a happy man.

Pretending stressed concern did not cluster my mind, I tossed jokes to the mob. Promising I carried no cash, I disappointed all by informing the loudmouths, "I need *your* money. I'm begging for charity." Meantime, I whispered to John to persist crawling forward, giving him the direction to veer left to avoid the jagged rocks. The anger escalated, and now our vehicle slightly rocked as those closest attempted to tip the heavy truck. Others focused on wrenching open the rear door, but thankfully the locks held. If the crooks scrambled inside the car, then John and I would lose the Land Rover. Why was I such a magnet for drama? Why had I been foolish when radio announcements insisted people stay at home? I should not have left the camp, but in my defense, how could I have predicted this mess? John continued inching forward, and although still surrounded, an opening between the boulders allowed an exit.

"Drive John!" I cried. He responded—stamping his boot upon the accelerator caused the diesel engine to snarl. The mob was caught unaware. Feeling the bumps, I imagine we ran over a foot or two.

Out of harm's way, I tuned in the radio. Kenya was boiling. 'Unless you have an essential reason, stay inside, lock your doors, and do not venture outside. We are in a state of emergency.' This announcement barked over the airwaves constantly. John—keenly listening in—revved the engine to its limits, figuring the sooner we reach home, the better. Fortunately, from thereon, the trip proved to be less stressful. At Kaptule center, a rowdy group hurled stones as we ferried through a wooden roadblock, yet not a pebble hit the target, and I appreciated John's rally car antics.

At the camp, a statehouse broadcast screened President Kibaki being sworn in to serve his second term. Another channel aired Raila refusing to concede and declaring voter fraud.

Disappointingly, neither man pleaded for peace as mayhem erupted like a volcano. Cries from the elder Kalenjin, recalling the days of the sixties, exclaimed, 'First you steal our lands, and now our Presidency.' They referred to the original Kikuyu government, which gifted plots in the Rift Valley to their supporters. In the book, 'Facing Mt. Kenya,' written by the founding President, Jomo Kenyatta, the author wrote, 'Nothing is more important than a correct grasp of the question of land tenure. For it is the key to people's life.' Kenyans are a nation of agriculturalists, and some folks in Eldoret talked fervently of reclaiming the forfeited land over bothering about a change in the presidency. If confusion and ethnic fighting began, the repossessing of lost pastures was possible.

Violence broke out right in front of our eyes, dividing the country in two. Like a trek for Noah's ark, a mass exodus of foreign workers and tourists began gravitating towards Nairobi's airport. Nationwide the stores, expecting—and experiencing—looting and rioting, hurriedly bolted doors whilst the opportunists overwhelmed the streets. On the national news, scenes showed hoodlums breaking into a Bata shoe store and having the gall to try on footwear before stealing. A different clip revealed a man struggling along the street with a large electrical appliance balanced on his back, looking much like a refrigerator. He had not been to the Bata store yet as he remained shoeless. The local news revealed bodies scattered on the ground in Burnt Forest, a village near Eldoret; the footage lacked any element of censorship. A reporter posed a haunting question, 'Who shall bury the dead of the fleeing tribe?'

Wangari Maathai, the Nobel Prize laureate, stated the clashes were an act of 'ethnic cleansing' whereas an international news agency termed the unrest, 'a near civil war.' As is often the case, the affluent neighborhoods were unaffected, but if you reside in poor or rural districts, then good luck.

By nightfall, Kenya became a country of conflict. Later, the news reported, the post-election violence led to a conservative estimation of 1,500 deaths and over 600,000 internally displaced people (IDP's) becoming hunted, hungry, and homeless. I, who grew up with Margaret Thatcher politics, miners' strikes, and poll-tax marches, was no stranger to demonstrations. Living in the social democratic stronghold of England, where protest rallies happened weekly and participating in a march could likely earn you school credits, disputes were nothing new. But the violence and bitterness, turmoil, and havoc, accompanying this unrest was horrifying. The strife was grievous and brutal and escalated by the hour.

On the night of December 30th, during mealtime, screams and hysterical wailing interrupted the usual calm. An enraged mob of people, sounding like a couple of hundred, approached the camp. Concerned, Pieter and I slipped out of the dining room and advanced the twenty meters to the compound gates.

As we lingered in the darkness, the night colors changed from violets and musky blues to brilliant yellows and oranges. Flames engulfed a building adjacent to the camp. A large complex housing eighteen families exploded into an inferno, and the occupants, hauling what possessions they could, fled for their lives. Iten was ablaze with a kaleidoscope of fiery colors, and the scent of smoke choked the air.

A local *matatu* driver darted inside our compound, blurting out the news that an unruly mob currently combed the town. The rabble hunted the Kikuyu people to incinerate their houses and properties. "That is why your neighbor's house burns. And if you shelter Kikuyus, yours will cook too. Then, if they refuse to flee town, they will roast. Right now, you can relax—your camp is not on the list."

These arsonists were the close neighbors of the people they terrorized. They knew precisely which families to target. "Stay indoors as the mob is armed," the driver warned before he sprung back to rejoin the gang and prove his alliance.

In the dining room, the foreigners still had not twigged on to what was happening, this despite the occasional volley of gunfire heard as the police, vastly overrun, clung to protect their compound where many Kikuyus had sought protection. I decided it would be best to muffle any outdoor noises and not alarm the guests. Removing a Spanish guitar out of its case, I struck up a tune. Rose Tanui and Dorcas Kosgei, two of the resident athletes at the camp, understood my motive and began singing. Before long, the visitors harmonized, and hearing yourself think became impossible.

Initially, Iten was labeled Hill Ten by the explorer Joseph Thomson, denoting the height of the location. From this vantage point, one can see a breathtaking vista of the surrounding villages. Later that night, in all directions, I saw a web of fires. Little dots of orange peppered the landscape like tiny stars against a moonless sky. Around Kenya, IDP's hid at police stations or huddled at churches, seeking refuge. International aid organizations closed down and evacuated their foreign workers. Ironically, the individuals claiming hardship/danger pay for working in Africa fled in the hour of need. Later in fundraising meetings, hearing, 'I do not trust the Kenyan government, the aid groups are the hope for the future.' I disagreed. When the staff of these teams absconded, it was the government who stood tall and stepped up.

The majority of citizens caused no trouble—only minor factions of disorderly rebels ripped up Kenya. The white canvas UN tents, routinely erected for refugee camps, now burst full of locals, and the army deployment focused on protecting fellow citizens. With the banning of live newscasts following Kibaki's announcement and foreign journalists ordered to vacate the country, impartial views became scarce. The TV aired gospel music, old news replays, and little else. Even living in an Internet world was useless because Iten enjoyed no real Wi-Fi access at this time, and few folks possessed a smartphone in 2007—certainly none of us who stayed at the camp.

On New Year's Eve, Pieter and Lornah, who lived a mile or two away, had dropped by to host a party. Pieter fried *Olli-Bollas*, a Dutch specialty of dough, dipped in a pot of hot oil. With popping sounds and remembering the earlier warning shots gunfire disturbance, I joked, "At least if we go, no one will be hungry." Since the worst had passed, or, so we thought, it was okay to have frivolity in a grave situation. Had I known what tomorrow would bring, that flippant statement would not have left my mouth.

On January 1st, a bombshell struck. The resident camp athletes and I sat shuffling cards when abruptly, the background music droning from the TV stopped. A newscaster appeared and read out a brief announcement. I have forgotten the exact horrifying statement, but the matter would cause even the steeliest of stomachs to churn. On the fringe of Eldoret town, twenty miles (32 km) west of where we sat, a church burned to cinders. Other religious buildings during this time were set alight, yet the agitators had sunk to the lowest rung.

The news related how a sizable mob had herded a group of women and children like cattle, young and old, inside the building and doused the holy structure in a wet coating of gasoline. The numbers were vague, but between thirty-five and fifty women and children perished in the flames. Betrayal had fallen on the bastions of religion—faith, love, and charity. The last colors of humanity descended from the flagpole.

What person would strike a match to ignite a furnace with intent to burn women and children alive and in a church of all places? That man, who is capable of creations, and gifted such potential, can stoop to the unspeakable defies all reason. Shocked by the news, I could not accept the words; the act belonged lost to the horrors of the savage era, not events that could happen in my neighborhood.

The crimes spread like a virus. Far east in Mombasa, eleven people roasted in a torched house, and out west to Kisumu, fatalities on this day hit fifty-six. A sisal ranch belonging to the former President's son, Gideon Moi, burned, as did a sugar plantation leaving hundreds of workers displaced with lives in tatters.

The violence of this day triggered evacuation flight procedures from multiple embassies. A chartered plane assisted the Dutch citizens, and with additional space, other nationalities could occupy the vacant seats in a jet leaving from Eldoret. Pieter confirmed passage for the foreigners residing at HATC, then Lornah telephoned the police to request an armed escort to the airport.

On January 2nd, the principal newspaper screamed out four words on the front page, 'A Nation in Crisis.'

Following breakfast, government vehicles rolled and clunked into our compound like tanks entering a battleground. With mobs ruthlessly enforcing the roadblocks by halting then looting traffic, the fortified protection was essential. Anxious foreigners, clutching bags and suitcases, breathed in relief when they climbed aboard the convoy. Yet seeing machine guns capable of firing three bullets per second mounted on the vehicles gave me nothing but the chills. Melancholy hung like a gray shadow over the camp, and the foreigners, now fully aware of the dangers, slunk around in drab miserable spirits eager to exit Kenya.

Lucia Kimani, a former citizen and Kikuyu athlete who resided in Bosnia, stood in line desperate to leave. Gripping a small rucksack, on the brink of tears, she waited to clamber onto the truck, but despite owning a European passport—and displaying it for all to see—the police refused her passage. Surmising it to be a ticket issue, I at once stated Lucia could assume my seat.

Already, I decided to stay in Kenya. At the camp, six local females were stranded and unable to travel on the roads. Hearing that a University Professor, Dr. Mengech, had struggled for four days to navigate the roadblocks to Eldoret extended no hope to these ladies. Professor Mike Boit faced similar frustrations, and both men were Kalenjin, not even Kikuyu. The mob, at their pleasure, ransacked properties and claimed possessions as the spoils of war. Should the controlling gangsters approach, since I was not a target, I might help to avert a disaster. With lives at stake, the January meetings I scheduled could wait.

However, the police commander expressed little interest in anybody's ticket. Speaking directly to Lucia, he reasoned, "We can't control the mob. The likelihood is they will scrutinize the vehicles at the roadblocks. Your presence endangers the foreigners." He contended the ruffians, who easily outnumbered the guards, would explode if they discovered a hidden Kikuyu—the facial features of the Bantu women are remarkably distinctive. Pleading, Lucia offered to sprawl flat, face against the dirty bed of the truck, and hide under the legs of the foreigners, but no concluded the police, it was too risky.

The Dutchman, Jeroen Deen, who was ever helpful at any Shoe4Africa event, trundled over to say goodbye. He posed a question, "Why not leave, or do you have a wish to die in Africa?" He thought it wrong I stayed, but to me, Kenya felt like home.

As the convoy departed, kicking pebbles, Lucia returned to unpack her bag. Beads of sweat rolled from her forehead, and I could think of no consolation words. That morning, a radio reporter declared in a town, fifty miles (80 km) to the northwest, the worries were not tribal violence; the danger was the louts targeted local women. With no Kikuyus left to abuse, the criminals attacked any ethnic groups, and the district hospital noted an increasing number of rape victims.

That night, under a shawl of darkness, a Kikuyu mother crept into the camp. With her home burned in Eldoret and nowhere to turn, she arrived alongside five young children and one baby. Looking at a point of collapse, I guessed the troop had traveled by foot. We prepared beds and brought buttered sandwiches, but the poor kids sat too distraught to eat.

After dinnertime, I tried elevating the gloomy mood of our growing team. Strumming national songs, I attempted to engage our visitors—but worries clustered the room like moths around a hurricane lamp. Naomi, a Kalenjin athlete whose brother perished in the 1998 Nairobi embassy bombings, did not help matters. Maybe frustrated by the situation, she drew her own conclusions, "Yes, Kikuyus are nasty, and they must depart from the Rift Valley. If they do not, they will get chased." As she spoke, she leered, curling her lips at Lucia, and I throttled the urge to fling her out of the camp like a tennis ball. Yet if Naomi fled blabbing to the mob in town, our building would be in flames tonight—a diplomatic approach was necessary.

The next day saw Pieter and me dashing through the cornfields when a mob of too many men approached the camp. Our spy, the rumormonger *matatu* driver, misinformed us reporting that foreigners now presented the prime target. Pieter had dropped by to deliver a flask of coffee when the driver rushed in, spilling the distressing news with half-sentences. He reckoned the armed insurgents were a couple of minutes away, "Get out, here, I'll tell, you Nairobi. They'll leave." Alarmingly, the hoodlums could be heard in the near distance chanting, 'Kill. Kill. Kill."

Chaining the gates so no one could enter the compound, we sprinted through the bush to gain a viewing point and work out why the focus had shifted to visitors. As we pushed past the overgrown foliage, we stumbled into Shaheen, the man I trailed at the roadblock. He confirmed the news, relating that George Bush publicly endorsed Kibaki; therefore, all outsiders became enemies to the ODM party. Fortunately, both men were wrong. Nobody pursued us, and another storm brewed, God knows where. Yet this little act exemplified how each day played out, with us waiting for the next disaster to occur.

Two days later, Lucia's luck changed. The police considered risking another armed convoy to the airport. This time the escort included nationals, so we smuggled Lucia into their compound.

The scene inside the station house was distressing. My eyes locked upon this grassy field. Like brightly colored tulips, forty-odd kids lingered on the green, not cramming in friendship but standing alone. Most youngsters wore soiled satin shirts and dresses of vivid colors clearly recognizable as their Sunday best. Arsonists must have torched their house, and the parents would have screamed to the kids to grab their smartest clothes, then flee for their lives.

I wandered around the field, and not one child spoke or fluttered an eye. Perhaps they had become numb to the bleak reality? As parents or caretakers bargained for a passage of safety in the limited vehicles, kids stood like wilting petals resting on dead stalks. Why did I witness this misery? Was I performing any good by staying in Kenya? Being unable to help felt like digging my fingernails into an open wound. I scoffed, reflecting on Dr. Mehta's hoity-toity words, 'There is a meaning *why* you came to Africa.' That sentence sounded ridiculous and redundant.

More dismal news followed, confirming the rumors that a friend, the former Olympian Lucas Sang, had been murdered. His hacked and charred body, discovered in Munyaka, was unrecognizable but for a shred of red cloth from his tracksuit leg. Two other Olympians, Kiprotich and Koech, both lost their fathers. Frustratingly for Paul Koech, he was away, campaigning for peace in Darfur as the murder occurred. Closer to home, Driver John's dad suffered ghastly injuries when escaping from a raid. Grim days transitioned to graver as the hooligans continued causing havoc. Tensions frayed, and each knock on the door rapped like a death threat. Buildings were burning, bodies severed, and countless destitute casualties piled up in the IDP camps. If people received a scoop of maizemeal per day at the help-centers, it would be a miracle as the rebels looted the Red Cross trucks ferrying donated produce.

Our supplies dwindled too—electricity outages became commonplace, and the drinking water was long gone. Boiling pitiful amounts of rainfall for tea meant personal hygiene took second place. Naomi's recommendation of being smelly together offered no solution, so becoming creative, I devised eco-bathing. Not for the bashful, at dawn—sans clothes—you rolled in the overgrown grass wet from the dew. After three rollovers to the right, you stop, soap, and lather the body. Then, you repeat the action to the left to rinse off. Surprisingly effective, and after much laughter and giggles, we all began smelling of roses.

11th of January 2008. Four days ago, Pieter flew to Holland. His text read, 'The route to the airport is terrible, hundreds of kiosks burnt—it looks like a war zone.' Now I viewed it for myself on the journey to Lucas Sang's funeral in Kuinet. In the more built-up zones—but now broken down—the roadside lay like a sea of breezy ash. Numerous cars, roasted to empty iron shells, already boasted a tint of stained rust. Driving with a talented runner, Solomon Bushendich, the word destroyed enveloped every sentence—homes, lives, and futures.

I reflected how days before the violence erupted, I bumped into Lucas Sang in Eldoret. Healthy, wealthy, and enjoying the farm life, he had spoken merely of his excitement for the Christmas holidays. A liked and revered man, Lucas represented Kenya in the 1988 Seoul Olympic Games and often frequented town for his agribusiness.

The funeral centered around an open field adjacent to Sang's home. Farm machinery, poised for plowing the fertile fields, made for a poignant reminder of an interrupted life. The who is who of the athletes' fellowship stood in mourning, and I estimated a crowd of 2,000 had gathered by the time we arrived.

Ushered to the VIP seats but envisaging lengthy talks, I opted for the dried grass at the perimeter of the field—this way, I could sneak out early. All around, it was a sad and somber affair. Listening to the speeches, I heard folks encourage men to auction their cows, purchase weapons, and avenge Lucas's death. The phrase *Love thy neighbor*, and *God has made of one blood all peoples of the earth* sounded scornfully forgotten upon this day.

Later, as the choir began chanting a melodious tune, the elders explained that, as the sun sank into the horizon, the coffin should simultaneously descend to the soil. But, at this moment, a ripple of panic occurred. The rumors spread a Kikuyu mob, knowing individuals assembled in mass, had prepared a nightfall ambush.

The attack was perchance gossip, but grievers hurried to locate their cars and evaporate into the dark—you do not gamble on a battlefront. Bushendich had disappeared, so I began strolling towards the tarmac. Ben Limo, a top athlete, hearing a local commissioner met an untimely death, rushed home but stopped to offer me a ride. Yet I felt an intense desire to linger and walk, to collect my thoughts. I could hitch a lift later.

Ambling absentmindedly, distracted by a strong waft of woodsmoke spiraling from a roadside home, I glanced around and noticed a troupe of kids offering me a shadow escort. I beckoned the shy teens forward. The youngsters, looking stressed and agitated, cut straight to the chase, "Sir, we are in fear. If children die inside churches, they will burn us in a classroom, right?" They asked with alarming frankness, terrified that as the school term began, their building might become a target. What could I say? Lie through my teeth and promise better times ahead?

Nobody had any idea what tomorrow would bring. One boy squeezed my arm, "You are the Shoe4Africa man. Will you help stop this fighting?" The words were not as much, 'Can you help?' but seeking what actions I took to help. But how? I had been asking myself the identical question every day. Even stepping outside for the funeral denoted irresponsibility when the sane advice recommended abandoning Kenya or at the very least hiding behind double bolted doors.

Raking my brains, an idea occurred to stage a peace march. Following 9/11, I organized a friendship run in Central Park. No medal, officialdom, or bib number needed, yet hundreds of runners united—the event presented quite a statement. Why not switch my shoe events over to promote peace? Glancing up, I noted darkness had descended, and black knotted clouds blotted out the purple dusk; it was time to return home. Thumbing down a ride from Katwa Kigen, a renowned lawyer, I thanked and assured the children, "You've inspired me. I now have an idea on how to help!"

The white SUV incident. Roadblocks were hard to navigate. Those arrowheads are dipped in poison. (Author, Thilo Thielke, mid/below).

Chapter 14. 2008

LOVE. PEACE. UNITY.

The real and lasting victories are those of peace and not of war. –
Ralph Waldo Emerson

The peaceful demonstration I planned promised to be the most prominent positive news event since the outbreak of the violence, so I craved extra oomph. The population should glance at the newspapers, and the concept of unity must pounce from the print. But how could I grab the front page of the nation's news? What might captivate the imagination of the entire country? Then, it struck me. Instead of concentrating on the Rift Valley runners, why not locate forty-two legends from across the four corners of Kenya to symbolize the country's forty-two ethnic groups? Starting with the 1950s, when Kenya initially assigned athletes to the Olympic Games, I could assemble medal-winning heroes from each decade. In America, this would mirror every NBA Hall of Famer throughout history, gathering onto one court.

Not stopping there, I would recruit 600 schoolgirls, adorned in the yellow peace T-shirts, to trail the runners, adding volume to the occasion and closing down the streets. The entourage could wave olive branches, instilling the spirit of peace and harmony into the children's hearts.

To date, two Kenyan men had won the world marathon championship title, and fittingly, each represented one of the warring ethnic groups. Luke Kibet, a Kalenjin and the current holder, had been caught in the crossfire of a stoning fight and knocked unconscious on the streets of Eldoret. Wrapped in a bloodied bandage, Luke pledged his support. The former champion, a Kikuyu, was nonother than Douglas, the athlete who battled Simon Robert Naali—the man I rushed to the airport. Perfect, they could both hoist the national flag, leading the march through town. That striking tri-color emblem, designed by the justice and constitutional affairs minister, Tom Mboya, in 1963, to display state unity.

The violence had boiled down to a discontented calm with minor outbreaks and skirmishes, but little had improved. Hatred and blame continued to simmer into the consonants and vowels of hushed conversations as hundreds of thousands of citizens remained depressed and destitute. Intertribal resentment seethed intensely, and the government collaborated with the mediator, Kofi Annan, towards resolutions of power-sharing responsibilities to appease both factions. Yet the cause, the underlying roots, would they be solved by Kofi's actions?

I believed the message of peace required better promotion on the community level. In China, over 99.25% of the population gains access to a television. Therefore, to transmit central government media via mainstream methods works. Yet in rural East Africa, where one in 200 households own a TV set, area chiefs and newspapers held the amplified voice. If the cover of the Daily Nation, East Africa's largest circular, captured a picture of kids marching in solidarity, flanked by the running legends of a united population and not of disjointed ethnic groups, the event was sure to soften and bond hearts.

Keeping quiet regarding the activities became imperative—if the day twisted into a political rally, it would constitute a disaster. Hosting a function celebrating so many major names, legends of the international sports world presented challenges. Knowing politicians, desperate for a platform, might arrive with authority for a hostile takeover was a worrying concern. Hence, precautions were paramount, like recruiting the schoolgirls two days before the event and selecting six diverse schools (eight would show up). Stating each kid earned a T-shirt and free running shoes proved an adequate incentive to attract numbers. Then, twenty-four hours prior, I requested, "Can kids bring olive branches? I'll explain why later."

As dawn broke, on the day of the race, shades of amber coated the town of Iten like a giant sunflower umbrella. Leave alone the thousand plus T-shirts I purchased, but because individuals understood the gist—they put two and two together and decorated themselves with saffron strokes. From all angles, people streamed like vibrant ribbons, and happy-faced kids clutched olive branches, or an equivalent, in their hands. Seventy-eight-year-old Nyandika Maiyoro MBE, the captain of the inaugural Kenyan squad traveling to the Olympics in 1956, performed as our Grand Marshal. Donning his original blue team blazer and clutching the battered leather suitcase purchased to travel to the 1954 Commonwealth Games, Nyandika arrived a day early. He insisted on standing roadside to welcome all guests, like Wilson Kiprugut, the first Kenyan to medal in the Olympics, 1964, and Tecla Chemabwai, a member of the original women's squad from 1968.

When the athletes reunited, deep emotions stirred as happy memories resurfaced. All of us rejoiced to watch heads roll in laughter and a backslapping that took place in the essence of harmony and love.

Before marching, the two marathon world champions hoisted the black, red, and green with a white trim Kenyan flag high against a dome of cobalt sky. The unifying image ignited a cheer swirling through the assembled crowd. Proudly, the two men stood ahead of fifty-odd world-class icons, fronting the rally. The energetic schoolgirls, dancing and singing, trailed the runners. Junior boys galloped forward to thread arms with the girls. On the kids' initiative, they began chanting, 'Shoe4Africa, Run for Peace. Shoe4Africa, Run for Peace.' Eyeing the crowd, I recognized a few Sudanese, Ugandan, and Tanzanian athletes rallying their support. The campaigners made quite the impression trooping through the unsuspecting town.

A girls' two-mile race followed, and the famous athletes graciously formed an extended line to hand-gift each finisher their first pair of running shoes. Two hours of inspiring speeches ensued, and Douglas rose beyond anyone's expectations. Mastering phrases in Kalenjin, he composed a ballad of peace to sing to the crowds in their local tongue. With the national media attending, we received TV, print, and radio coverage, and the following day we captured the back and center pages of the nation's premier newspaper. Unfortunately, army helicopters dispatched to squash a skirmish near the Ugandan border spoilt my scheme to steal the front page!

A touching moment came in the evening after the athletes had departed. Walking to present an athlete with a spare T-shirt, a familiar drunkard approached. Inevitably, his conversations involved an ask, and today must be for the colorful garment I openly carried; I was wrong. Stumbling forward, his alcohol-laced breath choking the air, he muttered, "I want to thank you for doing what you did today; we needed that." And then, with faltered steps, he staggered away.

With our success in Iten, numerous requests sprouted to duplicate the program. CNN's Inside Africa attended the subsequent event in Nandi County. The news channel admired the principle of providing shoes to the children to gain a running start in life. On the day, a correspondent David MacKenzie selected one random child from the large crowd for a pre-race interview. The chosen boy declared he longed for shoes to commence training; the footwear, he promised, would transform his life. Sure enough, young Barselius Kipyego did win a pair and ten years later became a talented runner winning a prestigious world championship medal alongside other accolades!

The following event, in Eldoret, was not without considerable risk and might have easily backfired. Twenty thousand people—mainly Kikuyu—lived in shabby white tents in a heavily guarded field within the city limits. I orchestrated a peace event at the largest IDP camp in the country; the plan was to march a school of Kalenjin children from Eldoret, wearing our peace shirts, along the main road for two miles (3.2 km) before entering the site. At the camp, the displaced youngsters would form two rows. The Kalenjin schoolers would enter, shaking each camp kid's hand as they proceeded down the lines, handing a second T-shirt to a new friend. Now, all united wearing matching peace uniforms, the 500 youngsters would run a race weaving through the overcrowded camp before the eyes of the bewildered adults.

My bet was any child participating might consider the other clan as friends. Their memories of the awful clashes could end on a note of grace. The Hill School, one of Eldoret's oldest, agreed to partner—the headteacher eagerly signed up for the kids to participate in such a transformative event.

As I did in Iten, I kept the plans vague, divulging the specific details to nobody. I could imagine the headlines if this backfired; 'Foreign idiot leads a school of kids into hostile grounds after months of fighting—what did he expect?'

Since January, countless times, I journeyed to this site hauling food parcels to the hungry residents. My friends living here were both young and old, and I knew I could rope in a team as on-the-fly volunteers. The heroes to inspire the children, as usual, reverted to the legendary athletes. Traveling west from Nairobi was John Ngugi, an Olympic—and a five-time world—champion. He admitted feeling cautious reaching the Kalenjin lands. "But I must be here to help you to promote your project," he asserted. Another Olympian arrived hobbling on a cane. Ben Jipcho, shot in the knee during the clashes, too insisted upon taking part in the reconciliation process. Despite the immense pain, he trekked one mile with the children before scooting ahead in a *matatu* to greet us at the camp entrance.

When the race began, kids quickly bonded by grasping the hands of their new friends. The adult IDPs, startled by the commotion, burst out of their tents. Joyful for any distraction after months of drudgery, they cheered as if attending a football match.

Spectating on that day stood the wiry thin Kimani Maruge, who first attended primary school when aged eighty-four, acquiring him the nickname of the world's oldest schoolboy. Why a Mau Mau freedom fighter, who battled for Kenya's independence in the 1950s, lived inside an IDP camp under military guard was pitiful. When Maruge watched the youngsters run, wetness crept into his eyes. At first, I thought sadness flushed his heart, but then I saw him break into a cheerful grin. They were tears of joy and hope.

⊱⊰

Claudio Berardelli, an Italian, is a longtime resident of Eldoret. Owning a fire-red Ducati motorcycle, as skinny as a broom, few folks can imagine his profession. Claudio is an internationally recognized distance coach who has guided countless obscure athletes to glory and prosperity. We initially met in 2004, devouring pancakes in Puerto Rico, and had been close friends since. Due to his time-consuming job, we often meet in the evening, and after dinner, I will spend a night at his house because the public transport from Eldoret to Iten ceases at seven p.m.

Early one morning, leaving Claudio's, I was tramping to the Iten-bound bus station. Except, an eerie sensation urged me to drop by the destroyed church that dominated the world headlines on January 1st. I cannot explain this impulse, but starting to trust in destiny, I reversed directions. It was a decision that transformed my life. Uncertain of the actual site location, I borrowed Claudio's driver, Andrew, and set out for the district of Kiambaa on the outskirts of Eldoret. After fifteen minutes of driving around in circles, we appealed for help. But to our surprise, the locals refuted that any such event had taken place. Worse yet, a couple of the men accosted us, threatening to strike the car's bonnet with sticks if we proceeded. Despite their warnings, we soldiered on traversing deserted dusty backroads. Andrew wished to turn back; knowing nothing more than the church sat in an arbitrary field with no street address was of little use. Stubbornly, not accepting defeat, I instructed Andrew to keep driving.

After another ten silent minutes, a scruffily dressed Kikuyu man jumped out from the side bushes and scurried forward. Flapping his arms like a windmill, he anticipated the object of our search.

He resembled an older man, looking around sixty-five years, and stated he was born upon this soil. "Like most, I lost everything. House burned, cows seized, and how you see me today is all I have. How can I start again in life? Every day I question myself, was my life worth living to reach this amount of misery? A lifetime spent toiling to end up with zero?"

He slept beside a temporary security structure the police erected after the church burning along with his nightmares and suffering. The farmer who knew too well what happened agreed to escort us towards the ruins. He had his reasons, "I want to show you so you will tell the story many times, so this never happens again."
He jogged in front of the car and refused to take a ride. Indeed, we stood 200 meters (218 yards) away from the land where the atrocity happened.

In a field of scorched grass lay the depressing skeleton of the destroyed building. Slag, rubble, and broken walling lay practically leveled to the ground. Oddments, like a row of burned bicycles, the blackened bedsprings of what had been piles of mattresses, and a withered wreath of dead flowers portrayed a ghostly picture. Health workers had removed the decipherable forms of beings, but the clear-up looked rudimentary. I heard most of the bodies were unrecognizable and charred to burned cinders. Nearby, in a bed of ashes, I spied a ruined shoe. With both the toe-box and heel part burnt, the charcoal remains of a shin bone protruded from the shell; that image left little to the imagination.

Our guide began weeping. Slumping shackled in a state of sorrow, he scrambled words in his dialect—I did not know what to say or do. I glanced over at Andrew and saw more tears falling. How did this happen? These souls must have been in agony during their last moments. To die huddled, barricaded, and caged inside a burning coffin of a church? I felt hopeless and stupid. Why on earth did I want to come here?

"You see this piece of a headscarf, the blue cloth, look," the man pointed to the toasted material where one scrap was surprisingly recognizable. "This belongs, belonged, to a sister who was crippled. She sat in a wheelchair. Her burned chair is right there," his arm gestured to a fire-ruined metal frame. "She aged over eighty years and injured who? You know, the youngest to die was three months old." Unable to stop himself, he broke into convulsing sobs. Tearful moans garbled his words, "If you want to uncover the truth of the happenings, ask Grace as she was inside the church as it burned."

Still numbed by the horrors, I turned in the direction he indicated; I had imagined we were alone. But hunched over by a pile of earth and rubble, where I presumed the church's altar once stood, squatted a woman. Had she been there all along?
A little apprehensive, I wandered forward to greet the lady. Honestly, I seized this as an opportunity to distance myself from the grieving man. I felt responsible for rekindling his troubled memories.

Approaching the crouching woman, I inquired if she could describe why and how this event materialized. Nothing made sense. She gazed over with faraway eyes as if weighing me up, and ten good seconds passed before she climbed from her knees, and I stood face-to-face with the flaccid shadow of a human. A blind man could have sensed the leaden yolk of grief languishing upon her drooping shoulders. She introduced herself, "My name is Grace Githuthwa, and I am a woman without the will or reason to live." Wiping the grimy soil coating her hands upon a stained olive-colored shirt, she narrated her devastating tale. "It was near noon, and since the 30th, we slept here because our houses burned. When the homes caught fire, we dragged out mattresses and possessions to camp by our church for refuge. For two days, it sufficed as shelter. Then on January 1st, as we sat chatting, we heard blood-curdling screams. A mob approached, so we dashed for the church—It was dreadful. They fired the arrows at us, and those sharp tips carry poison. You will be dead in two minutes if that arrow strikes. The furious people waved machetes and flung stones, anything at us. 'We are only women,' we screamed, and 'leave us because we are harmless women and children.' Our men were away and unable to help."

Grace spoke of how she huddled with other ladies, shaking in fright, inside the church. "Outside, they hauled our mattresses, blocked the entrance, and jammed the windows. Instantly came the smell, the foul stench of fuel." She stopped talking and reflected as if trying to connect dots that did not make sense. "Definitely, they transported the fuel with the intent of arson. Very soon, the church caught fire, and the smoke dragged like a fog. I was so frightened because no one could understand why they wanted to burn us. It was terrifying seeing more than one woman's clothes catch on fire. Then the burning roof beams fell in on us."

She paused; the emotions became overwhelming, and the skin around her eyes tightened. I fumbled for words of consolation, but she extended a calloused hand—she was not finished,
"When the mattresses burned down, boys scrambled, climbing through the windows. Others darted for the doorway, but they faced flying arrows. The confusion became crazy, and I heard a Kalenjin man standing near the entrance bellowing for the madness to stop. He cried the mob had gone too far and to let us out of the church, 'Enough,' he screamed, 'Enough.' Seeing a chance, with my daughter following, we hurried for the doorway, but outside, Miriam, she is three, was missing. I wrapped a blanket around my head to filter the smoke and went searching. I found Miriam by the altar."

Grace's unblinking eyes now left mine, and she turned her gaze. I presumed to where she had last seen her daughter stand. After clearing her throat, she continued,
"I snatched Miriam's hand and ran. At the church entrance, one elderly lady caught my clothes. She had fallen on the ground near the flames and held tightly to my skirt. I screamed, 'Let go,' but she refused. I do not know why. Did she fear being left behind? I do not know. But, picking up Miriam, who was small, I flung her out on the grass. Then, I frantically tried to release myself from this woman's grip, who had become crazy, believing she now burned. She clung so tight the dress ripped. But the people there,"

Grace trembled, tears flooded down her cheeks as she lost her composure, "the mob, who were our neighbors, our very neighbors, they had snatched my baby and hurled her into the fire, to die, in the worst of the flames."

The image of a three-year-old burning, a child who played games instead of politics, who laughed and learned in place of arguing and fighting, was horrifying. Faintness and dizziness cuffed me like a barreling truck, and tears stung my eyes. Little Miriam's face formed, fighting for her last breath whilst the flames carried her to a terrible and tragic death. What type of man flings a helpless child into a furnace? Oh my, how could I offer comfort? I mumbled words, "It's senseless, shameful… it's."

Grace looked up and cut me off, "No." For the first time, she appeared a little hopeful, clasping her hands together. The following words escaping from her lips surprised me, "There is a meaning for this happening."

When I spat out the word "What," it was not because I misheard, but Grace repeated, "There is a meaning for this. God knows. He knows there is a meaning."

The last time—the only time—I heard those words, insinuating a tragic event held a practical meaning, came from Dr. Mehta. In my circles, if a terrible act occurs, we blame humans, animals, or nature. Grace repeated the exact sentence Dr. Mehta spoke when I came within an inch of dying. What kind of faith did these individuals retain? Was it a coping mechanism that Grace must believe Miriam's brief life was not in vain? Or had religion brainwashed her, and the Doctor, to deem that everything of significance—despicable or not—happens for a meaning? I did not understand. Furthermore, I am listening to the mother of the dead child speaking? Show me any sense or reveal a valid reason.

I left Grace standing alone, suffering in an insurmountable stage of grief. Losing a child goes beyond the term labeled as devastation. Watching your infant roast in the most chilling of murders must be like bearing a sentence of execution for every waking day of your life. Stuffing notes in her hand, uttering useless words that seemed to fall like stones from my lips to the hard soil, I hugged a listless and wrecked woman. Walking across to the car, the phrase, 'there is a meaning,' looped like a broken record inside my head.

Leaving Kiambaa, confusion racked my brains. A need to help kicked in, but my part was organizing the peace march—this church business appeared way too heavy. Briefly, I wondered; should I raise money to renovate the house of worship? Yet, I knew that act would backfire. I already ran into trouble two weeks ago for trying to help after purchasing a bicycle for a fifteen-year-old boy, Philip Kimunya.

Clambering through the inferno, crawling out of a burning church window, Philip had confronted the mob. He received a thrashing but somehow had survived. When I bumped into him at the general hospital, his body had scabby burn scars smothering his arms and legs. When I inquired what he yearned for most in life, he responded to own a bicycle, though it might be months before he could ride it.

Hurrying to the supermarket, I purchased a bike, the best on offer, which drew the rage of a crowd who witnessed the gift being wheeled into the hospital. The idlers had lingered until I exited, then hollered, "Hey white man, are you buying bicycles for our children stuck in Kikuyu land? Why are you not choosing to help them? You are a traitor, a bad man. Go home." And so, the insults flowed. Explaining I cared not for ethnic preferences would fall on deaf ears. I just heard a boy escaped from hell and desired a gift, and I simply wanted to help. Was that so wrong?

Next page: 1. Marathon World Champions Douglas Wakiihuri, a Kikuyu, and Luke Kibet, a Kalenjin, lead over forty-two Kenyan legends symbolizing the forty-two different tribes on a peace march.
2. Six hundred schoolgirls completing the Run for Peace event.
3. Wilson Kiprugut was Kenya's 1st medalist in the '64 Olympics. Nyandika Maiyoro, was on Kenya's 1st Olympic team in 1956. The two men served as the peace run's ambassadors.

281
300

Shoe4Africa
run for Peace
Shoe4Africa
run for Peace

CHAPTER 15. 2008

EAST & CENTRAL AFRICA'S 1st PUBLIC CHILDREN'S HOSPITAL?

History will judge us by the difference we make in the everyday lives of children. – Nelson Mandela

Driving back, neither Andrew nor I opened our mouths as if we concealed a despicable secret. Only when we approached the town center did I speak. I requested he drop me at the Gran Prix café, as strong coffee, the strongest, might prevent my head from swirling. Did I want Miriam's face appearing with charcoal lips and smoke filtering through her eye sockets spinning inside my mind? Of course not. But how could I forget? Hopefully, the owner Moses Tanui was around—a man I met during that first run in Kenya twelve years ago. Ordering a drink, I occupied a garden seat in the shade of an overgrown tree bending like a weeping willow. Scratching words on a notepad, I composed a poem for Miriam because what else could I do? Perhaps I should invest in a gravestone, but where would I place it?

As the waitress handed me the cup, Pieter and his wife Lornah entered the café. Lornah stood locked in conversation, but Pieter ambled over in my direction. When he approached, he tossed a blue laminated folder on the table and asked, "Hey Toby, do you want to do this?" But it was scarcely a request since before I could respond, he brushed the document aside like dirty crumbs off the tabletop. He began rambling about the car he had recently purchased. But the wording on the pamphlet diverted my concentration, "What on earth is that document about?" Pieter sighed, tossing back his head, "You remember my friend, the doctor? I hinted, hinted only, I might be willing to fund a modest charitable project to the tune of a couple of hundred dollars. Well, that doctor went crazy. Completely crazy."

The doctor returned with a monster of a pitch, not for 200 dollars, but requesting a multi-million-dollar hospital. Pieter was likely to chuck the document in the wastepaper bin. Holding the papers, I read the bold typeset words aloud.

A PROPOSAL TO BUILD EAST & CENTRAL AFRICA'S 1st PUBLIC CHILDREN'S HOSPITAL.

"Wait," I could not help myself. "Let me," my mind flowed faster than any tongue could click with an imagination spinning in cartwheels. A slideshow of events slammed against a blank screen. This experiential life, green satchels, and Major Ramachandra's free spirit. My wonderful treatment at the children's hospital in England. Starting to run. Dropping out of school, Amsterdam poverty days, and again starting to run again after recognizing Carl. The Nike sponsorship race, inferring—like Mr. Matthew indicated—that running could launch exciting adventures. Bumping into Simon Robert Naali, then Noel directing me to Eldoret. Kibera, the Crocodile Christmas & the Machakos shoe race. The Swedish woman at the airport, gifting her footwear. Authoring a book about Kenya, and by fluke, having the manuscript published. That horrendous attack in Zanzibar and witnessing firsthand African healthcare for the locals. The healing of Dr. Mehta, his belief, and his conviction. An unknown travel agent. London Charing Cross surgeons, saving my life. The NYC Marathon, Karen dying, and the terrorism of 9/11. The forming of an official charity, the clashes, the peace movement, and now

Miriam. Grace lived six miles (9.6 km) away at the IDP camp, and only by chance had she decided this morning to revisit a site of gruesome memories. All these circumstances spoke like bold statements provoking me to ask, is this proposal scripted for me? Even bumping into Pieter carrying the file in a random café signified an improbability; this was the first time I had ever seen him walking in Eldoret. Furthermore, had I swigged the coffee ten minutes ago, the moment would never have occurred. A public hospital for children, how perfect, a center to gather regardless of culture, class, sex, or creed.

The forces combined, at least for me, and I knew beyond doubt, this opportunity presented a calling. But wait, hold up, I had committed to the marathon. I realized I stood at the most diverse of any crossroads—the weightiest decision of my professional life. Accepting the hospital scheme remained impossible as an ancillary project to the Manhattan Marathon. Both required a laser focus, an over-the-top full-time commitment. What a choice, 7,000 miles (11,265 km) apart, two separate continents, and two diverse tasks. Which should I do? Go for a dazzling career job where I named my salary or stick to the unpaid volunteer work?

The running event suggested the logical occupational choice. My life, all my contacts, were immersed in athletics. I could purchase a car instead of pedaling a bicycle and secure an apartment—my expertise promoted one choice and canceled out the other. Plus, If I dropped the marathon project, fat chance Shmuel would lounge around waiting. He had already invested considerable capital establishing the company. I could hear the rasp of any financial advisor, 'Toby, choose the hospital, and you will be penniless for the rest of your life.' Yikes, which should I do? As I juggled the two options, the melodic strains of Dr. Mehta bellowed in my ear. Without any doubt, eliciting the words of the doctor, this must be *the* reason why I came to Africa. Instantly, I decided, "I will build this project." And I whispered, for little Miriam. Pieter winced, issuing one of those, *'Are you crazy?'* frowns.

Only later, in Iten, did I pause, breathe, and think. My qualifications for this gargantuan task were hardly impressive. I had no training in fundraising or construction. No team of workers or even one staff member waited in the wings to support me. My medical experience, although considerable, originated from the wrong side of the bed. My finances barely kept me afloat, let alone suggesting that I should embark upon such a project. Parental aid ended when I left home—no old family money, or indeed new, would cushion this ride. Since I never graduated, no school alumni would rally at my rear. I lived in America as an immigrant on a temporary residence permit, residing in an illegal sublet—had I selected the rational choice? Was it judicious to say no to a billionaire partner?

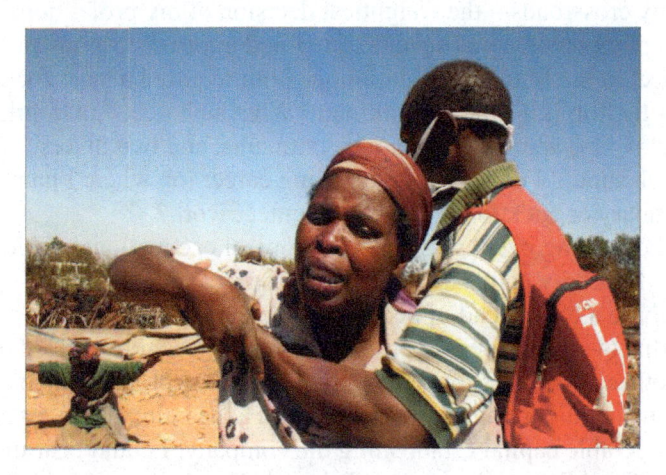

Grace was insistent that there was a meaning to her daughter's death. Philip's grandma sinks to her knees behind. Photo: Thilo Thielke.

Thumbing through the proposal, I began searching for loopholes. If any item appeared dubious, I would jump ship and step back to the Manhattan Marathon. But turning the pages, each line of the preamble coaxed me to understand I had chosen correctly. How could it be, in sub-Saharan Africa's forty-six countries, there stood just one public children's hospital? The Red

Cross constructed a facility fifty years ago in Cape Town, South Africa, yet no other country followed suit? The report recorded over thirty pediatric institutions in the UK and 250 in the USA. Therefore, one dedicated public hospital for an estimated 500,000 million youngsters in the sub-Saharan, whereas one per 290,000 kids in the USA? Calculating the economics of this venture, both in construction and in service, the center would create a profound impact generating thousands of local jobs. The concept certainly aligned with my aspirations for our newly founded charity.

Kenya, like many developing countries, had yet to prioritize pediatrics. Maintaining the healthcare system was the goal. 17.5% of the U.K.'s GDP channeled to medical, whereas the number hovered around 5% in Kenya—funds for new hospitals were unavailable. Children attended general hospitals, most of which lacked pediatric specialties, and naturally, these complexes, especially with booming populations, became overrun. Stories circulated how parents might hear no bed space was available for their child.

Once, in Nairobi, I confronted a doctor who offered this harrowing explanation, "We are constantly above 150% occupancy, so hard choices happen. Keeping an adult alive means ten orphans stay off the streets, but if we prioritize a child and one adult dies," He never completed the sentence. The words struck me as a heartbreaking reality and the cycle of life in reverse to my childhood. Simon Biwott, whom I had gifted shoes to in 1995 before he exploded into his world-class marathon career, included his experience: "Even if your child is fortunate and sees a nurse at a general hospital, you will rarely discover syringes, or any equipment, sized for kids."

From personal experience, I could attest to a country requiring a quality public facility dedicated solely to the children. I cannot imagine the trauma for kids to witness sick adults inside the same premises, wailing and writhing in pain. Kids required a stand-alone separated building.

Dr. Okwiya, a Kenyan US-based doctor, one of my helpers on

the Marathon Monday, related this telling story of his youth, *"I was admitted with severe osteomyelitis to the left leg as a ten-year-old. Later, an adult patient was admitted to the bed next to mine, moaning in pain through the night. The following morning after a commotion, his lifeless body was taken away. I saw and heard it all, lots of blood on the floor. The experience was quite scary and disturbing, vividly remember it to this day."*

༄༅

To commence my work, I thought it judicious to gen up on African health facts. Pouring over the websites of WHO, UNICEF, and Save the Children, I unearthed some mind-blowing statistics. Over one billion people live in sub-Saharan Africa, and it is the region of the world with the largest public health crisis. Although sheltering 11% of the world's population, this area carries a quarter of the global disease burden. How could it be one in eight sub-Saharan kids died before reaching the age of five, and two-thirds of those deaths proved to be either treatable or preventable? And, shockingly, 80% of kids who died did so without ever seeing a health care provider.

The last matter I read on the Internet stunned me—I did not walk alone. I enjoyed the eminent company of Nelson Mandela, who, unbelievably, embarked on a mirror mission in South Africa. Here are his punching words from 2005, *"(A public) Children's Hospital, will be a credible demonstration of a commitment of African leaders, to place the rights of children in the forefront, nothing less would be enough."* His foundation strived to achieve the same objective and would later open a children's hospital in Johannesburg in 2017.

If my energies poured into this project, it must be the best effort possible. Not a partially used building, a white elephant with vacant floors and invisible patients, but a bustling center that drastically upgraded pediatric public healthcare for the region. Starting date 2008—my personal development goal should be in 2023, that I would have contributed my part to help obliterate the sorry ⅛ mortality statistic. Each issue I unearthed demanded research, like, why was a patient treated in a private hospital admitted for three days, yet the public institutes averaged nine? What represented the ultimate design for a children's hospital for maximum airflow, preventing the spread of infectious diseases? Where to begin? Which elements might initiate a systematic sweeping change?

Back in New York and eager to share the news, I convened a board meeting. Announcing our tiny nonprofit planned to gift Kenya—and East & Central Africa—its first Public Children's Hospital was electrifying. I could hardly wait to spill the beans.

The board aligned with most small-scale charities—friends who gathered around a kitchen table three or four times a year. Representing the entire staff, I listed progress updates, reports on finance, fundraising, and upcoming goals. These meetings took less than an hour, and that included the mandatory small talk.

Anthony, who joined our directors in the spring of 2007, embraced the hospital idea and could not have been more supportive. However, all other members voiced the opposite view and collectively resigned the following day. In fairness, it is impossible to know anything about an organization, or its workings, unless you have a hands-on position or put in the hours. Therefore, to attend a meeting, expecting to hear about shoes sent to the post office and happy recipients, and listen to such a radical suggestion as I presented, it is no surprise my announcement backfired.

Reflecting, I do not blame the members and might have quit myself. Where indeed was I qualified to conduct such a development? How did I plan to oversee the task and to raise the millions? Wasn't I struggling with funds for our events, scholarships, and the mere postage to mail the used shoes? Additionally, I had no intention of terminating or curtailing our current projects. On the contrary, I aimed to start more programs, namely the anti-FGM scheme. Hm. Maybe I should keep quiet for the moment about that plan.

"And who will provide the fifteen million?" Someone questioned.

Grinning, I explained the funding strategy I was sure would work, "I will invite a few millionaires to chip in," I mentioned how the children's agencies would be scrambling to help. Organizations I read on the web sought creative schemes to help persuade African families to birth fewer dependents. But if ⅛ kids are dying and kid's health facilities were lacking, wouldn't the parents play the survival odds? If the agencies wished to encourage lesser kids, then supporting public pediatric healthcare centers became paramount. "We are achieving the first step one. Who won't want to join us?" I cried, but I sensed my plan did not stimulate confidence in the room.

One board member challenged me, "I've just googled and found one kids hospital in East Africa, and it is actually in Kenya." Yes, but an exclusive *private* facility for the wealthy children, located in Muthaiga, home of the old colonial British. A public-relations officer I knew rushed a sick child here, and she cried that her baby's bill, admitted for one night under observation, cost $220 *before* any medical procedures. In 2006, I read the Kenyan median monthly income stood at $359, so who exactly did this center service? Okay, so I lacked a board of directors, but I could not help myself; even if it meant crawling along alone, I committed and would build this hospital.

Although I sprinted out of the blocks after one hopeful month, the bank balance hovered at an uninspiring zero. Right away, a fairytale helter-skelter journey of jolts, furrows, and fireworks began—please bear with me as this story sparks in all directions—the craziness and disorder, the crude and shameless begging had started.

Naturally, my wealthy friends ignored the unedited one-paragraph email that requested a six or seven-figure contribution. Hope, albeit free, is a careless emotion when appealing for funds, and I doubted a second email would sway people's opinions.

However, at this time, Senator Barack Obama, chiseled with lofty dreams, orchestrated his presidential campaign. I kept on hearing, donate—cents count—$10 or $20 donations can carry him to the White House. Hmm, I concocted an idea. Being HTML compliant, in the year 2000, I coded a basic website. A friend Peter Farago, who graciously printed all the posters for the Shoe4Africa races, never charging a penny, had recently gifted me the Photoshop software. This program allowed slicker graphics, and I launched a page where I could inscribe personal names onto images of bricks. Inspired by a presidential campaign, I lowered the request—considerably—to one hundred dollars and emailed six friends, 'Let us place our names on the foundation stones.' Marty Levine, a good pal, promptly sent double, then Chris Bilsky obliged, and with my donation, that totaled 400 dollars. No one else responded. Okay, reverting to Photoshop, I stretched the pixels width for those bricks to fill the base. Perseverance is what I required, but how many $100 donations would it take to raise the millions? Golly, I would need buckets of unwavering stamina. But, for a runner, the journey to gain stamina is a treasured gift, not a deterrent. Besides, the lasting memory of quitting lingers longer than the stubborn ache of enduring, and $400 for a simple email request gave me hope!

What next? What trick could I use to get the ball rolling? An official announcement enabling people to learn about this project might be a smart move. The Internet bubbled over with exciting schemes, and any news, especially for a distant African venture, was hard to amplify without paying for media, which I flatly refused to do. Charity events in NYC happen daily, and each week races for a cure or cause take place. There are over 1.7-million charities in the USA and the borough with a glut of them? Yes, Manhattan. But how many nonprofits are there in Reykjavík? I figured few, and searching the Internet, no East African healthcare projects popped up.

Bouncing the idea off Ivar, he offered to launch our grand project during a fundraising dinner at an Icelandic hotel. Soccerade could foot the bill, and he invited all my board members for an all-expenses-paid week of touring Iceland. The company had recently signed up Felipe Massa and Alvaro Parente, Formula 1 & 2 drivers; already, Parente, with a Shoe4Africa logo pasted on his racing car, had won the Barcelona GP2 event. For

Soccerade to promote its affiliation to Shoe4Africa, was an easy decision, and they could write off the costs as business expenses.

Since my board resigned, Anthony, Jeanine, their kids, and I flew to the Nordic capital for the event. However, things did not look promising as Soccerade stewed in the launch mode, and worryingly, the Icelandic kronor crumbled daily. As the country hovered on the brink of bankruptcy, there could not have been a worse time in history to request donations.

The Icelandic Minister of Health, Guðlaugur Þór Þórðarson, did everything he could to spruce up the evening, but the timing was wretched. However, as I had worked out a deal with Ivar that Soccerade would donate a minimum of $30,000, I can state the launch was a big success.

✧

A chance meeting led to an opportunity to elevate the charity to the next level, but it came at a price. Steven Goldstein, an EVP at a blue-chip investment firm, kindly gifted a cash donation. But there was more. Steven functioned as the Wall Street Journal spokesperson during the kidnapping of their writer Daniel Pearl in Pakistan—he is recognized as a savvy strategic advisor. His company had hired a renowned team of Boston consultants, and Steven recommended I chat with the experts for an hour.

Great, question number one, how could a minute charity of one worker raise a few million dollars to build a hospital with no track record, experience, or credibility?

The suits, all ten of them, swung open personal laptops, fired up projectors, and started the show—geez, had someone told them Shoe4Africa was one guy who was yet to purchase his first cellphone? After retelling the Zanzibar story, the professionals, pitying me, became fixated on how powerful the charity could become *if* I reverted to only footwear. The way forward meant hiring a team, a big team— 'Scale up' was the hip buzzword of the day. Then, after investing a substantial amount in promoting an image and changing the charity name, I should home in on just shoes. To summarize, I should entitle the cause *Sneakers4Africa* because shoes are dirty. "But you did a great job in identifying an object to ship over to Africa that everyone can offer up."

"No," I interjected, "Shoe4Africa denotes one special shoe. Footwear comprises an element of a broader mission."

"Then make it totally sneakers and learn from the evangelists. Speak by using quotable soundbites and guide the conversation back to sneakers. Repeat that sneakers change lives. Sandwich the word sneakers into every sentence. Oh, rent office space in a fashionable district, be trendy. Impress donors as they approach your agency. They don't understand charities with no workplaces, makes you appear amateurish."

The suggestions flowed, "Partner with a delivery service, as you do not want to touch the dirty shoes. They could even sponsor the operations so the donations can cover the sneaker events. Donors do not care how huge and obese your overall operating costs are, as long as they assume their personal donations roll directly into project overheads. Pay yourself whatever you desire—use partners to cover wages. Employ a social media team of videographers, and photographers, to create beautiful brand-name recognizable imagery—fundraising centers around selling stories, not talking about the work. Buy ads. PR and advertising staff are project costs, so you can legally pay these folks from your general funders. Build a mailing list and spend 20-40% of incoming revenue on creating adorable content. That is how 80% of the donations will gush in."

Wow—in one hour, I heard the dummies guide to build a profitable nonprofit. According to the experts, I wasted too much time on the ground in Africa with the African people.

"You should be flying around America, telling *your* story. Pay a third-party team to perform the work over there. Why go to Africa? Africans won't give you donations. Follow the money, man."

The specialists continued, "And hold galas, preferably at the Met or at destinations that thrill your donors. If a person contributes money, then shine a spotlight on their table as it encourages others. And do not, no matter how compelling the offer, partake in any venture apart from the sneakers plan."

I asked the obvious, "And my big idea, the hospital project?" "Heck no, it confuses the donor. People do not understand when you sidestep from a cause, like when you refuse to accept a salary. Who works for free? Jesus freaks or retired folks. Hey, on that subject, tell donors you are working to end a problem—people like believing in a finish line. Set a date, fifteen years from now."

End what? At this stage, my concentration had slipped—what was wrong with me? Why didn't I want to make a profit from the nonprofit world? I must say, I chuckled at the notion of stopping poverty in Africa by hiring troops of Americans. Has any charity truthfully recruited staff to attempt to put themselves out of business?

One sticky problem remained—all the advice related to shoes and how to expand. Nothing addressed my intention to construct a hospital. That conversation lasted two minutes—to the experts, they imagined an asthmatic one-legged ant hiking Mount Everest with an oversized anteater in his backpack—stay small, alone, and thrifty but generate big bucks? It is not going to happen, they promised.

Nobody voiced a clue on how I could convince foundations, companies, and organizations to contribute money. Applying for grants, typically, you list people, not a person. Your development director, executive director, regional director, overseas director, program manager, and information officer. Who is the communications lead, donor relations, accounts manager, label your top five paid staff, and who directs your PR team, which staff member monitors grant support or matching gifts…? Yikes, did I need to drum up a host of fake names? How could I entice individuals to help me without compensation?

Volunteers and interns, I found, inevitably failed—you enthuse over coffee, spend hours educating people on issues and tasks, and start. Then, realizing there are no trips to Kenya and safari included, the intern silently fades out of the picture. I heard it said—If you do not pay, they will not play.

However, that corporate sermon provoked me like a man

shoved off a deck chair. Charity, for me, involved people pitching in. Therefore, if I begged for donations, then what would I give? Enrich myself with a hefty paycheck? I vowed to work every hour possible without compensation until completing the funding to construct this hospital. Of course, we needed at the very least one full-time staff, but it should be a person without a salary, so let that person be me.

The challenge remained to channel all the donations to this one project and not give a penny to a single person before paying the architect and contractor their dues. Was it possible? I could squeeze in early dawn coaching and evening sessions to supplement my living expenses. Any person prepared to follow suit, please sign up. Acting alone had never bothered me—the problem rested that I shuddered to solicit strangers for donations. Accordingly, if I could not offer substantial money myself, pledging work hours would be my sales pitch.

The ambitious scheme of working full-time sans pay caused an earthquake split in my personal life. Dropping the marathon project failed to be understood by any friend—but this no-pay pledge exasperated those closest to me. My girlfriend, visibly upset, used a fluorescent marker to highlight a newspaper article, thrusting the journal into my hands. The story reported that a fellow New Yorker, depressed and drowning in debt, burnt out by the business world, had launched a charity proclaiming to *Save Africa*. "Why don't you mimic him?" she hinted at breakfast. "He's including his partner, salaries, and bonuses to boot, and the two of them are raking in almost half a million dollars. Clever young Turk's saving himself! What is amiss with that? But, no, you aspire to play the pious volunteer. Have you questioned me about what I think? Nobody cares if you compensate yourself or not. You will wane in your petty martyrdom. How are you planning to survive? Do not expect me to bail you out and clear your bills. How can you fundraise when you are competing alongside charities consisting of squads of skilled salaried staff?"

This relationship dissolved instantly, and the subsequent one turned out to be no better, "Carry on like this, and you will be bagging groceries in a supermarket as a pensioner. Focus on a career like every responsible person half your age does."

Since reaching sixteen, I had slipped through an uninterrupted series of sinking relationships typically enduring a year or two—I held onto library books longer than love affairs. Half-listening, I recognized the steadiest girlfriend, for the time being, might be the hospital project.

Not helping matters, the financial sector in the United States collapsed. A sledgehammer slump smashed the market in a fashion not witnessed since the great depression eighty years ago. The 10128-zip code, where I lived, albeit in its tattered corner on First Avenue, portrayed a wealthy and generous district, but tax-deductible donations trickled to a halt. Nobody wanted to hear that word donation uttered by anyone—especially for an obscure country in Africa.

Friends employed by nonprofits stated similar sob stories; charity had died. On a personal level, my income took a hit. For anyone in my coaching groups, unemployed or in hardship, I waived their fees. I began wondering who would fail first, the organization or myself?

But an economic crisis is an opportune time to re-evaluate, and if I wanted to achieve this project, certain adjustments might be a wise idea. Honestly, I understood; I knew I had problems as I am an attentive listener.

Reaching out to donors invariably, I caught three fundamental questions. 'Are you a doctor?' Followed by, 'Are you an Architect?' And the third strikeout? 'Well, you are African, right?' In one fundraising meeting, a disenchanted woman stared at me, unable to shield her dissatisfaction. Flinging her arms to the ground, she moaned, "I thought you were an African woman, the name Toby." I fell short of expectations in a myriad of ways. Oh yes, and the fact that I neglected to craft a business plan seemed to faze prospective donors too.

The project bank account paddled in molasses rather than spiraling skyward. So, searching for a gleam of inspiration, I attended an African health event at a New York hotel.

Wandering the floor, I bumped into a warmhearted Somaliland lady, who, in 2002, established a women's medical center in her home city of Hargeisa. Although diminutive in stature, her actions transformed a nation. Showing me pictures of her project, Edna Aden narrated that she initially dreamed about building a maternity hospital when she was aged eleven. Today, she bore the face of a lady in her seventies. She cried that few donations arrived until she neared the finishing post a couple of years ago. "The journalists, the press, they never wanted to recognize me or help to recount my story in the early days. But when they saw the building near completion..."

Meeting Edna yielded feelings of both encouragement and worry: She was African-born and bred. Her father a notable medical doctor, herself a registered nurse, a former Foreign Minister, and a wife of a Prime Minister and a President. In short, a world health rock star with enviable connections. I, on the other hand, held fewer qualifications. Not surprisingly, I could not even receive an email response or callback from the UN general inquiry desk regarding my mission.

Too bad I undertook my project in my late thirties—I would impersonate a nonagenarian by the day of groundbreaking. Moreover, my project cost significantly more than hers. Had I bitten off too much?

Desperate for any idea, I wrote a book for Westholme Publishers entitled *'More Fire. How to Run the Kenyan Way.'* Where I found time to write, I do not remember. Mary Darling, a good friend—and my fourth board member—tried to purchase a copy of *Train Hard, Win Easy*. She noticed the first edition currently sold for $300 and higher online, "What is in that book, gold dust?? Produce another." So, I did, pledging 100% of my royalties to Shoe4Africa. One more drip in the barrel.

Representing a minor author who refused to cough up for a publicist/marketing, I did not reckon upon sales but who the book could reach. In this respect, I succeeded with a few readers making notable contributions after learning of the book's charitable mission.

In August, I visited the Moi Teaching & Referral Hospital (MTRH) in Eldoret, one of two national hospitals for Kenya. Built by the British in 1916, the center had undergone decades of upgrades, yet I still saw sick men, women, and children mingled into one cramped complex. The kids' quarters were slotted inside the women's ward. The catchment territory for this hospital stood at an overwhelming 24+ million. Shuffling around the congested female ward felt like navigating a busy village market. I discovered two ladies and two children in most beds—with at least two family members for each patient. How doctors unearthed the space to breathe, I do not know. These were dire conditions, and the risk of cross-infections from patients inside the same bed was frightful. Life camped on a jammed mattress must have been unimaginable, but the overcrowding of public facilities is customary and inescapable in developing nations.

The purpose behind this investigative trip related to the presentation I received proposing that we build our project in the neighborhood of an existing general hospital. Why not partner alongside a functioning facility and have one team run the whole shebang? The affiliation to MTRH would directly promote our hospital to a teaching institution attached to a medical university.

The concept presented would be a private to a public partnership. Shoe4Africa takes possession of the site, hires a team to construct and complete a kid's-only building, and then after opening the new hospital, gifts the site to the Ministry of Health. A partnership alleviated the most significant of costs. Land in Eldoret is horrifically expensive as a quarter-acre city-center plot sold for one million USD—and I wished for five to ten acres. But, if I allied alongside the government, we could utilize unoccupied public land—just like Edna's plan. Right away, the project estimates would slash drastically by sixty percent. As alternatives, two Kenyan household names offered sites in central Nairobi and Kakamega—yet Eldoret shaped up perfectly.

Recent projections estimated that in a decade, over half a million people would crowd this metropolis, and compared to Nairobi, the city did not enjoy an inch of the capital's resources.

Eldoret sat upon the Nairobi to Uganda throughway, threading trunk roads to Ethiopia and Somalia, and boasted an international airport—the site location offered, smack in the city center, was ideal for a national children's hospital. Right away, I exchanged conversations with the Deputy Director, Dr. Wilson Aruasa, and we began a marathon deluge of emails to cement the partnership. The Doctor estimates we exchanged a million emails, but I am sure it was two million!

Furthermore, the credibility of a coalition to a government was timely. Behind my back, I heard frienemies voicing suspicions about the enterprise. They implied that my scheme was a scam. 'He begged for our used shoes yesterday, and now talks of a national hospital? Really?'

A video statement on our website would be a prudent move, so, carting a camcorder to Nairobi, I contacted the Minister of Medical Services, Prof. Anyang' Nyong'o, asking for an interview (the father of the actress Lupita). With his visual endorsement, the Minister composed a letter proving the validity of the project.

On occasions, potential donors questioned, 'If needed, then why hasn't the country built it?' The Government of Kenya is not a bottomless pit of capital. Fundraising practices happen the world over—a month ago, I attended an aid concert in New York to construct a health center in the Bronx organized by the singer Paul Simon. But to bolster the reasoning, I quizzed Kenyan students, why should foreigners endorse this project? The pupils were the recipients of comprehensive scholarships to Ivy League schools in the States. A young chap named Brian chimed up,
"The expenditure on pets in America exceeds ours on healthcare. More funds transfer to cosmetic beautification and weight-loss reductions in the USA than this continent budgets for the basics of keeping citizens alive. Nobody elects to be born into poverty. Is it not an unwritten obligation to serve the underprivileged child?"

Forget the pets; my English neighbor fed his lawn more nutritional supplements than any kid consumed in Kibera. Had I gone with the baseless suggestion to 'leave the mission to the Kenyan government else they will never take responsibility,' that plan of inactivity achieves nothing. I validated a plan of action, and on a note of action, an art dealer suggested he run the New York City Marathon and cajole his friends for donations to support the hospital fund. As such, Lord Anthony Crichton-Stuart unwittingly launched a stream of runners who, over the years till this day, would complete marathons to aid our cause.

At this time, sunbathing on the African coast, the Edwards' household holidayed in Lamu—considered the St. Tropez of Kenya. With a proposed site pinned down in Eldoret for the hospital, I wondered if Anthony might be interested in flying west to view the area? Not only did he agree, but he stepped up unexpectedly. Returning to the states, although his character in the ER series died six years ago, the screenwriters requested he perform a flashback appearance in the show. With extraordinary generosity, Anthony & Jeanine donated the entire fee, $125,000, to our cause. Was this a lottery win? Yes—ER producer, John Wells, followed suit and wired a generous donation of $50,000.

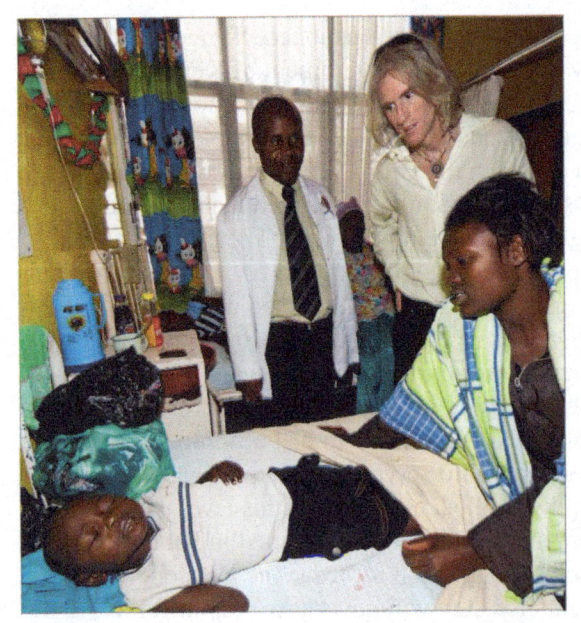

Being a complete novice in health matters, I spent a lot of time talking with experts and visiting any place where a sick child could be found.

Having been an in-patient at a beautiful public children's hospital in England I knew the importance of creating a kids-only hospital building.

Chapter 16. 2008

KIBERA REVISITED, WITH 5,800 FRIENDS

We make a living by what we get, but we make a life by what we give. – Winston Churchill.

Now, surpassing $295,000 in the hospital account, I bounced along in optimistic spirits when planning the handout for the footwear collected on Marathon Monday. Not touching the hospital funds, Soccerade and two individuals donated the costs to host the women's event. The logistics looked onerous. Nobody had ever staged a mass race inside Kibera involving a few thousand ladies, and nobody has done since. For good reasons—compactness, confusion, and corruption framed only part of the obstacles to hurdle. According to the media, we organized the largest gathering of women in the history of the slums. But a critical friend remarked, 'Who else would encourage 5,800 ladies to run through a trash-filled shantytown but you?'

The clashes forced us to postpone the delivery of the two containers, and the summer would be the first shipping date. Given the magnitude of the post-election violence and our involvement with the reconciliatory process, I opted to dedicate the event as a peace celebration. The date preferred was the Saturday closest to the Kenyan Independence Day—December 13th, 2008. Presuming I worked with a healthy leeway, I had not allowed time for the shipping swindles and stolen paperwork; the shoes finally arrived from Mombasa at the last possible moment on the morning of the event at four a.m. How we managed to clear the customs a day prior on a national holiday to release the containers would be a chapter in itself.

What a day! After handing out almost 6,000 free T-shirts, the run played out to be a huge hit. Due to the narrow track impeded by trash mounds, slum dwellers, and hand carts, the leading woman breasted the finish line before the last entrant started the race. This congestion created a magical amber ribbon of peace T-shirts streaming throughout the slums like a solid yellow brick road of unity.

The swiftest lady earned footwear donated by Bill Rodgers, the sole person to win the NYC and the Boston Marathon four times each. Loice Bunei, a blind woman who today works for Standard Chartered, claimed Paula Radcliffe's shoes for her courageous efforts of completing the run. It remained a minor miracle she did not tumble over the heaps of garbage.

Handing out the footwear caused an eruption of excitement. Women hustled impatiently, refusing to stand in line—elbows and arms flew in all directions. Paul Tergat hopped on the bonnet of his silver Land Cruiser, awash in a sea of ladies, pleading for order. Pre-race, I did my utmost to accommodate any requests, and two of the area chiefs wished I included their friends among the volunteers for the shoe distributions. A couple of those rogues surreptitiously lobbed a pair or six over the school wall for a later pick-up. Rather than fight, I dispatched a bunch of women to gather the items. Guessing I may have been a bubblegum gangster—had I lived in Kibera—I admired their ingenuity.

The soccer game was rambunctious. With shirts sent by Cristiano Ronaldo, it appeared the whole slum longed to enlist on the team. The superstar had kindly personalized a bunch as keepsakes. The opposing squad, Soccerade, compromised of athletes. In the words of the national newspaper, *'An*

embarrassment of talent was on show with a galaxy of the world's top marathon stars on parade for a sports-for-peace mission.'
I figured once the runners toed the ball, no one could halt them—the tactic worked. Highlights played on the television news for days, and folks concluded Martin Lel, bagging two of our goals, deserved a soccer career *when* he quit winning major marathons. Not forgetting my Sabella skills, I netted the third.

The Shoe4Africa Eleven. *Ruth Mueni, Lucy Akinyi, Haram Ali, Susan M, Edith A, Hawa Yusuf, Alice Nyaboke, Sorophine, Josephine Adiambo, Mercy, Beatrice, & Coach Arafat M.*
The Soccerade Ten. *Goalkeeper, Olympic Steeplechase Gold, Matthew Birir. Defense NYC & Boston runners-up, Chris Cheboiboch. World, NYC, & London champion, Douglas Wakiihuri. Daily Nation Sports Editor, Elias Makori. Midfield NYC & World record marathon holder Paul Tergat. Anthony Edwards. Toby Tanser. Attackers, 4x Boston champion Robert Cheruiyot, and 3x London, 2x NYC winner Martin Lel. Super-Sub, the Chairman of the NYC marathon, George Hirsch.*

Work conflicts carried Salim overseas, but his assistant stepped up nicely. Cantar, a Kibera resident who offered a bed for the night when I required a sleepover, voiced a request. Why not form a women's slum soccer team? As the ladies were a squad of diverse ethnicities, they could play as ongoing peace ambassadors. Returning to New York, I would gather thirty cleats to carry over on a subsequent trip. Soccerade provided home, away, and even branded training kits alongside stylish tracksuits for the ladies. Over the next couple of years, the team performed like champions.

Leaving the slum, we partnered with Cisco by handing out a hundred tiny video cameras to women aiding them to record stories. Documenting their version of a situation in disputes, where a masculine voice boomed loudest, these pocket recorders were priceless in the days before smartphones. The Kibera project, start to finish, proved to be an enormous success.

Flying back to America and into NYC, Mary Darling kindly suggested lunch at Pastis, a chic French restaurant. Mid-afternoon, I discovered I fell afoul of a pickpocket. I reddened, recalling how an Eastern lady had pressed vigorously against my chair—she must have slipped a hand into my jacket. Signed traveler's checks, cards, ID, and around $500 in cash were all gone. How ironic, wandering around Kibera for weeks, with nothing worse than a parrot bite at midnight, then fleeced in Manhattan.

The following day, outside the 92nd St Y, a misplaced wallet lay in the gutter stuffed with cash. Woohoo, karma. The Y located the individual's address, and after placing the billfold in a sealed brown envelope, I cycled to a nearby apartment block. Refusing to leave a name with the building's doorman, I sought no compensation. All this Maasai hoopla and providence proved a reward would arrive in the shape of my returned pinched wallet! Stepping back onto Park Avenue, I spied someone had removed my quick-release front bicycle wheel—karma indeed.

A stream of yellow shirted ladies made a two-point-four-mile solid ribbon of peace looping around the Kibera slums.

CHAPTER 17. 2009

THE BENEFITS OF BEGGING IN MANHATTAN

What we have done for ourselves alone dies with us—what we have done for others and the world remains and is immortal. – A. Pike

After one year, in 2009, I wondered, is Manhattan, considering the outrageous expenses, the appropriate location for me? But New York Toby fueled the life I conducted in Kenya. Residing in the sticks, rarely do you bump into individuals like George Bush, Novak Djokovic, or Usher. New York remains a city where meeting anyone and everyone becomes possible. Eight million citizens equal buckets of prospects and possibilities. If I had to solicit one hundred people to reap one donation, I did not care, as I relished the chase. For the following year, my fundraising schemes sprouted like wildflowers. Most failed, but thankfully, others succeeded. One lesson that runners learn is that not every training run will deliver the result that you desire. But each run will carry you forward.

So how, as a New Yorker, *did* I beg for money? Frankly, I attempted every trick. I began by dabbling in the music business, envisioning people donating $10 to receive an individualized e-card, a downloadable Christmas tune, and a brick symbolically placed in their name at the hospital centered around an end-of-the-year drive. According to reports, over 30% of donations occur in December, so I planned to be ready.

Nobody I knew had attempted this musical concept, and I was certain it would reap in the riches. Song4Africa could be the acoustic version of White Christmas.

Bob Dylan's son, Jesse, had recently created a three-minute infomercial for Shoe4Africa after Anthony and I had connected with the filmmaker at the SoHo Grand Hotel. Jesse skated on the clouds after directing the music video, *Yes, We Can (Barack Obama song)* that received a gazillion social media likes—would he volunteer for a second project for us?

In Britain, there is massive hype about who lands the Christmas Day #1 soundtrack. I set my sights on gaining that top spot as a tune with a charitable twist represented a media magnet. The question remained, which vocalist attracted the most attention? Subtle hints suggesting Father Bob for a voiceover for the first video had flown over Jesse's head—therefore, I imagined Santa Bob was out of the question. But a month ago, when interviewed for a magazine, the journalist provided an electrifying tip. The lady had schooled alongside Beyoncé, and they shared a mutual friend. In return for a recorded and produced song, why not offer the superstar and Jay-Z the naming rights to the hospital?

At this moment in time, Anthony invited me to travel to Las Vegas. He, and a delightful lady, Uma Thurman, starred in 'Motherhood,' and his PR team scheduled a speaking engagement at a tech conference. Creative Artists Agency arranged for Anthony to perform a tweet on stage, and he agreed to type in a request for a donation. The concept, which failed, would be asking the audience for an on-the-spot contribution to the hospital. In those days, tweets linked to an electronic payment platform were a novel occurrence.

Following the event, Anthony conferred with his management team, so I went wandering. Possessing an insatiable appetite, I noticed a vacant hall containing a lavish breakfast buffet. What do they say, eat promptly and beg for forgiveness if caught? Grabbing an overflowing plate of food, I sat at the farthest table to hide in the corner of the room. Five minutes later, two men followed suit and surprisingly joined my side. Ignoring me, they discussed wireless laptop connections, which then was cutting-edge technology. Had I known the gentlemen's names—Jermaine Dupri and the second man, an agent for Jane Fonda—I may have requested their help. They soon attracted the attention of a lady. I began to wonder should I move to an unoccupied table, but since I arrived first, I stayed put. Besides, the woman, Robin, who introduced herself as a Pussycat Dolls founder—whatever that was—graciously brought me into the conversation.

The space was deserted bar our overcrowded table, with one stool vacant. Sure enough, a good-looking guy approached and claimed the last chair.
"You must be someone—who are you?" he asked. I laughed, I was Toby-Nobody, and we hit it off immediately. During our conversation, he mentioned once selling out Wembley Stadium. His name? Matt Goss, the headliner of the 1980-90s band, Bros. Wow, back in the day, the band was the bomb in Britain. Now, with months of sold-out shows at Caesars Palace, he had climbed back into the limelight.

How fitting, *White Christmas* plays in the film *Love Actually*, and the movie portrays a retired musician's comeback seeking a Christmas hit. Perfect, I could turn film fantasy into charity reality. Matt gravitated to the idea immediately, even inviting me to visit him in Hollywood. Encountering such extraordinary individuals is a true blessing of this world.

Yet unfortunately, I hit roadblocks from his general manager. He understandably expected a certain level of professionalism and did not appreciate the 'let us record in the cheapest studio, and it will be all right on the night' ethic. But as this door closed and as I did not receive a peep from the Beyoncé management, a lady I coached, Chrissy Morgenroth, proposed that I reach out to her uncle.

Thus, one month later, I found myself dining with a Motown

legend and his wife Carol on Park Avenue South. Two bites in, Leon Ware announced he would, and I quote, 'love to be the voice of Shoe4Africa.' Leon had long desired to be a part of a project connected to giving back to kids and thought this concept very doable. He revealed he had written and produced songs for luminaries like Tina Turner and Michael Jackson. "Hey, you know that song *I want you* by Marvin Gaye?" Sure, who in the world does not? "Yeah, I co-wrote and produced that one." I was flying high until Irving Berlin's estate nixed the use of their Christmas anthem.

Next, albeit briefly, I attempted an intricate tennis strategy to capture funds approaching Heward Packard. After a breakfast date with 39-time Grand Slam title winner Billie Jean King, then bumping into Novak Djokovic a couple of times during social events on Seventh Avenue, I concocted another brilliant hair-brained scheme. But, as the idea floundered rather than soared, I wondered, should I dial back and pick a traditional method of hunting donations? Be realistic and attempt a proven plan.

During the summer, I shot footage that the owners of The HATC camp submitted to the KLM airlines for a charity clip to air on the Dutch planes. I thought, why not present a similar concept to a different airline?

British Airways, my preferred carrier, supported numerous Kenyan charities, so I checked out Virgin Airlines who marketed flights to Nairobi with what I deemed were dull commercials. For Virgin, I imagined a scene involving the reigning Olympic marathon champion, Sammy Wanjiru—one of our ambassadors. "Hey, what is the fastest way to travel to Kenya?" Asks a cute Kenyan flight attendant. Meantime Sammy is sprinting through Tanzania's Serengeti, outrunning a chasing cheetah. A jet zooms overhead, "In comfort," she giggles, cuddling and caressing one lucky commuter inside the first-class cabin.

Combining the visuals of a plane wing and a hospital wing, the care-wing airline could donate a modest pledge. Then, over time, collect unused foreign coins in envelopes during their flights to recover the donation. BA had garnered millions for charities using coin collections. Why re-invent the wheel, or in this case, the wing? Virgin's CEO, Mr. Branson, was a billionaire with profitable commercial properties in Kenya, and his daughter trained as a pediatric doctor—this promised to be money in the bank. The stumbling block? How to contact Mr. Branson, but as I say, look no farther than New York.

Tegla Loroupe, a former Kenyan world record holder, came to town for the marathon. Breezing into her hotel room to say hi, I slumped onto a comfortable chair and struck a rigid object. Leaping up, I realized I sat upon a book,
"What is this?"
"Branson gave me his paperback." She grinned.
Perfect, now I had the mogul's personal email. The following week, during a conversation with an Upper East Side financier, he advised me to BCC the request to Mr. Branson and channel the ask through his number two, who oversees Virgin Unite.

So, dragging Anthony along, we cycled to Virgin's Manhattan offices, but I discovered business and charity could be an awkward marriage. If I understood correctly, Shoe4Africa would furnish a substantial payment to Virgin, allowing us usage of their brand, and naming the hospital 'Virgin' would somehow generate funds.

Not once was I demoralized at any rejection, and a reader might enquire, why list all these failures, where is this story heading? The truth was, in every venture, I gained knowledge even if I did not collect a dime. Failure, for me, is in failing to try. The virgin lesson helped me to navigate the corporate world. Could I drum up a scheme to earn money for a company before requesting a contribution?

A runner, and a COO of an underwear company who knew of our programs, offered to donate men's undies. Hesitant that I wished for the handle of a male underclothing patron, I persuaded the corporation to produce a line of branded undergarments in bold striking colors. If a pair with the Shoe4Africa logo on the bum sold, we would receive a donation, and both teams would score. The C-IN2 Shoe4Africa glitzy underwear line looked a fantastic fit in all departments and could potentially cover up for the Virgin disappointment. Yet, despite being a grateful recipient of a dozen pairs of these items twelve years later, I still await the first disbursement from the scheme.

One NYC event we could bank upon was a team of twenty kind souls, running the marathon clad in hospital scrubs (albeit designed by Paul Marlow, a Marc Jacobs consultant). Each runner had been graciously soliciting funds, and Tegla tagged along as a celebrity participant. Her youngest sibling perished after he was misdiagnosed at a rural clinic. Running to improve pediatric health in Africa became a heartfelt cause to this Kenyan lady.

On the race day, Tegla and I paced Sarah Jones, a Tony award-winning actress I had the pleasure of coaching that year. On the finishing line, Tegla—the first African lady to win this marathon—was interviewed by NBC. '*Tegla, how does it feel to run for Shoe4Africa?*' And she responded, *"It means something special because I always run for myself. This time I think of how many children I am saving. It means something more than winning this race."* Tegla and Sarah's participation, and of course, Dr. Mark Greene, who signed up, earned us much-needed free media. James LeGros, an actor impersonating a doctor (on NBC's Mercy, Dr. Dan Harris), also kindly donned our green scrubs.

Anthony sent out a bunch of emails that summer soliciting support for his marathon. Mark Webber (his friend), the F1 driver, made a PayPal donation. Seven days later, karma struck, and Webber won his first F1 event. Coincidence? Donate, and try your luck!

From running, we shuffled to cards. A friend, Frank Furlan, organized a poker game sponsored by Omega at an exclusive store on Wall Street. The watchmakers generously donated a chronometer and gambling chips used in the James Bond Casino Royale movie to the tournament winners. If a timepiece sold, Shoe4Africa would receive a handsome commission. I was an atrocious salesperson and forgot to inform any of the guests to consider a purchase. Then again, doubling between the coat check and the door check-in, I neglected the seller's duties. No watch left the building. But at least the game accrued another $10,000 for the hospital fund.

Like magic, our bank account mushroomed to $700,000, but I would not contemplate placing a single brick until we approached at least a million dollars. Any lead or possibility that emerged that might lead to more money, I said yes to, remembering the Wayne Gretzky quote, *'You miss 100% of the shots you never take.'* Therefore, when a dinner invitation arrived where I reckoned on a hefty donation, I committed at once. Requesting funds is tough, but I relished the opportunity to sit alongside seven others for a private party with F.W. de Klerk, the Nobel prize-winning President.

De Klerk, of course, commandeered the conversation, and I bid my time to execute the 'ask' for Africa. The night was illuminating, hearing firsthand tales I read about as a youth in the newspapers. Being an avid supporter of the Free Mandela movement, purchasing a campaign T-shirt, and mailing protest letters to South Africa, I had regarded this man as the enemy. Regardless of my beliefs, I would accept his contribution. Then, as I eyed the chocolate cheesecake, de Klerk tapped his silverware on a crystal goblet, requesting silence. Gosh, even he pursued donations, begging like a poor man, just like me.

Numerous ideas did not pan out, often because I adamantly refused to spend a penny chancing to raise a dollar or that people merely reneged on deals. But the diverse opportunities explained the compensations of residing in Manhattan. I mean, strolling to a running race in New York, meeting Joan Rivers at the crossroads, it transpired her apartment peered directly into my friend Shmuel's. Relaxing at a post-run brunch, Bobby Kennedy Jr. grabs a chair, complimenting my Train Hard, Win Easy T-shirt, asking for the back story.

Although impromptu meetings seldom funneled directly into dollars, referrals from a personality opened up doors a lot quicker than if I initiated a request. All I required was a durable plan on how to survive in one of the world's priciest boroughs. This bold pledge to live from early morning coaching proved unsustainable. I miscalculated the budget—my piddling earning capacity was half of its initial projection due to my frequent travels to Kenya. So, how could I further slash already frugal costs? Carving out a $5 a day food allowance, I dieted like a Tibetan monk, but a better step would be relocating from the Upper Eastside of Manhattan and finding inexpensive digs. Settling on a tiny studio in Harlem, the two-mile uptown hike reaped a significant saving.

Life in Harlem entailed a competition of expense cutting, and each month, the contest was to trim a little more. With few electronics, my monthly utility bill hovered around twenty dollars; not bad considering this one room served as both living quarters and the Shoe4Africa office space. My house phone, on a cheap plan, allowed local calls only. Calling out-of-city meant I needed a stack of coins in my pocket, and to find a non-vandalized phone box in Harlem was near impossible. I stole the Internet connection from a school opposite my apartment and became a champion super saver. Venturing up north gained a grace period to let me continue working full-time for Shoe4Africa without pay, but three years later, this location switch almost killed me.

Matt Goss of Bros, and Robin Antin, the, founder of the Pussycat Dolls.

Chapter 18. 2010

NOW A SCHOOL?

Educating the mind without educating the heart is no education at all. – Aristotle

Skipping school did not underline how highly I valued education. A recent Zambian book entitled *Dead Aid: Why Aid is Not Working* did little to promote fundraising efforts. People glancing at the words scorned, 'Look, even Africans write they do not want our donations.' Yet, the author, Ms. Moyo, did not dispute humanitarian relief—both she and her father applied for and received aid from overseas. My wish would be for every child to gain free healthcare and quality schooling—investments in these sectors are the broad pillars of how any country strengthens its economy.

One day, holding a running event for kids in Nandi, I announced I would supplement school supplies to the awards. In 2003, President Kibaki abolished tuition fees for public schools, but parents must provide uniforms, shoes, schoolbooks, pens, and pencils. I pitied the elders who frequently struggled to afford these items. Children regularly missed a month of schooling in January as elders scrambled for funds after Christmas.

In my second 'Education Run,' a mature man in his twenties stood among the boys to collect his rewards. One head taller than the nippers, he drew my attention immediately. Pulling a local aside, I enquired, 'who is the lanky interloper?' The tale I heard described the man-boy as just another unschooled youth, nothing uncommon. Yet to me, this was unusual.

Wishing to help, the following morning, I set out with a school uniform to visit this chap. It was an enjoyable trek, meandering through the sweeping, immaculately trimmed tea fields.

When I arrived, Man-boy was chatting to two friends. He lived in poverty on squatters' land in a mud and wattle makeshift hut. Over a cup of sugarless black tea, he explained his parents never believed in education. Every day his job entailed walking, be it ten paces or ten miles (16.1 km), to scavenge for food,
"Relatives provide, or I search for the weeds called *managu*, that we eat with *ugali*." After gathering firewood to sell and burn and fetching water from the river, he returns home to nurse his invalid parents. Man-boy said he longed for school, but how?

Hearing of our race provided his get out of Alcatraz plan. However, unlike me, who would be screaming out *my turn*, Man-boy related his good luck now aided others. "I divided the pencil into three and have split the book pages. If you assist me with two pairs of shoes, these fellows can join me at school." Man-boy had borrowed a rusty blade, sawed the one pencil, and sharpened the ending stubs to form three mini-pencils. The exercise book, split into three piles, looked a delightful mess; no teacher would accept this muddle. But his actions humbled me.

No wonder he pined for schooling—educational centers and churches in rural areas represent the social hubs. Few families own televisions, so by default, the public buildings are the trunks and branches of community life. The state of the local school near where I held the previous race was horrific. The mud walls crumbled, windows resembling carved holes and held sticks for frames, and boggy dirt floors upheld the structure—rickety, misaligned iron sheets managed to cover most of the roof. Hmm, I wondered, could I upgrade this community? The construction constituted nothing more than a decaying mess. Talking to the kids, they had complained the teachers' attendance remained spotty, quoting an hour a day at best. But probing the tutors, they countered with compelling explanations.

"When it rains—which happens often—the children dash from the classrooms and dart for the trees, or home, whatever is closer. If their exercise books get wet, they risk a beating from an irate parent. You can observe the ceiling leaks, and would you teach in there?" The educator then pointed to a sloppy, grimy floor, "Try standing in that puddle of muck—this is a place for pigs, not learning."

Today, the wind whistled through the gaps in the walling, spiking a chill. With no electricity, the room hung in dark and murky shadows. Once a week—on a Friday—the children collected buckets of stinky cow dung to smear over the mud classroom floor. The manure produced an impenetrable temporary surface to combat dust, worms, and allergies. Too bad I visited on a Thursday, and each shoe sunk like a house brick into the dirty muck. Poor kids, what miserable conditions. I wanted to provide the children with a better studying environment by building a decent structure. An educated village has far-reaching implications, but I needed to be careful approaching my new board. Recollecting how the last team fled, they may consider the school as a slight distraction to the hospital project.

'Is it shoes, athletics, scholarships, empowerment, AIDS awareness, FGM, or hookworm? Or hosting peace events, and now, a hospital? Where is your focus, Toby? What? What did you say, something about building a school? Stop accepting more tasks.' Cringing, I dreaded the feedback. Yet, the dots are connected in the approach to lifting people out of poverty. I cannot concentrate on a singular aspect. You provide healthcare, but there is no food? You distribute water, but you do not educate? How can one operate without the others? Stating, 'That is not my problem' went entirely against all instincts and my upbringing.

At once, the notion of constructing a proper facility became a crucial task. No surprise, summoning a community gathering, I pledged to the delighted teachers that I would strive to establish a new school for the community.

Upon returning to New York, I emailed friends who had dodged harassment when I hounded folks for hospital contributions. Furthermore, I had convinced myself establishing a crew for this mini scheme should be critical homework for the hospital. Being illiterate in construction matters—and soon to spearhead a mammoth project—meant I must understand the ins and outs of the business. The dummies guide to building a hospital is yet to be written. I needed to learn the lingo of the architects and contractors, visit the public works office, and understand how to gain permits; these were necessary skills. Interpreting the rules of the environmental impact folks, reading the bill of quantities, and studying pricing costs was all new to me. Hiring quantity surveyors and sub-contractors would be priceless for the big enterprise and help to ensure the wool was not pulled over my eyes by providing required hands-on experience. The tricky issue might be the school construction money. But sure enough, out of the blue, the funds arrived.

Conversing in a Manhattan bar, I launched into coaching a team of guys aiming to complete the Paris Half Marathon. If presented with a workout plan and fundraising pages, could they contribute any amount to the school construction fund? Any amount, at this stage, I would accept gold teeth. Weeks went by, and I sent out emails and updates but did not hear a peep—all the subtle hints were ignored. Not once did they participate in offered complimentary training classes—had they ditched me? Winter turned to spring, and I practically forgot about the group. Other leads looked promising, and by luck and piecemeal, the school money dribbled in. Hoping for an $80,000 budget, already I had stockpiled twenty percent—besides continuing to fundraise for the hospital. That account displayed an attractive $795,000, which elevated us to a whole new status of smiles at the local bank.

The group* resurfaced days before their departure, 'Can you bring T-shirts to our offices?' I figured they might announce the fundraising had failed—that played as the measure for most of my

little schemes. But handing over the garments, a check slid back. Feigning politeness, I tried not to stare at the digits and expected a modest contribution, but I was stunned. Glancing down, I noted the amount swallowed all the cost of the construction. Explaining my own fundraising efforts, I expected a deduction. Their leader, whom I shall entitle Mr. Schools, who is a dear friend today, winked, "Why not retain it for a second project." One indeed became four in the next three years.
*With big hearts, the team wished to donate anonymously.

The first of six schools we have built. Today, thousands of children have passed through our classrooms. Furthermore, at other sites, including the hospital, we have built classrooms and facilities.

Koitalel's legend, his impact on the local culture, proved unforgettable, and I planned to link the Shoe4Africa schools with homegrown heroes. American kids worship music or movie stars, yet most of the youngsters near the location of our building site had never seen a TV set, and although names were vague, many children knew 'the glory of the Kenyan runners.' Better yet, kids understood these champions entered life lacking silver spoons—just like them. Martin Lel had campaigned for a school for his community, and as I thought about it, the discipline, determination, and dedication of an athlete are the ideal tenets for a student to emulate. I devised a model: We fundraised for the construction costs and then selected a local athlete to honor who had shone in education *and* sports. Today, Martin Lel and Janeth

Jepkosgei in Nandi County, Moses Kiptanui and Sally Kipyego in Elgego-Marakwet, and Mary Keitany in Baringo County are the beneficiaries of our Shoe4Africa schools. With our latest—the All4Running School in Nandi—there will be around 2,000 kids attending the tuition-free government-accredited schools we gift upon completion to the local communities.

৽৽৽

After launching the first school, I deposited another unexpected generous donation to the hospital fund. Pedaling on the bicycle, I delivered a letter of thanks, and inside the card, I requested, could I convey my gratitude over a coffee?

Stacey kindly agreed to meet, revealing a friendship with Jeanine and Anthony. She directed a charity and distributed Christmas presents to kids, not a few either, the amount Mr. Santa delivers. For her foundation's anniversary, they planned to gift 10,000 children. Stacey suggested partnering—could I manage a couple of thousand kids?

I had recently launched an anti-malaria campaign to help the most vulnerable folks, gifting bed nets to the deaf and disabled communities. I enrolled kids in various schools to be awareness ambassadors and educate their classmates about malaria. I could order small gifts and include family bed nets for an impactful Christmas parcel. Yet Kenya struggled with a crisis, and the country was locked inside months of a devastating drought. Hunger stung as the burning issue, and the basin of the Rift Valley, lacking rainfall for seasons, bled in a disaster zone. Just forty minutes' drive from Iten, barrel-bellied cows now resembled rib cages on broom-poles. I heard reports that some residents were spotted gnawing on rats for sustenance in desperation.

Meanwhile, down in Kibera, people I knew whisked a sprinkle of flour into a jug of water for their daily meal. With crop failure, an economy nationwide sunk. The idea of buying Christmas presents paled in comparison to providing life-saving nourishment. With Stacey's aid, I could dole out over two thousand gift parcels to the kids. Inside each Yuletide sack would be a 2.2 lbs. (1 kilo) of sugar, rice, and flour, a bottle of cooking oil, a tub of fats, and a box of tea. The children would become heroes, bringing an unexpected blessing home.

Athletes in Iten, like always, volunteered as the free workforce for Stacey's event. We divided the wholesale food into individual packages—that arduous task took over twelve hours for fourteen people. The next day, before dawn in the darkness, cramming everyone inside a dilapidated seven-seated Nissan *matatu* with a defective suspension, we trailed the food truck to hunt out the kids. On the agenda were five rural centers—Likwon, Barwesa, Keturwo, Muchukwo, and a place whose name I forget. The rule ordered the kids must collect the Christmas parcel, and after informing the village elders in advance, the events ran smoothly.

Since my initial visit to Kenya, my heart has cried for the impoverished child. Here in Likwon, I saw worse than anything I could imagine. Rags slipped off the shoulders of malnourished kids. Children too weak to walk, eyes almost popping out of their sockets, patiently stood in line to collect the food parcels. This work ripped my soul, and if I had shed tears, they would have been blood-red.

Various individuals—never the hungry ones—will promise you that nutrition drops perpetuate poverty as they waffle on about schemes of 'teaching a man to fish.' Other people advise finding a wonder crop that might grow in the sand without water. Digging wells can be helpful, but not a single solution either. Holes dry up, and the International Institute for Environment and Development estimated up to US$360 million has been spent on rural water supply schemes that are now dysfunctional—today, thirteen years on, estimates say that number to be over a billion. A well does not tap into underground ever-flowing rivers as donor's hope, and drilling can cause over-exploitation of natural aquifers. Arsenic and chemical elements can rise to harmful levels destroying landscapes in the aftermath. Think of fracking and how drilling unearths more than worms. Regardless, whether these schemes worked or not, I became compelled to address the immediate problem of people starving for the need of basic food.

How many people relocate for a job, an opportunity, or just because they wish for a fresh start? Me, for one. What number of those people moved from one habitable area to another? Me. There are regions of the world where only the poorest of the poor reside, folks who can never dream of moving. Everyone I questioned during this day pleaded to transfer to Eldoret if given a job. 'Poverty alone traps our feet from traveling,' explained a withered old man.

Decades ago, these dilapidated resourceless areas recognized pastoralists only as passersby—nobody sunk roots here. In America, with milder climates than Kenya, over four-fifths of the country is urbanized, but two hundred years ago, that number fell at one-fifth. Africa slowly shadows this direction, and if balanced with a leveled birth rate, the trend will save lives.

Today's method constituted the best I could do right now. Yes, my heart broke, leaving Purity and Ben behind, five-year-old twins whose mother blended soil and watery flour, mincing in earthworms for protein, for their nourishment. Yes, the donated food would only last for the next week or so. No, it is not the ultimate solution, but it is better than doing zero. But imagine this, if Stacey fed five communities of hundreds of families for a week, what could a united world achieve?

The heat thrashed inside our minibus on the ride home, which of course, lacked air conditioning and functioning windows in the rear. The van's ventilation ducts teased and taunted by blowing boiled heat and itchy dust into our lungs. Nevertheless, as I loaned the vehicles without charge, I could not complain. Two staff members fainted, and Precious Boit, a girl we sponsored during the clashes, vomited repeatedly. Today signified an aid project at its best—one hundred percent of the donation went to the kid's gift packages. Pulling into Iten, Christmas was over, but I would not have swapped the day for any other. My phone vibrated, and I recognized the number—it was the preacher who had introduced me to Purity and Ben. "Toby, you will not believe it. After you departed, a farmer spoke with us. Observing your team today inspired him, and he has agreed to donate maize every month."

Eighty-five percent of Kenyan Children attend primary, but only thirty percent attain a secondary education.
Caroline Maritim thought her schooling days over after finishing primary school. She started a family and mothered four children. When she heard we were building a free-to-attend secondary, she came dashing despite being in her mid-thirties. Today, with a degree, she is back teaching at our school.
With our new All4Running/21Run partnership, we opened our sixth school; eighty students enrolled for class one in the first five days! Everyone in Europe who purchases shoes from these stores will be contributing to help Kids Education in Kenya. Purchase shoes with purpose!

Chapter 19. 2010

FROM THE SEA TO THE STARS

Luck is what happens when preparation meets opportunity. – Seneca

Wide awake at three a.m. one morning, I rehashed a vivid dream. Two years into the project, and the donations waned horribly, and I lacked inspiring creative ideas. Fumbling to the notepad, I sketched out a vision to run from a sandy beach to the peak of a towering snowy mountain. The Sea marked the spot of my attack, an absolute low, whereas the mountain characterized the high of touching the stars and establishing a hospital to help others recover.

Now, caffeinated and hunched in front of a computer, I began browsing maps. I could depart from the coastal city of Mombasa, jog across the Taru desert, and run over the Taita Hills. Next, traverse two game reserves—where wild animals roam—before entering Tanzania. Finally, zip up the slopes of Mount Kilimanjaro—the tallest freestanding mountain in the world. From the Sea to the Stars would average forty-odd miles per day (64 km) of running over one week. Scant research showed no one had attempted to run this route with its dramatic climb on the last day, attaining an altitude from sea level to 5,895 meters (19,341 feet). The venture coincided with the tenth anniversary of the Zanzibar attack and hopefully could raise considerable funds. If I collected over $120,000, our bank account would topple the magical one million dollars barrier. That elusive figure loomed like an imaginary road bump, and hopefully, the next million would be easier. A million? Not bad for a couple of years of clumsy begging.

※

Rodney Cutler, a good friend, owns a string of fashionable hair salons in New York. He clips the heads of folks like Paul McCartney and Emma Watson. Trimming my own hair, Rodney shakes his head when I swing by for a coffee and insists on awarding me a free prune. As his scissors snipped my scruffy mop, he decided then and there to accompany me to Africa, offering to launch a promotion at his Broadway parlor. All this sounded wonderful, but I thought I should check on the logistics before inviting others. Although I have never enjoyed an authorized safari, driving through the game parks to meetings with Mike, I read the blaring warning signs. 'Stay in your car—Man-eaters on the loose.' So, I mused, are humans permitted on foot in these parks? And what regulations surrounded the mountain? There I discovered official rules stated one must commit to a minimum of five days for a Kilimanjaro summit attempt. The duration helps prevent any adverse effects of the altitude. Attempting a single-day run-up meant staying under the radar. Rodney acted with positive intentions, but now as he invited others, I wondered if numbers might draw unwanted attention?

Rodney, too researched and argued people died each year of acute mountain sickness, and my idea presented too much risk. Why not switch the format by running to Kilimanjaro before stopping at the foot of the mountain and waiting for more US-based friends to arrive? The following day a group could embark on a weeklong hike. He hinted that an Esquire magazine writer was on board and promised a published article, surely fundraising would improve with a social expedition.

However, I had chased donations for several weeks, and my

boast stated running, not hiking, from the Sea to the Stars. With an animated video produced by Pilar Newton-Katz, I had gathered over one hundred pledges, so I could not recant and rearrange the plan. My single-mindedness and stubbornness gained the better of me, and regrettably, I lost Rodney's friendship that summer, though I am relieved to say not for very long. He recommitted to join me in November, then reaching Kilimanjaro, he would drive to a hotel in Moshi and wait for his friends as I continued running to the peak.

৩৵৶

Arriving in New York after the millennium, Dick Traum—the founder and force of the Achilles International—requested I join his charity's board. The team aided disabled athletes to enter mainstream sports. Later, I became the director for his premier event, the Hope & Possibility run in Central Park. Why not—one more responsibility to add to the pile. Dick feared the race was doomed to die. Mary Wittenberg of the NYRR and most others in the know assumed so too. But I managed to overhaul the event, increase the signed-up entrants from 1,500 to over 8,000, slash costs by over eighty-five percent, and maximize the revenue by thousands, upon thousands, of dollars. The annual run transformed into a fixture on the city's must-attend races, with marque sponsors, a sold-out field, entertainment—like the NYC Knicks dancers—and qualifying entry status for the NYC marathon.

In 2007, I added an obesity awareness theme for the Youngsters. Kids would earn a pair of new sports shoes if they completed the free-to-enter fitness dash and pledged to exercise. Passing health messages through running was a practical way to address the accelerating trend of children's obesity. And alongside health tips and nutritional advice, I delivered fitness info-packs to the class teachers. Again, I tried relaying the gift that transformed my life—Running. Childhood obesity awareness held little traction in the mid-2000s—Michelle Obama and others had yet to adopt the cause. Like AIDS in Africa, it stood out as an awkward, ignored term, and I attempted to introduce the problem into daily school conversations. Our event flourished, and the following year Mayor Bloomberg awarded the obesity initiative and the open race, each with a prestigious 'Office of the Mayor's Proclamation.' I could not help dwelling on the irony of gifting shoes to Americans in a campaign against an increasing inclination of obesity, yet over in Africa, supplying shoes to the underfed kids to help them run out of poverty. I truly existed in two separate worlds.

The event boasted a reputation for being star-studded, particularly in 2010 when a gentleman called Harry participated. Many celebs have attended, like Anthony Edwards, Armie Hammer, Cara Buono, Casey Siemaszko, and Jon Stewart, to name a few. Furthermore, politicians, such as State Governors, laced up their shoes. One intimate moment fell when the fabulous Gloria Gaynor appeared. As her iconic anthem, *I Will Survive* thundered over the event's P.A. system, she greeted Mery Daniels on the finishing line. Daniels, a victim of the Boston Marathon bombing incident, demonstrated although an act of terrorism blew off her left leg, it had not stolen her spirit.

However, the entrant whose appearance required six months of planning was for a prince. I went to great lengths to ensure the royal entourage depended upon my leadership for Harry's trip. A prince seldom runs in open places, especially in the highest-profiled public park in the western world—*after* the media have published the precise location and exact time of his presence.

Receiving the Prince, the night prior upon a ship's deck, his engaging personality struck me at once. The next day, to a larger degree, when we ran together. Whilst exercising, Harry spoke deeply of his commitment to charity work and his passion and love for Africa. The continent remained a place, maybe the only place, where he noted he could genuinely be himself.

Another equal highlight of that summer was the progress of the classrooms and administration block of The Shoe4Africa School. Turning up to the site unannounced to monitor the team, I noticed the work crew under scrutiny. Despite it being the holidays, kids huddled by the piles of bricks and lumber. They took pride in inspecting the construction and offered to help, be it fetching a shovel, or carrying a bucket of water. The children's joy of witnessing the community benefit was so inspiring to see.

This location lacked a public secondary facility, meaning after primary classes, the kids' education finished. Discussing with the juniors, they yearned to attain inspirational careers. One boy announced he wished to study aerospace engineering if provided a chance to attend a secondary school. He enrolled at once alongside a woman in her mid-thirties. In poverty and a mother of four, Caroline Maritim presumed her learning days had passed. When she heard of our plans, she came dashing. Years forward, after graduating, she attained a degree from Kenyatta University and today is a teacher back at the school. And Boniface Kipkosgei? Well, he did graduate from university as an aerospace engineer.

During the construction, I again learned the lesson of not bringing my Western thinking to Africa. The workmen labored at a lackadaisical pace. Paying per job and not for the hour, I did not care. Whether they placed ten bricks in ten minutes or per day made no financial difference. One morning, I criticized the team, offering what I presumed should be words of encouragement, "Build slow and finish in twelve months. Or, if you operate faster and complete two schools in a year, you will earn double." The foreman, an ever-smiling man in his fifties, put me in my place, "The wages are sufficient. We have a job. I am employed. I hope to work for you for two years and accept less. Securing a job is greater than the money, and my wife is enormously proud of me."

☙❧

All the stories telling of people, like me, who pursue life journeys, include gatekeepers. These aides randomly appear and assist you in achieving the quest. Having glanced at the map, after the town of Voi, there were several ways to meander from Mombasa to Kilimanjaro. Which provided the most scenic, safe, and passable route? Searching the Internet was useless—I saw only direct car highways. Were there stretches where I could venture off-road, and what about purchasing food and supplies? Who on earth might facilitate with such a unique request?

That summer, in NYC, I met the charismatic Italian author of *I Dreamed of Africa*, Kuki Gallmann. Passing her table at a function, she held on to my hand and remarked a couple of inspiring words, "You know I came to New York to meet you. I am certain."

I should add, at a black-tie event on Park Avenue, I had omitted reading the required dress code remarks, and my turquoise shirt matched Kuki's shawl! We exchanged contacts because her words intrigued me. She retains a reputation as a change-maker.

So, a month later, in Kenya, I dialed her cellphone. She at once inquired, "What are you doing Saturday?" Replying I possessed no plans for tomorrow, she answered, "You do now—you are coming to visit."

Martin Keino, the son of the renowned Olympian Kip Keino, offered me a ride, and the drive to Kuki's estate in the Laikipia Highlands was nothing less than enchanting. Stupendous nature on the four-hour journey along the Great Rift Valley had me mesmerized. After entering her ranch, we followed the lengthiest driveway I have ever taken. Passing by tangled bushes, dams, and dirt-hewn airstrips, we drove for four miles (6.4 km) before arriving at a clearing circled by an enclave of thatched huts serving as guests lodges. Kuki, who lives much further down the road, waited for us, revealing a friendly smile.

Clambering from the vehicle, I witnessed a hefty elephant, with a rigid clumsiness, scratch his mud-caked flanks against my designated hut. Kuki drew a tanned finger to her lips, "Ssh, you must-a wait-a until he moves." No arguments there; I gave him all the time he needed.

Inside one of the huts, I splashed chilly water over my grimy face to rinse off the vermilion-colored dirt from the travel and then took a brief tour of a sliver of Kuki's property in her jeep. My eyes scrutinized the landscape, searching for the boundaries of the 110,000 acres estate—it was shocking to imagine one person held custody of this grand expanse of land. Wild animals roam freely inside the protected domain, and her garden is truly one of the unspoiled wonders of the world.

    Four enjoyable hours later, following a nourishing outdoor meal, Kuki departed, and we lounged with her staff as the final flickers of the campfire embers crumbled to ash. Why do the flames of an open fire trigger deeper emotions in discussions? The conversation overriding all others was listening to a slight lady called Lilian Kamaitha. After explaining my purpose, she gazed for a long time up at the sky before remarking, "A place dedicated for the poor children is so needed." Nobody spoke, and she continued, "Have you ever noticed how sickness for your child arrives mostly at night? You lie in bed and pray as if your life depends on those words traveling up to heaven. You implore the sickness will miraculously fade away because that is the only option. You have spent every penny, begged each of your neighbors, and pawned your last possessions. Prayers are what remains—that is the healthcare for destitute people like me, prayers. We get chased away from private facilities, and pharmacies aren't charitable."

    Her tender words stung like the lash of a cane. How do you address a sick child when you have nowhere to turn and no medicine to provide? I envisioned Lilian as she collapsed to her knees, sobbing silently in prayer, and I could virtually hear the muffled cries of her child. I thought of my brain surgery in England, which had cost me not a single penny. I felt incredibly grateful for being born in a country adopting a national health service—birthright stood as the greatest divider I had ever met.

    When the fire died to a pile of white cinders, I noticed Lilian's eyes glistening in the moonlight, no doubt recalling tough memories. Nobody offered small talk to lighten the mood. What could anybody say—the night was over. Retreating to our respective quarters in the pitch-black, I shuddered. The temperature dropped dramatically, but it was Lilian's haunting words that inflamed me with shivers.

    Back at my hut, I shouldered the door shut and dove under the heavy woolen blankets. Five minutes later, the wind whipped the door open a crack, as darkness had concealed a latch. Undressed and reluctant to stand, I inched the covers tighter—I was warm enough. After ten minutes and in the bush nearby, I heard the throaty grunt of a lion close enough to catch his post roar panting. I assure you I jumped from the bed pronto and secured the door. This life may be la vita normale for Kuki, but wildlife and I, do not mix.

Eager to exercise the following morning, I questioned if anyone wanted to go running. Martin considered it unwise, and Daniel, a staff member, point-blank refused, "A lion wandered around the compound last night. Lots of prints." Okay, not wishing to sound like a dumb tourist, I stuffed all the syllables up my sleeve and kept quiet. But by mid-afternoon, my feet itched like a nettle rash, and the enticing trails emitted a magnetic force. I had queried Kuki when we arrived if it was safe to go running. In a lilting Italian-English accent, she replied, 'Fine, it's a-fine.' On reflection, did she interpret my question correctly?

Initially, I cautiously jogged adjacent to the camp. As the incredible vista lured me in and lost in the beauty, I strayed further. Striding along the undulating dirt paths in an undisturbed nature of paradise proved an inspiring way to pass the afternoon. I aimed to complete a loop course, but after fifty minutes of jogging, I realized that all the trails looked identical. Clambering a hill, I tried to regain my bearings. No luck, and as I descended the rugged slope, I admired a herd of galloping impalas bolting through the bush. My initial thought was, what a breathtaking moment and having been in Kenya long enough, 'Yikes, run!' I certainly had not provoked any fright.

As the toffee-colored creatures vamoosed, I figured it made sense to follow their direction. Thus, by pure luck, the impala provided guidance.

Five minutes later, I recognized the roofs of our huts half a mile ahead. Glancing at my watch, I blushed, knowing others waited for my return.

After quickly showering, I greeted two new guests, Jamie and Mike, and we hastened to Kuki's home in a green battered Range

Rover for a special dinner with our hostess. Not even one hundred meters (109 yards) from our camp, I saw two imposing black-maned lions obstructed the path. The fiercer looking individual scornfully stared straight at us, refusing to budge. Jamie, not batting an eyelid, steered to the left as if sidestepping a pothole. The second lion rose, threw back his ruffled fur scarf, and revealed an impressive jawline before kindly permitting us to pass.

I related how fortunate I had not bumped into these beasts ten minutes ago, on foot. Jamie inquired why I ran in the wild, and I explained I skipped yesterday's exercise. Fitness is tough to gain and effortless to lose—I must keep in shape as the longest run of my life was coming up. The story of the Sea to the Stars spilled out.

"Oh, a wonderful trip. I can tell you the best roads to use, which to avoid, we recently drove over that exact route," said the second man, Mike Korchinsky, the founder of Wildlife Works. "We'll show you very detailed maps at breakfast as we carry them in the car."

What a crazy coincidence! Like in Tolkien's Hobbit—trust, and you will receive guides, you shall encounter people on your journey who play their part to help you overcome obstacles. Destiny, a person's purpose, rings as a solitary call, but as I sought to unearth Kuki's story, she had furthered my direction.

⋧⋨

October saw the Seas to the Stars idea collecting over $100,000 of donations. Kindhearted donors latched onto the fact I threw my heart, legs, and life into this cause.

Further funds rolled in, and two weeks before flying to Mombasa, forty runners assembled for the NYC marathon. Good souls responded to the call, friends like previous race winners Liz McColgan and German Silva. Liz provided a thoughtful interview to The Herald,

"Toby has done a lot more for a lot of people in his life than most folk would even attempt to do in a lifetime. I have no desire to run 26 miles again. I am doing this for Toby and his Kenyan charity."

Naturally, we decked the team out in Shoe4Africa gear to promote the cause. The Kenyan Edna Kiplagat offered to display the logo on her singlet—we trained together in Colm's group fifteen years ago. Regrettably, I did not find time to iron a logo onto her singlet, especially since she ended up winning the whole race! Chrissy, Leon Ware's niece, did collect a logo. She decided to wear her own singlet and requested the stencil transfer. Hand ironing all Shoe4Africa merchandise, I was well-practiced and instructed her to press forcibly, else the stencil peels off.

Chrissy enjoyed a splendid race until running out of steam at mile-21. Sobbing, she cried, "I only managed to hobble through Harlem because of the spectators. The S had dropped off my shirt, and it read HOE4AFRICA. I got the loudest cheers."

Throughout 2010, donations continually revived my spirits. Most gifts did not include letters, but when they did, I could cry reading the messages, like the one below from Kenya, containing eighteen single-dollar bills. The barely sealed, crumpled brown envelope held a brief letter.

Dear Tobby, God bless you. If you over in America can make this happen for Kenya, then it is for us here also to do something. You may not remember me, but it is I who have seen your work in Kibera. Love Lucy, mother to three.

Lucy peddles tomatoes, and she told me an excellent day would be earning four dollars. Between mud walls and the crude sofa acting as a bed in the night are eight to ten soil-filled rice sacks. These containers keep the earth moist for cultivating plants. In the daytime, she drags the bags to the doorway for a splash of sunlight. Feeding four hungry mouths and servicing rent, I do not know how long she must have labored to gather the funds. Or how she received the dollars, but her donation, all donations, fueled this journey.

Leaving Harlem to commence the adventure, the donation thermometer on my Sea to the Stars page, added to the earlier total, meant we shot over the magical million-dollar mark. The run alone garnered $134,311. A pleasant touch was receiving a good luck letter the morning of my departure from a prince—all boded well for a memorable trip.

After landing in Nairobi, I taxied to a coffee shop to meet the gentleman who arranged the ground transport, Cliffe of Micato Safaris. Micato is, without any doubt, Africa's premier Safari company, and the owner, Dennis Pinto, who lives in New York, had generously given us a walloping discount for two minibuses to trail our journey. And, because Micato does everything better, they roped in a police escort to allow our convoy to motor without stopping in the congested traffic of Mombasa.

Wrapping up the meeting Sammy Gitau, the first man from the Mathare slums to earn an MBA, slipped by the café—Sammy and I were planning a music recording project for the Mathare kids. True to form, the Nairobi resident is prouder of an iron bridge he had erected for his community than of his degree. Tottering on a cane, dressed in scars, Sammy related a car driver had struck him when crossing a road by a school stop sign,
"That woman did not stop. Our roads are treacherous, take care, or you gonna be hit, man." Geez, what a sendoff.

The following dawn, I relaxed high in the clouds flying to Mombasa. Upon landing, the heat on the coast was stifling, which did not bode well for our run. Rolling down the windows in Kalamazoo's taxi made no difference; my lungs could barely absorb the soupy air. Mombasa is an ancient 1000-year-old city of African, Asian, and European heritage. With a tropical climate, it is one of Kenya's most popular destinations. However, I had no time for tourism—Operation Sea to Stars commenced tomorrow.

Initially, I aimed to set off and, when exhausted, camp by the roadside, but instead, I structured the days to accommodate Rodney's team. The curveball glared on the final day's run with the acute elevation. Last month, a Spaniard, Kilian Jornet, zoomed up and down Kilimanjaro in less than eight hours, albeit aided by a team offering support along the route. Kilian, two decades younger, born in the mountains, spent 10-days before attempting the run camping at extreme heights on Kilimanjaro. My plan, slightly less glamorous, relied on hope. Fast times did not interest me, just fast money. Actually, the loftiest heights before my run involved an elevator ride to Sandy Weil's office in an NYC skyscraper last week, unsuccessfully begging for donations from the billionaire's assistant.

However, retaining no team, at the least, I required a speedy guide. Through running contacts, I learned of a Tanzanian claiming the fastest unassisted runs up and down Kilimanjaro. That impressed me—climbing without a team. Simon Mtuy was the man, and fortunately, I secured his services.

I checked into the Baobab Hotel—the friendly establishment stood 200 meters (218 yards) from the lips of the Indian Ocean. Then I ambled to the beach to designate the exact spot for tomorrow's launch. Could I invoke old emotions to add motivation for my run? Though today, watching the unrelenting rhythm of the tide, it was impossible to imagine I had once staggered along this coastline, desperate to save my life. With salty sweat trickling into my eyes and my neck damp from too much unruly hair, the blinding heat disturbed every thought, and pumping myself up for an endurance run proved impossible. Under the sun for hours of exposure, I feared I was in for a roasting tomorrow. Even for this brief twenty minutes, my pale skin baked and blistered.

Strolling pensively back to the hotel, I ordered a chapatti and waited for my New York friends to arrive. What crazy task had I signed up for?

Rodney turned up as promised, midafternoon. His posse included Mike and Dean, employees at his salon, and a writer called Mina and her partner, David. Mina would run alongside Rodney with Mike, Dean, and David, working as his support crew. Their gang required one vehicle and me the other. Dean packed camera gear and intended to record Rodney's trip. I looked at hiring a documentarian, but the offer of free Nike's and splendid company engaged no takers.

Documentaries cost way beyond what I imagined. I had attended a film featuring a paraplegic man scaling Kilimanjaro. A request for donations followed the viewing—not for any charity, as was the original intent, but to offset the substantial cost of the man's biopic.

That evening, noshing down a Chinese Chow Mein and sharing stories of our preparations, I realized I did not belong in the gladiatorial ultra-sports arena. Rodney's confidence developed from crushing Ironman competitions, whereas Mina had trained for hours, conquering mountain marathons at lofty heights in Colorado. My faith was inborn—self-assurance is an odd attribute, and I had more than a fair share. Life's stories provided bruising reminders regarding the power of the mind over the strength of rubber-band muscles. Preparing by clocking eighty miles (128 km) a week, which doubled my usual mileage, I was confident of my fitness base. The issue, I believed, was not endurance training but managing the searing temperatures and preventing an injury. Plodding along roads mimicked an inborn skill I knew all too well.

Our conversation veered to the logistics, and the group waited to hear of the locations for the day's meetups, meals, and lodgings. Surprised looks spread around the room when I remarked I proposed arranging all this on the run. None of them had holidayed using Toby's Tours. The fact I selected the route and organized the vans in time was a minor miracle.

Day One. At 6:25 a.m., as the orange sun peeked over the horizon, we stood in the rolling surf of the Indian Ocean for a photo before jogging up and running onto Malindi road. Upfront, the lead police bike wobbled precariously, so I upped the tempo to appease the rider and found myself running alone.

Inside the trailing support vehicles chauffeured by local guides, both named Mohammed, sat two policemen. I had complained bitterly of the unnecessary security expense till Rodney mentioned the run memorized an anniversary of a brutal attack—touché but scrimping to save every cent I only backed down after hearing their daily fee was equal to a fancy Starbucks drink.

Door to door, the entire trip, inclusive of NYC to Nairobi return flight, and three African flights, my personal minibus, ten days accommodations, and mountain/guide fees, cost under 4,000 dollars. Sponsoring myself, I whittled down every penny. I planned to stay in the dingiest of hostels and eat roadside foods. But unexpectedly, Shmuel offered support. Possibly he did not believe the expedition cost so little because he donated a check for 10,000 dollars. Instead of upgrading the trip, I dumped $6,000+ into the hospital fund.

    Weatherwise, with vivid azure skies, it looked to be a magnificent morning, a typical African summer's day—glorious for those who adore lazing on sandy beaches. The sky gleamed too blue, undiluted, with not a chance of any cloud cover. Although the hour was untimely, the tin-shack shanties lining our route were already open for business. Store owners, hawking trade, eyed me with a sneer and suspicion when I jogged by. The cabbages and trash rotting in the sun from yesterday's market, jamming the roadside gutters, offered recollections of the ghettos, not of a holiday resort. People, cats, and cars—my eyes darted anywhere except upon the long road ahead.

    I had run in locations over five continents, but Mombasa's heat and humidity beat them all. Especially when you mixed in the truck fumes that I sucked in with every mouthful—fuel regulations and omissions controls are somewhat foreign to Mombasa roads. The traffic crawled like a clogged drain, and cars nudged against the fenders of the vehicles ahead. Revving motorbikes crept into any nook, and if room allowed for one lane of motors, I saw two droves. Breathing in, I must be slurping pure grime straight into my lungs. Thank goodness my escort, sighted through a cloud of diesel fog, was a police patrol bike, else I would not know where to turn at each junction.

    Half an hour later, I gagged for a drink. Where the heck is my support van? Conceivably traffic caused the problem. I pushed on. After one hour, now really parched, I peeked again and recognized nothing but a trail of chugging cargo trucks. With 240-miles (386 km) to go, no way was I running backward, so I footslogged on.

As I ran, I reflected on my gains from this journey. Not in the sense of raising funds or the diverse scenery, but I pondered if my perspectives might alter. Running has consistently been a reflective time, and I thought of my life's steps leading to today. Where did my compulsion to partake in charity work stem from? And if I did not see Carl, would I have started running anyway? Probably not. What about traveling to East Africa? Was there an alternative way to unearth this purpose? What other goals would I have obtained?

All the answers were uncertain, but the delightful part of being here was everything felt right. Why question that? There was not a single shred of doubt in my mind this work reflected what I should be achieving with my life. I trusted in destiny and felt liberated. I recalled the sage words of the philosopher Emerson, *'We acquire the strength we have overcome.'* Oops, I stopped daydreaming as my grandiose philosophizing should wait for later—*if* I accomplished this task.

After one hour and thirty minutes of running and countless stray musings, that I craved fluids remained an understatement. The traffic had thinned, and jams could not be thwarting the driver. My throat, feeling like coarse sandpaper, needed fluids. Head pains caused by severe dehydration, was ruining the day.

Lumbering along in the baking heat, as much as I tried distracting myself by glancing at the surroundings, the lack of water swamped all my thoughts. The landscape, scrubbed out by the sun, revealed dust and barrenness, and the views evoked memories of a road trip I took driving from New Mexico to Las Vegas. I saw no scenery to shift my attention from the overpowering thirst. The others should have twigged if they had commandeered both vehicles, then I was running without any support. What happened, day one gremlins?

After two hours plus, I decided to catch the police rider and request that he U-turned and locate my driver. Forty miles in this temperature without water would kill me. It was a gamble as I had no idea how I could contact anyone if, he too, disappeared.

Thankfully, the scheme worked, and fifteen minutes later, after passing twenty miles (32 km), Mohammed and his van appeared. Instantly, I chugged back two liters of water and orange juice. Understandably my stomach writhed in knots, so I added three Clif Bars, decided to call it lunch, and relaxed slumped by the roadside.

In Mombasa, 2007, during the colder month of March, the world cross-country events changed from the usual morning hour to the late afternoon. The organizers acknowledged the destination presented issues for distance running, and they attempted to avoid the worst of the heat. Even so, sixty percent of the competitors took to recovering in ice baths after running for just thirty-odd minutes. Mombasa recorded the highest dropout rate of any world cross-country championship in history. The tough Ethiopian men's squad, acclimatized to the heat, failed to register a finishing team for the first time. Who but an idiot would plan an ultramarathon in Mombasa?

Climbing out of the van to begin running again, Rodney and Mina staggered into view, looking like roadkill. Disbelief almost popped out of their eyeballs as they combated this incomparable weather. I am certain I looked terrible myself, but the nutrition had performed magic. We exchanged encouraging words, and following my lead, they too stopped to refuel as I pressed on.

Trundling off down the road, people yelled a cordial greeting and, when I passed by a school, hundreds of children scuttled to the playground fence. "Where to? Where to?" they screeched in unison. When I replied, "Tanzania," they cackled till a couple of the kids bent over, doubled in stitches. I could not suppress my laughter either. The concept I might run from here to Tanzania sounded ridiculous, let alone jog up the continent's tallest mountain.

Pressing on under a sun that pierced my body and drained my soul, I knew I would finish the distance, but at what cost? After twenty-two miles, stiffness crippled my strides. Watch any marathon race, and most runners scowl with a pathetic 'help me' gaze at this point. Your body becomes depleted of glycogen, which is the fuel for the legs and the energy needed for the brain. So, how do you keep moving forward on zero power? Typically, I focus on the finish line, but today there was no finishing post. Where does the resolve come from to continue, and what force drew me onward? I labored on two rigid stumps that failed to function as legs, and yet, somehow, I surpassed the twenty-six-mile mark, a marathon of torrid heat. The following job was to not concentrate on the fourteen miles (22 km) ahead—or that I must repeat this ultra-distance throughout the week.

    Running the old hilly cobblestoned Rome Marathon course used for the 1960 Olympics, the invited field received instructions to place electrolyte drinks along the route. Too bad I forgot to drop off my bottles with the race director. At five km (3.1 miles), I discovered the only public refreshment offered was carbonated water. Try swallowing bubbles when racing flat out—it is impossible. The day would be a scorcher, 75°F. We whipped by the Trevi Fountain, featured in La Dolce Vita—had I not been in the prize money, I promise I would have dived in. For just under two hours and twenty minutes, I ran with a fireball burning inside my throat. Today felt worse, and those flames scorched like a furnace both in and outside my body. Could I continue?

    With thirty-one miles (49 km) accomplished, I now covered virgin territory. My record had stood at an elongated marathon training run in Spain after being chased by a long-horned bull, and later a grisly toothed wild boar high in the Andalusian hills; that day, I hit the magical thirty. Would I collapse after thirty-one? Somehow, I reached thirty-five, and each stride I took hurt like the chin-up you attempt after reaching bodily exhaustion.

    Why am I putting myself through this discomfort? Did I reckon the run would be enjoyable—well, Toby, what did you expect? When coaching marathoners, I offer caution, wait for the pain, and as it appears, embrace pain—like a medal of honor—it is validation you are achieving a formidable task. Only after blood, sweat, and agonies does the reward worth collecting arrive. I had been hauling my medal of misery since mile twenty-two and was ready to toss it away. We expect discomforts in long-distance running, and in a macabre fashion, before hurt occurs, the expectance of pain impels us to believe we are the warriors we dream we can be. So why, when groaning aches almost cripple us, should we complain? Suck it up, Toby, and run on. God, some days running really stinks.

Mohammed, having motored ahead, scrambled out of the van and screamed like a banshee, "Congratulations. Here marks forty miles (64 km), forty, you can stop!" The poor chap was bored senseless driving so slowly for hours. He knelt to sketch a chalk line on the road for the next day's start. Grinding to a muscle-locking and cramping halt one short meter after his marker, I volunteered to die. Slumping to the ground, I spread both hands over the road as if trying to absorb hidden energy from the earth. Had I chewed off too much? Tomorrow the schedule asked for forty-three miles (69 km), and I must maintain the timeline to reach Tanzania on Friday morning to meet Simon, the mountain guide.

Peeling myself up from the baking tarmac was like scraping the burnt residue off a frying pan. I knew I must hurry to arrange our lodgings for the night before Rodney's group arrived and complained again of my lack of preparations.

Since the Kenyan highways include an abundance of roadside motels, this was a trivial task, and after a brief scout driving to a neighboring town, we located a guesthouse and reserved rooms for 200-shillings ($2) each. The owner, Margaret Wanjiku, threw back her head in disbelief when I informed her of New York prices. Explaining I resided in Manhattan, where the average monthly rent hovered at $3,500 for a one-bedroom apartment, she skipped away laughing in disbelief.

On the shabby wooden veranda, zapped of energy, I relaxed, dozed, and gulped endless cups of tea from a thermos, utterly understanding the word shattered. After draining the flask and its droplets, I shuffled to my room, right as the other minibus arrived. The motel walls were paper-thin, and I heard complaints from Rodney and Mina—then a hush. Mohammed rapped on the door,

"Your friends say they will not stay here. They are complaining the rooms are unclean, and there are no private showers. They expected something," he could not grasp the precise words. Finding Margaret, I paid her a token and explained her guests wanted pricier lodgings. Now she looked really baffled.

After driving to the neighboring town, the others twigged the selections were few. In America, if you mention a Motel 6—named after the original nightly cost—certain connotations drift to mind. The hotel we departed suggested a Motel 2. Scouring the stables, hotels, and butcheries, the team finally agreed to a slightly upgraded motel at $3 a pop. The joint looked pretty similar, though rooms included personal showers. After traveling on the cheap for years, I forgot to respect what services a westerner demanded. I did issue a pre-trip warning back in America, stating prepare for rudimentary conditions on this expedition, but their parameters must have differed from mine.

Munching down a supper of boiled rice mixed with mushy beans, I observed couples traipsing in and out of the courtyard. Super, we had booked ourselves into a brothel—so much for the upgrade. I suspected the others, too tired, were oblivious to the prostitutes' hustling.

Our group held the vibrancy of a plate of burnt toast. No one related positive stories from the day, and Dean mentioned that Mina quit running after lunch developing colossal blisters—three became two on day one. Hopefully, the sores would heal before her mountain stage.

After eating, I excused myself, eager to limp into bed. Honestly, I wondered how I could wake, let alone run tomorrow.

Once inside the bedroom, the humidity hung like a steaming, sagging sauna towel, and a swarm of buzzing mosquitoes practiced spitfire plane maneuvers. Not unexpectedly, I had skipped any medication against malaria and hoped the ancient torn bed netting sufficed. I had begrudgingly taken the required yellow fever injection that is mandatory before crossing between Kenya and Tanzania, but I did not want additional drugs. The nurse at the inoculation center recommended using Diamox to address the altitude on Kilimanjaro, "It helps to increase your breath rate," she explained. "But wouldn't jogging on the mountain produce that effect?" I replied. My medical plan after the jab was a toothbrush, toothpaste, a bar of soap, and two disposable razors. With burning taught skin and a strong hint of sunstroke, sunscreen and lip balm might have been sensible additions.

Day Two. Throughout the night, bizarre dreams revealed visions of dying legs survived by a beating heart. Climbing out of bed took three times longer than usual. Deflated like a floor mat, I could not even muster up the energy to be cranky. Before the sun rose, we gathered our belongings and loaded the vans. Rodney, looking drained, voiced his doubts about completing today's stage and was recalculating the daily mileage expectations. Fueled on energy drinks and hopes, I recognized his crash before it happened. Dejection and exhaustion veiled his eyes as he kindly provided me with a generous squirt of his sun lotion before we split up to drive to the start line. Meantime, the sun scorched the horizon line with little pity for us fools.
"Yikes. It will be hot, hot, hot," smiled Mohammed as we returned to yesterday's ending point.
"Well, ensure you stay, stay, stay close to me today then," I replied because running sans water again might finish me off.

Twenty minutes later, ready to begin, I found myself tightening and double knotting my laces—any reason to delay the torture. Recently, aligning with the rest of the planet, I purchased a mobile phone and receiving a text message of another sizable donation lifted my spirits. Contributions always consoled me, and my mantra became money over mileage.
The others trailed our van and had opted to use my chalk line for their start. Dean, rolling the camera, suggested we jog together for a photo op. Yet after less than a mile, I ran alone, out on the road to Tanzania. Back in New York, Rodney's pace might be swifter than mine, yet here he stumbled. My muscles tightened and squeaked as I tried to match his fatigued stride. I desperately

needed to avoid injuries, and chopping my gait offered a surefire route to stressing a tendon. After years of training athletes in New York, I discovered running at another's pace often causes hip and knee issues. Better I push the guilt aside, be selfish and press on alone.

When running, I listened to churning thoughts jumbling inside my head. With long-distance jogging, once your mind drifts, the miles melt away. Not all of my ruminations were cheerful, and I reminisced about a friend's child who died when a medic offered treatment for malaria, and the toddler suffered from pneumonia. I played stupid mind games, thinking if I established the hospital sooner, then Ibrahim may have chosen to escort his daughter to our facility, and the baby might still be alive. Then I thought of Miriam, burning inside the church, flames snatching her breath. Each time my limbs creaked or moaned, I reflected that whatever pain I experienced, it remained incomparable to the pains those children endured.

Trying to elevate my mood, I thought of the paradox of running. I entered the sport believing the aim should be to defeat others, but the genuine challenge becomes the competition against yourself. For example, compare two opposing football teams—they will never share refreshments on the pitch. Then observe the major marathon leaders fighting to win a single purse of hundreds of thousands of dollars. During the race, athletes frequently pass drinks aiding the same competitors they aim to defeat. The antagonist of running is yourself. There is an unspoken guild in the sport, and the membership is simply bonding through participation. Running elevates you to an acuter state of being, not just physically but mentally.

Speaking of mental issues—and why my analogies either focused upon refreshments or ill health—the heat was causing my brain to sizzle like a fried egg on a red-iron skillet. Could there be at least an inch of shade on today's run?

At lunchtime, Mohammed yelled out of his window, suggesting I stop at the crest of the upcoming hill near the Tsavo East Game Park offices. Then, he sped off to seek a sheltered space in the parking lot. These acts of thoughtfulness caused a considerable difference. He constantly picked spots clear of noise and cars, so I gained the maximum rest. I was appreciative to have this considerate, benevolent man as a companion.

Jogging to the parked van, I noticed Mohammed shaking his head. I overheard him conferring with our other driver. I gathered Rodney, staggering left and right, had quit running, suffering from severe heat exhaustion. "One left," Mohammed grinned, "and, no pressure, but the burden is entirely on you. Don't you quit, or I will be unemployed."

I would not quit, but let me drag out the lunch hour, chewing twice as long for each bite and gain much-needed recovery. As I refueled, I hoped the warmth would abate before the following stage of exercise—but it did not. The dashboard thermometer hovered menacingly over 113 degrees °F (ca. 45 °C) and, that was when parked under the umbrella of a shady acacia tree.

The afternoon trek across the Taru Desert would prove more demanding than any other—the egregious exposure and roasting heat became torture. Undoubtedly, there must be easier ways to earn donations—no level-headed man, beast, or reptile would ever agree to join me. The road ahead, crusted sand and stone, stood without a hint of life. The crème lathered on my face and shoulders at dawn had long evaporated, and my light skin undertook a thrashing. Nobody stepped out walking, let alone running, as I set off running beneath the shimmering sky. The effort felt like skipping inside an airlocked oven. Why didn't I sign up for a bank robbery?

One hundred years ago, when the British Army trampled over this stretch of an unforgiving land, soldiers dropped like flies and died of heat exhaustion. The route soon became waymarked a no-travel zone for pedestrians, and a railway was hastily constructed to provide a passage. Mombasa represented a stroll in the park compared to the Taru Desert.

Joseph Thomson, the famed explorer, described the wasteland, *'Eerie and full of sadness as if here is all death and desolation.'* Taru is where the earth buckles and cracks and is destroyed beyond restoration by the furnace of the relentless subversive sun. My non-athletic friends think I love every run, that I leap out the door at dawn with a smile plastered on my face. Ha, if they could only see me now, grumbling like a penniless street tramp.

After an hour or so of drudgery, nature called, and I detoured off-road to hide behind a bush of shriveled stunted shrubs.

To my horror, instead of urine, out trickled crimson blood with streaks of pee. Oh, shoot, what had happened? Google Search, the poor man's doctor, was unavailable as my cellphone could only receive calls and send text messages. Imagining festering ruptures, like a foot-long butcher's knife slicing a tender steak, I dreaded that a river of blood gushed haywire inside my body. Perhaps I should not press on for too much further and risk exacerbating the wound?

How would the others react? Would they intervene and force me to stop? Being the last man standing, if I quit, the Sea to the Stars adventure was over. That could not happen. Inexplicably, the need to complete this quest overrode commonsense. Let us keep the issue secret, I decided.

With one hour scheduled to run, I slashed thirty minutes for a precaution and expected to regain the miles tomorrow. Relaying the adjustment to Mohammed and Martin for a rendezvous at thirty-nine miles (62.7 km), I crept off on a cautious jog. Swallowing a fly, I coughed to spit out the bug, but I discovered no saliva in my mouth. Instead, I tasted the scorched earth's dust that had caked itself onto my dehydrated dried-out lips. Well, at least I did not taste blood!

Thankfully, I completed the day without further incident. Battered, beaten, and barely able to muster a sweat, my withered body resembled the sole of a tramp's old boot. Finishing the run made me reexamine the hackneyed phrase, 'on his last legs.'

David had taken charge of the lodgings because of yesterday's kerfuffle, and Mohammed called to discover the group's whereabouts. Wow, we upgraded to a swanky safari lodge where the western guests graced ironed khakis and wore buttoned-up collared shirts—what a striking contrast to the frothy brothel. Rodney kindly shouldered the extra expense for me, calculating the price would exceed my miserly budget. After greeting the others, I dashed straight to the showers for a soapy scrub-down under the piping hot water. Under the nozzle, I noted my quadriceps, still quivering, looked bruised and discolored to a dark purply-brown shade. Crikey, my body began disintegrating, and I still had four more days of agony remaining.

Day Three. Despite the comforts, I could not sleep. As in Zanzibar following my attack, I propelled like a yo-yo between hot and cold flushes. Heatstroke, I guessed, caused the discomfort. Too quickly, a thin line of reddish-gold dawn streaked through the dainty cotton lace curtain. Rising slowly, I limped to the bathroom. Unable to pee since yesterday, I held my breath—though thank goodness the regular color replaced the blood.

As the sun boosted itself over the horizon, Mohammed and I departed alone. I apologized for the early start, "I am sorry, no lounging in luxury. You selected the wrong runner to shadow." The others had chosen the cozy comforters, a buffet breakfast, and a safari excursion over lacing up their running shoes.
Yet to my surprise, Mohammed disagreed, "No, I am happy being here because it assigns me as part of your mission to establish the hospital. I am honored to be involved and will not forget this memory ever. You, and me, to the mountain. Maybe it is my choice to trail you." His words juggled with laughter, and a shaft of sunlight splintered the windscreen, landing on his face to illuminate a beaming smile. Despite the unearthly hour, a fire burned behind his eyes, and I knew each embracing word flowed straight from his heart.

Today, I stood face-to-face with a formidable adversary called distance. Knowing I portrayed the weak opponent, I convinced myself I must run to be a victor, not like the victim yesterday. As if I was a wooden puppet, but without strings to pull, I ran stuttering along the road, motivated only by fundraising dollars. Instead of lifting a shoe, my strides shuffled over the tarmac.

Michael in Kibera discovered his drive and placed an astonishing effort in training to run out of poverty—finally, I equaled his passion by craving funds for the hospital. Running for a purpose was propelling me forward. But would my body hold out? The odds looked out of my favor because I now developed a worrying throb. Stress fractures in the foot begin as dull aches, usually over one toe. Wiggling my toes, I sensed a crack forming. Please, no injuries today—I concocted deals, promising myself, if I completed this challenge, it would be my last ultra. Keeping moving would be my plan until forced to stop. One stride forward means a stride closer to the mountain. Do not think; place one leg in front of the other and hope the pain passes. If troubles halted my progress, it would not be for lack of gritty determination.

Keep moving had been Al Gordon's favorite motto, my eldest acquaintance, who sadly died last year at the ripe age of 107. Sitting on two nonprofit boards alongside Al, he narrated stories to me of how and why philanthropy mattered so much to him, and he drilled that motto of keep moving into every discussion. Now represented the time to honor Al.

Sandy dustbowl beige and browns swept to a greener canvas as I approached the town of Voi. Now I thought of my N'gong days. Denys Finch Hatton, Out of Africa's protagonist, had perished here, crashing his biplane near the Mwakangle Hill. More relevant to my journey, last night, a cook narrated a friend of his was devoured by a lion in Voi a year ago. "He was mauled alive when the head fell in sleep, and the legs became unable to escape" was the graphic description of the poor man's demise. Another sturdy reason to keep moving!

The terrain took a twist, or should I say a steep rise, when I entered the region appropriately identified as the Taita Hills. Diverting off the roadside, I jogged along vibrant orange dirt trails. The cut against the walls of the dark olive bush looked unreal. The colors, so abstract after the bland tarmac, served as a welcomed reprieve to the eyes. The disadvantage to the beauty of these back paths became the continual undulations. Climbs completed led to a downhill dip, and then the next ascent would immediately pounce into view. Up until this point, the route rolled out pancake flat. Yet ironically, with the hills, the indestructibility of belief began creeping in. Whether it was the peaks changing out which muscle groups I used or because of the soft cushioning underfoot, I am uncertain, but I guess the latter. If you drop a golf ball on both concrete and grass, you recognize the shock absorption benefits of landing on softer surfaces.

Running in Africa provided a colorful meaning to a nature run—a variety of unique distractions appear before your eyes. My daydreaming jolted when I spotted a snake. I dislike snakes; fear is the more truthful word. The coiling reptile, if outstretched, looked as long as me. Descending a hill, I saw the fiend only five steps away—I almost froze. Freezing did not help my vertical lift as I am the basketball player who jumps, and his shoes do not leave the court.

Somehow, probably skimming the snake's noggin, I cleared the enemy as the serpent presumably dozed. Mohammed, who navigated the tarmac road, remained far out of sight; what happens had I been bit? Did I require a plan for snake bites?

Another infuriating hurdle was crossing homesteads. The locals constructed *boma's* made of impassable prickly thorns (barricades around homes) to hinder lions and other predators. Although the detours were minor, one step sideward brought an exaggerated groan accompanied by an exhausted huff. When you over-stress your body, petty issues become substantial problems. I tried laughing off the minor obstacles, but honestly, these diversions drove me crazy today.

Several miles later, I rejoiced to spy the town of Mwatate. Hurrah, Mwatate signaled the point at which I clocked back on schedule distance-wise. I had instructed Mohammed to wait for me a bit past the town, as ending the mileage in a populated area always caused delays with umpteen questions from well-meaning locals. Mohammed had parked in a breathtaking spot, and I yearned to capture the panorama on video.

Rambling into the bush, I scouted for a suitable elevated rock to stand upon for a sweeping 360° shot. Forty meters in front of where I stood, a pale and pockmarked mane-less lion sauntered by—thankfully not in my direction. The animal, shoulder blades hunched and scowling, glaring straight ahead, failed to spot me. But how?

Disregarding any advice, I cowered in a stance of fear. I swear I stopped inhaling, especially as a second followed its route and then a third. I regretted my stupidity of wandering into the bush. Obscured by a tree, praying I stood upwind, I recorded the moment on camera. Three became more—nine fancy cats!

Five minutes of silence passed before I risked sprinting back to Mohammed's vehicle to playback the footage. Having witnessed a zillion lions, Mohammed barely cocked an eyebrow.

He reversed the car as Rodney re-booked for a second night at the same lodge. And then, after a brief radio call hooking into the local safari guide's wavelength, he detoured to reveal more lions on the drive back. Like observing a sheep in England to a Kenyan guide, a lion is nothing exceptional.

At dinner, I discovered I captured better footage than the others who registered for the safari drive. Describing the snake, did I hurdle a highly noxious sleeping black mamba? Hopefully, no more animal or reptile sightings for me on this trip. Devouring plates of carbo-rich food alongside Mohammed and Martin, for once, I listened instead of speaking. Drifting off inside their stories, and hearing their aspirations for life, was pleasantly relaxing. That night I slept like a pea in a pod and rose fresh and perky in the morning.

Day Four. After six tough miles (9.6 km), the contours leveled out elevation-wise. In rhythm with the run, the journey now felt enjoyable. Although my lower body continued to groan and grumble, my lungs and heart purred like a cat on this scenic holiday. Somehow, I was beginning to enjoy ultra-jogging.

Today, the dirt paths switched to reddish volcanic dust, and the skies turned to a wild explosion of the royalist blues. Our route threaded us through the prairie location chosen by Michael

Douglas, an American actor/director, to film The Ghost and the Darkness. The narrative told of the two man-eating lions who guzzled a staggering number of humans one hundred years ago. Those beasts had prowled near Tsavo East's savannahs, where I had tramped on Tuesday. Now, as I cautiously ran in Tsavo West National Park, I would be grateful if I did not encounter their grandsons.

In the coffee shop before I flew to Mombasa, and unsure about the illegalities of running in the parks, I rallied friends with wildlife connections. Mentioning a contact helps to defuse tension, and that person could be on duty when I entered the park. Google revealed Daniel Woodley to be the senior warden, so I rang his number, and requested permission to travel through Tsavo West. Hearing I was not new to Kenya, he relaxed, "Okay. But keep the car near at all times." I reckoned receiving Daniel's word was my passport. No one in their rational mind chooses to run alone inside a game park, but it was the only route to accomplish my goal.

Although I kept my eyes peeled in case any ferocious untamed animals appeared, instead, indifferent zebras, grazing tawny giraffes, and apathetic elephants' way off in the distance sweetened my day. A perplexed monkey hot-footed it into my path, but as he caught my stretched shadow, he bolted like a chased rabbit. Apart from a couple of times, Mohammed hung consistently within a hundred meters should any fierce animal approach, and I did not feel endangered in the slightest.

Then, on this day, I noticed the prize. Coruscating on the horizon, titanic, imposing, and unlike most of the world's mountains that are perched among a range of peaks, Kilimanjaro, with a snow-capped crown, juts out majestically alone. Kilimanjaro, that towering challenge I initially spied in N'gong and later aimed to vanquish at the millennium. If so, I guess I would have never traveled to Zanzibar.

After completing the day's mileage and calling to locate Rodney's group, we doubled back to a place called the Lion's Bluff Lodge situated inside the 48,000 acres LUMO Community

Wildlife Sanctuary. Built on a ridge, the wooden, thatch, canvas, and stone camp allowed visitors to gaze for miles over the savannah at an impressive, vaulted viewing deck. Yet, instead of lingering and enjoying sundowner drinks with the New Yorkers, I desired recovery and rest. Consequently, I unzipped my luxury tented hut and took a pre-dinner nap. What a dreary companion I was proving to be. Run, eat, sleep—I bet the others thought me boring.

Later at night, under the twinkling stars, gobbling down bowls of carbohydrates, I again thanked Rodney for allowing this extravagance of upscale camping. One day, I must return, and instead of galloping through the landscape, stop and pause to admire this patch of nature's heaven.

Day Five. Although we left before the allotted breakfast hour, the staff had kindly risen at the crack of dawn to prepare sandwiches. Despite possessing no appetite, I accepted the food feeling bad since a person labored for our benefit. Stowing my bag, I discovered my camera mysteriously disappeared from the room. I hinted to the receptionist if the memory card resurfaced, I would be appreciative and silent. A cash reward above the value of the item did not help, and the equipment never resurfaced. Losing the camera stunk, but those images were irreplaceable—dang, I have always preferred door keys over tent zips. Fortuitously, my bulkier Handycam captured stills, and miraculously, that had not vanished from the room.

Where I ran today lay near the borderline separating Kenya from Tanzania. The same countryside on which the British had fought the Germans in the First World War. Crumbling remains of station houses, built as defense posts by the soldiers, still existed. The structures reminded me of the old grandfathers of Kibera and their sacrifice to defend the British Empire. As I learned, in 1886, Britain and Germany divided lands to establish two countries. Eighteen years later, both entities demanded the same people—many without weapons but acting as bullet shields—must battle each other in the Great War. Britain had declared that the larger ethnic groups should submit hundreds of 'fighting men' to protect the crown. It was bad enough you were conquered, colonized, and labeled as 'savages,' but now you were ordered to risk dying for a foreign cause and expected to slay your old peaceful neighbors?

After the war, the soldiers were dismissed from duties and sent home without fanfare. Imported Nubian soldiers, lacking dwellings, gathered in Nairobi, and the military doled out swampy plots as compensation for their service to the British crown. Shamefully, the administration failed to issue title deeds. Resourceless, named after the Nubian word Kibra meaning a forest, the boggy donated land became a congested slum.

My investigation constituted a google search, but I could not find one Kenyan honored by the British, or even mentioned by name, for his service during that war. Sadly, of the 250,000 enlisted Empire troops of 1914, only 35,000 survived by 1918.

Wildlife confrontations doubled today. I encountered an oversized scorpion giving me the sudden leg-lock, though happily, the specimen was lifeless. Cape buffalo, impala, and yellow baboons, by the roadside, went virtually unnoticed. Passing by a Maasai *Manyatta*, a makeshift encampment of packed mud and wooden huts, I heard shrieks of excitement. Spontaneously, a man draped in his vibrant red *shuka* (robe) dashed out to accompany me, cheered on by his nomadic neighbors. Three giggling youngsters bounded after the *moran* (warrior), giggling. They clutched sticks sported for goat herding and wore miniature shukas. The strides of the Maasai appeared effortless, like swans gliding over the surface of a lake.

We shared company for one memorable mile before I returned to the solitude of the valley. As the Maasai turned and departed, his three whispered words faded into the waves of the wind, "*Kwaheri.* (Goodbye) *Karibu Tena.* (Welcome again)."

While researching my latest book, *More Fire*, I enjoyed fascinating conversations with Archie Evans, a man who was instrumental in developing competitive running in Kenya. In 1947,

Colony Sports Officer Evans recognized impressive talent and planned to formalize a national track and field team. Archie aimed to build a squad and attend the necessary smaller competitions, enabling him to apply to allow Kenya to compete in the Olympic arena.

Considering the British-led government fought the Mau Mau rebellion, and the country flailed in a state of emergency, the task presented looked unsurmountable. Yet somehow, Archie achieved his ambitious goal. After escorting a squad to Kitwe, in Zambia, in 1952, he received an invitation to the 1954 Vancouver Commonwealth Games. Finally, in January 1955, Archie scored gold—admission to the 1956 Melbourne Olympics Games. Team member Nyandika Maiyoro explained Archie rose way above his role as a running coach, "He accomplished everything, the paperwork, the training, he became the father to the team—he taught me how to eat with a knife and fork. When I found myself disorientated on the streets of England, it was Archie who organized the police search."

Archie chatted fervently about the Maasai, "They demonstrate immense athletic abilities. But their passion for the land and cattle far outweighs the will to run in pursuit of tin cup prizes and paper certificates. They ran more than other ethnic groups in daily life yet refused to enter competitions. Maasai lived for the day and expressed no interest in leaving their land to play sports."

The Englishman, who had named his Keswick English house Nandi Estate, sadly died last week. Running with the Maasai and embracing Archie's spirit, I fully understood what he indicated in our final conversation, "When the Maasai run, you see the most natural of all of nature's movements."

Today I included an extra mile for the memory of Archie Evans.

On this running safari, the route traversed the old rusty railway tracks the British erected to cross Kenya in 1896. Coiling 600 miles (965 km), Winston Churchill labeled the line 'the most romantic and most wonderful railways in the world.' Hurdling the ancient irons, I relived Koitalel's story, how he crawled in darkness, wrenching up these hefty intrusions hoping to preserve his unspoiled environment. My mind then coasted to Karen Blixen, who, after boarding the train that ran along these tracks, commenced on a journey that would define her life. Although born to a privileged society in Denmark, Kenya was where her character bloomed. Then, my thoughts wandered to the troubled writer, Ernest Hemingway. When he had traveled along these tracks and gazed towards Kilimanjaro, what fancies flashed through his mind? Hemingway, recognized as a wild hunter, embodied far more than a famous gun-wielding sightseer. Like Blixen, he studied ethnic languages, fraternized alongside the people of African blood, and absorbed the pulse of the land.

The theme for Hemingway, Blixen, and indeed Harry stated that Africa presents both a promise and an escape— 'A place where I can be myself,' the Prince had claimed. The sentiment was perfectly framed by Karen Blixen upon arriving in Kenya, 'A new kind of freedom which until then one had only found in dreams.'

Slipping into a mood of reflections became easy because nothing bar beauty and history disturbed this glorious setting. The scenery was harsh yet heartening, and those Maasai, humble but headstrong, were timeless, like my imagination. Suddenly I was twelve years old again and running free—I could feel the guarantee of adventure rising from the skin of the soil underneath my feet. Why do I run? Here lay my answer.

Now, entering Taveta and returning to the asphalt roads, I noticed too much distraction to wallow in dusty daydreams. Sweaty, sunburned, and sand blasted, I tramped into the last town before the borderline, letting go of my musings and notions.

Entering a hubbub of activity, the rhythm of running disappeared, dissolving into an abrasion of noise pollution. Ironically, to anyone but a runner, passing from the embrace of exposed wilderness allowed me to feel isolated in the congested company of others. Like the writer cramped into an abandoned attic, who craves only the fountain pen as his companion, the runner alone is never alone.

Weaving my way through the tangled urban zone, I cringed in the confusion of having to dodge between *matatus*, motorbikes, and meandering handcarts. After the celestial cradle of the barren wilderness, Taveta resembles a shrunken Times Square without the obnoxious overload of wasted lightbulbs. From inside crowded shops, music blared from the boomboxes blown speakers, and each unit was cranking up the volume to outdo their neighbor. The cacophony of reggae, country music, and local twangs became ear-splitting. Hand-painted signs promising a comprehensive list of services slapped over the entrances of the abodes. One entrepreneur's artwork offered such a jumble as, 'Head shaving, boot polishing, music listening, braid patch-ups, and battery charging—each ten-bob (10-cents).'

Reaching Kenya's end, Mohammed, my trusty friend, turned back. I had reserved the vehicle till Sunday, but as Simon intercepted me tomorrow, Mohammed could depart three days early to enjoy an important family function. We promised to breakfast in Mombasa—a decade later, still in touch, it is yet to happen.

As I crisscrossed countries, I imagined hearing a barrage of queries. However, no one thought that a foreigner jogging to the customs office clasping a passport looked abnormal. Waiting for my passport stamp, I perused the map on the office wall; Taveta appears to be a Tanzanian town and Kilimanjaro Kenyan instead of vice versa. Either way, the borders are piercing visual reminders of the abstract land carving of the old colonialists. An unsubstantiated rumor suggests Queen Victoria gifted the mountain to her nephew, Kaiser Wilhelm II, the crown prince of Germany.

Now in Tanzania, David located a guesthouse in Marangu. The hostess greeted us, hollering out, 'Happy Thanksgiving.' Gosh, how many thanks must I hand out? Millions. I even thanked the schoolteacher who flung me out of the class years ago. Having resided in five countries, I typically forgot the national days, but the notion of one dedicated to giving thanks was timely.

Later in the evening, resting in a broken wicker armchair in the tranquil gardens that had once housed a coffee farm, I gazed directly at the looming challenge. The departing sunset cast a coral husk over the snowcapped peak— what a glorious finishing post. The magnitude of the mountain caused me to blush when recalling how I had dressed up the word purpose at the proposed millennium ascent. I know I wished only to be purposeful. Was that not the universal question, 'Am I heard, will my life count, and what is my legacy if written today?' Well, here I am, still trying to be of use and aspiring to conquer the climb as a different person. The new me was the same old river.

Seasoned by the years, unable to cling to the flowing water, time alters everything. The bones of my body, sculpted and scarred, were now ready for the challenge. Conceivably I fooled myself, slotting events into places where they might fit, but the fulfillment I recognized today was more worthy than what I imagined back then.

Maybe, I had to suffer the pains of the millennium, face the enlightened Dr. Mehta, for me to accept the hospital over the lucrative marathon project? I used to presume destiny nestled inside a person like a hidden gemstone, but that rock appears more of an onion—you either peel back one layer of skin or keep on peeling. Unquestionably the climbing would be more meaningful for the adversities encountered and the decisions I have applied since the millennium.

Day Six. On Friday at the vaulted altitude and before the sun rose, the air carried an unpleasant chilly nip. A web of frost coated the car windscreen, and I yearned to add a second layer. The early morning is my preferred time, the moment before the school blackboard becomes covered in chalk and dust and when the mood of the day is at its purest. Shivering, I could hardly wait to start the run.

Rodney, never beaten, had not quit. After Tuesday's blowout, adjusting the goal, he still clocked miles on his legs and planned to accompany me to meet Simon.

If not for Simon's guiding skills, this run concept was unachievable, so let us hope he remembered our date. Sure enough, as we parked, a car approached us at the border, and Simon climbed out with a smile but burdened by a heavy heart. A road accident occurred that morning involving his friend's wife. A bus crashed and burst into flames, killing and burning passengers. At the local clinic, the staff urgently arranged an airlift to Nairobi for the severely injured. Naturally, this catastrophe preoccupied his mind. Asking him if we should postpone, Simon shook his head. Then, as he promptly broke into a quick tempo, he uttered, "No, running will help to clear my thoughts."

The terrain in Tanzania started on leveled, well-maintained asphalt. If I daydreamed, I could be in Europe with painted markings, cats-eyes, and all. Soon we swung right at the Himo police station, ushering us onto a grinding incline to the Kilimanjaro National Park. The plan stated we aimed straight to the peak—thirty-seven miles (60 km) with a 5,141-meter elevation gain—but Simon was not emotionally ready. He concluded he needed time alone today. Maybe to contact his friend, I do not know, and I did not wish to pry. He suggested we complete the twenty miles (32 km) of climbing to the official gates and address the mountain the following morning. We could detour and run to his home, conveniently situated a few miles to the west of the gate.

The ascent to the park is brutally steep. *Matatus,* with squealing tires, hurtled down the narrow road at breakneck speed. None gave us a decent berth, and a couple of times, I found myself leaping into the bushes for safety. Describing the scenery, I might have been jogging in the English countryside—I found it hard to believe I approached Africa's grandest mountain.

David and Mina, who lingered at the hotel, enthusiastically waved as we passed. They hiked by the roadside, and I wanted to pause to brief them how grateful I was for their company and kindness. Both had been delightful companions, and knowing I may never see them again, I felt despondent for my constant goodbyes—a dismal theme of a traveler's life.

Reaching the gate of the mountain reserve, I intended to wait for Rodney. But Simon was antsy for a medical update—I would make it up to Rodney later, back in Manhattan.

After traversing fields, ditches, and forest, we arrived at the tranquil green estate of the Mbahe cottages. Incredibly self-sufficient, Simon cultivates the food he consumes, the coffee he brews, and even handcrafts his house furniture. A highlight of the day was slumping at a sturdy table carved from the dusky wood of a dhow boat smoothed by the salts of the seawaters, chowing down lunch, and chatting to his farm workers. But as peaceful as this sanctuary might be, I could not stop fidgeting—the object of my desire towered right before me. My leg muscles, with a mind of their own, twitched to add twenty miles (32 km) to the day's total.

Wandering to the cottage rooms, I flipped through a rack of outdated magazines. After reading a paragraph, I impatiently tossed the journals aside. How could I distract myself? I noticed the driver who dropped Simon off this morning had kindly delivered my luggage. Bored, I tried to unpack my bags as slowly as possible, but like a magnet, I returned to the compound to gaze towards the towering challenge. A worker, crouching in the garden, hands lost in the green weeds, spoke in Swahili, telling me the mountain perched high, maybe too high to run? But the Gods will decide, he concluded.

He stated his people's sun god, Ruwa, resided on Kilimanjaro. All Chagas (ethnic group), when buried, must face the precipice as the land is sacred. Would I be trampling on holy ground? Did the locals resent the tourists, like me, who came here to cross an item off a bucket list? My Swahili was too basic to phrase that question.

As the sun set, after devouring a wholesome vegetarian casserole and slices of warm banana bread, I retired for the day. The moment had come to define the trip as a success. If I failed to reach the peak, the journey from the turquoise ocean mattered little in the eyes of my supporters, and I feared donors might claim refunds. They knew nothing of the last week's escapades and anticipated a picture of me sitting on Africa's highest peak.

Simon, who disappeared after dropping me at his home, returned late at night and popped his head through the door to announce a departure set for seven a.m. My heart thumped like a skydiver's—would I make it to the top of the mountain?

Day Seven. Nerves, I rose early and spread my possessions on the bed, deciding what I required for the ultimate stage. Not much, just enough for a day. Surveying the skies, I did not see a cloud in sight—perfect for the run. I packed the bag as if preparing for war, picking a shirt, glancing at it, tossing it aside. Adequate clothing is a must, and I maintained a sorry record for often forgetting the significant items.

Once, when dizzy and drunk, after partying all night with the stunning contestants of a beauty pageant at the Pegasus Hotel in Jamaica, I rushed to collect my race gear at daybreak. Entering the hotel room, I congratulated myself on having the commonsense to lay my costume on the bed the night prior. I grabbed the items then dashed to the starting line wearing shorts, and fortunately, the Carib Cement Marathon started adjacent to the hotel. Scrambling to pull on my race singlet with a pounding hangover, I realized I held a pillowcase. Let me not make a similar mistake today.

Following breakfast, we jogged over the fields and forest to yesterday's finishing point. The immediate task required signing in with the chief warden and purchasing my permit, but to my annoyance, the director was absent. Striding around outside his office, a staff member informed me he habitually arrived late on the weekends,

"What is the hurry?" he asked, "the mountain will wait for you."

I found no amusement in his dry humor. No one volunteered to contact the warden and urge him to hurry like I kept on demanding. Our schedule required us to leave right now. Where was the idle warden?

When he did appear, over two hours late, he became suspicious at my three-day permit application (the cheapest, but not allowing climbers beyond the halfway point).

"Are you sure you are not here to reach the peak?" He smelled a rat, "You look fit, so why not to the top?"

Not wishing to waste money on the pricier permit, I informed him I planned another adventure next summer alongside friends. I coughed to feign ill-health. The chief bit his lip, peering at me with hostility. Unlike other climbers, Simon and I wore light running clothes. He dilled and dallied, vacated the office, and returned at 10:30 a.m. to finally sign the paperwork wearing a 'do not believe you fooled me' scowl.

Right from the get-go, we made haste overtaking what I determined to be the prepared people—those smarties who collected their permit ahead of time, or hikers on day two of their trek. Jogging by the lush foliage of the sub-alpine montane forest, the footing proved much easier than I expected—the pathways were well-trodden and clearly marked as if in a public park.

Passing the rim of the Maundi Crater, we paused to hydrate at the Mandara Huts. Two years ago, I had trained in El Yunque's rainforest in Puerto Rico; the environment was remarkably similar. This climb was undemanding. Reading a sign, 2,743 meters (9,000 feet) altitude, produced a confidence booster because I suffered no adverse effects at all.

The word mountain draws certain connotations, but, to my surprise, various paths even offered well-worn iron handrails. I would not be wandering in the wilderness eyeing a craggy peak, as I envisioned all mountaineering should be.

Hikers typically reach the Horombo Huts, 3,718 meters (12,200 feet), on the third day—but it took us under three hours of jogging. My pulse pumped at a moderate 120 BPM, indicating I did not exceed any limits, so far, so good.

The terrain now took a turn to Icelandic emptiness and sprouted low-growing tufts of vegetation. Rocks and stones replaced the greenery and, the temperature dropped to a cardigan chill. Simon advised we stopped jogging because we were way, way, ahead of our porters. "Let us rest at these wooden buildings," he suggested, pointing to a cluster of drafty-looking structures, "our friends (referring to the porters) are lagging miles behind."

In less than three hours, we conquered half the distance. The peak remained within reach, yet it would be pitch black by seven p.m. Even lollygagging at a stroll offered the porters no possibility of catching up. The notion of lacking food presented only the initial problem, but when darkness fell, what about torches, tents, or jackets? Once again, why do I overlook basic planning?

Simon deliberated that the sensible action was to relax, rest, and then complete the climb in the daylight. "From the start to the summit will total twenty-four hours, including a night's kip," he smiled, "and that is not shabby for your first mountain."

Sheltering inside the rugged dining area, nestled in a commune of inverted V-roofed huts, hikers milled around as if we socialized at a college-based Starbucks café. Groups of climbers munched bowls of what looked and smelled like chicken noodle soup. To pass the time, I chatted with Italian trekkers, and none believed we ascended so rapidly. Regretting my loudmouth, I diverted the conversation to Simon's astonishing record—to prevent anyone mentioning our feat to their guides. I did not know if the Chief Warden's henchmen might appear and demand a return to the base.

Sure enough, when twilight fell, the porters rambled into camp. Within minutes, they whipped up tasteless noodles and offered up dried banana bread, and I ate more for thinking of tomorrow's adventure than any hunger.

By eight p.m., I retired to a wooden bunk in a Norwegian-style mini-cabin as the others continued chatting. With frigid weather and physically shivering, I wistfully craved the Mombasa heat we left behind. Having no flashlight and without electricity in the tiny room, I fumbled in the dark and hopped straight into the bunk.

D-Day. Predawn, waking from a fitful slumber, I noticed my high-tech sleeping bag was inside out; no wonder I suffered throughout the night. At least a brilliant sky was breaking out; the sun would soon warm my blood. Disappointingly, my planned early departure backfired as the porters soundly slept in a maze of sixty-odd identical tents. Who were my porters? How come no one else bothered about time? If I heard one more, 'relax, slow down and acclimatize,' I would explode. Inside the maze, how does one locate your guide and heck, where did Simon sleep?

After an agonizing hour, I spotted Simon squatting like a yogi and admiring the view. Exasperated by my constant desire to hurry on and finish the last skimpy 2,194 meters (7,200 feet), he did not appear delighted to see me as I greeted him with a request to get moving. Perseverance pays, and at probably my eighth impatient appeal to rouse the porters, Simon clenched both fists.

"Okay, okay, if you insist, let us leave and go for it. We can connect with the porters after summiting on our descent—they can meet us at Kibo." However, a problem presented itself. To lug the food, water, rain jacket, trousers, spare shirt, gloves, and a hat was impossible. My sling-sac was tiny. Let alone the videocam and standard camera I rented from Simon's friend at the park entrance. But I would keep silent, or Simon might backtrack. Improvising, after noticing the cloudless blue skies, I slashed the possessions by tossing all the spare clothes.

Leaving the Horombo camp shortly after 9:30 a.m., a Belgian, Max de Caritat, who I also met on my descent and his ascent, witnessed our departure. In an email, he later wrote, "Everyone is on the mountain carrying two ski poles, hats, goggles, proper rucksacks, and big jackets and hiking boots. Then, you run by wearing running clothes, a string bag with a tall African man trailing you. I thought he's crazy."

Impatiently, I clung to a compulsion to conclude what should have been a memorable hike as quickly as possible. Why did I not enjoy the moment and appreciate nature? It was plain and simple; I was already planning the next fundraiser.

Kilimanjaro carries the climber through five vivid variations to the earth's scenery and four seasons of weather. The savannah plains of green bushland surrounding the mountain complement your 'English countryside,' they then yield to the 'Puerto Rican' rainforest with exotic foliage and overgrown plants. Next comes the Icelandic treeless expanse, hedgehog grass, and splintered stones before moving into the 'Venezuelan Andes' alpine zone covered in larger Andesite rocks and loose shale where nothing grows or speaks. Lastly, there is the 'North Pole' arctic freeze at the crest. Here was the idyllic destination for a Phileas Fogg mockumentary. Right now, I jogged through Venezuela.

Soldiering on, Clif Bars provided a reward after a forty-five-minute effort, and upon the hour, I enjoyed 200 ml of fluids. Rationing became vital, having brought just a one-liter water bottle. Gladly, I still did not notice any altitude effects, and steadily climbing at a jog, I realized summitting was a done deal. How differently I acted now from the wimp who collapsed at the Mombasa brothel. Today my ship bore a strong tailwind steering me home.

We reached the last shelter on this route, Kibo huts, with ease. Heartbeats per minute? 125. Typically, hikers relaxed here—at 4,876 meters (16,000 feet)—for a day before tackling the last leg to the crest. But with only 1,005 meters (3,300 feet) to cover and carrying a quarter of a liter of water, I anxiously pushed on. Kibo represented the location where a frozen leopard was sighted in 1926 by Donald Latham. The leopard spotting story appeared in the Geographical Journal and inspired Ernest Hemingway's literary reference in the fictitious *'Snows of Kilimanjaro'* written a decade later. The writer poses a question, 'No one has explained what the leopard was seeking at that altitude,' and now I likewise began wondering. Kibo, beyond scrubby rocks, was as full of nothingness as nothingness could be.

Around 5,486 meters (18,000 feet), the terrain to reach the peak finally became steep and slippery, and jogging proved impossible. On the scree, as small stones shifted, the footing had me floundering. I searched for a marked trail and found myself slipping and sliding down sections of the slopes I had frustratingly scrambled up. Having been 200 meters (218 yards) behind, Simon deftly overtook me at Gillman's point. He knew exactly where to tread, and I should have shadowed him. My slapdash slithering and stumbling gave him a few laughs. I secured the ultimate guide in the business, yet my impatience ran ahead of logical thinking. Can I blame it on the altitude?

Simon recommended we paused at Gilman's point, and I took the break to devour my last apricot Clif Bar, saved for this moment, before pulling out the video camera for an interview. Simon opened with a thought-provoking phrase, reasoning it was the spirits of Kilimanjaro that had guaranteed our success today only because the mountain was in full support of our mission.

Past Gilman's point, it became possible to jog again. So, before reaching the peak, I handed the camera over to Simon to film the last quarter mile of our run. When I saw the battered wooden signpost that marks the highest spot of the mountain, I felt an outpouring of relief—not emotions of a celebration.

Curiously, standing on the roof of Africa, I had no wish to linger. Not even to bother casting my eyes over the view. After collecting the validation stamp (a signpost photo), we commenced the descent as if I had passed on a relay baton to the next athlete. I felt no euphoria, but instead, a sense of satisfaction that we continued to progress in the proper direction of fundraising.

At the precise moment of turning our backs to the summit, the heavens split, and heavy snow, sleet, and hail fell with the freakish force of a plunging hurricane. It was spectacular to witness those rolling clouds crack open, as though the Gods had strained to hold back the curtains until I touched the stars. I have never beheld a swifter climate change—just five minutes earlier, I had captured blue-sky pictures at the peak.

Simon, who stands two meters high (six-foot-five) in bare feet, instantly broke into a long loping gallop reminiscent of a charging giraffe. "Oh no, a blizzard. Let us get out of here. Run like this," he hollered, cascading down the mountain using far-reaching sideways steps. Meantime I stumbled, tumbled, fell, froze, and banged limbs and bones, bouncing down the slope like a deranged ping-pong ball.

I struggled to keep Simon within sight when the storm raged as the drifting snow cut the visibility to a few meters. The only appealing aspect of this horrendous weather was, having drunk all my water, I could now refill my bottle with the drinkable slush. On occasions, I thought myself utterly lost. I guess Simon seized his revenge for the push I delivered on the uphill, and yes, I did trail the man claiming the fastest unaided ascent and *descent* of the mountain. Soon he vanished, and the landscape turned to a blanket of pure white. OMG, what about the story of the Andes plane survivors—cannibals in the snow. Was I lost forever? Recovering my senses, I figured I should stop being a drama queen. There was only one direction possible—down!

By luck alone, I located Kibo Huts. Simon, who arranged for our team to rendezvous here, had already arrived and changed into dry clothes. The porters, grinning like Cheshire cats, presented me with a bowl of steaming noodles, "We wish all clients were like you. Before this trip, it has always been us who must encourage the people to climb, not the other way around!"

Inside the cabin, an open fire cracked and roared, and I inched exceedingly close to the yellowy flames to warm my wet skin. Thank you, Simon, for this once-in-a-lifetime experience. On the peak, he had clasped my shoulder, "Today, your dream is my dream." It was all of us; every donor stood by my side. I thought of my late friend, Richard Chelimo, and the night when he broke the world 10,000m record on the track. Before that race, in a thickset forest, he mentioned the key ingredient to his preparation, "Never train alone, or you will not make it." Wasn't that a truth of life itself?

Chapter 20. 2011

STONING IN TURKANA

The reasonable man adapts himself to the world. The unreasonable one persists in trying to adapt the world to himself. All progress depends on the unreasonable man. – G. B. Shaw

One day later, I flew back to Kenya. Pieter and Lornah kindly hosted a celebration party at their Iten training camp with the resident athletes, including Mo Farah. Mo, a four-time Olympic gold medalist, has been a regular visitor to Kenya since 2007. I remember the evening he initially arrived, lugging along a pronounced London accent, and enjoying a brisk run with him the subsequent morning. Even then, relatively unknown, he differed from others. He is a driven outlier who trained harder than anyone I have witnessed in my years of observing athletics in Kenya.

"I thought Toby's run was amazing. It has never been done, and he's not doing it to be the best or to just do something, he is doing it for charity, to help other people." Sir Mo Farah.

The party celebrated the crowning cap of completing the challenge. The concept to run from the lowest point of the earth where I practically lost my life to standing perched on top of the world's highest freestanding mountain as I surpassed a million dollars in fundraising for a public hospital held a glorious ring. Three years later, I heard about a student graduating from a New York State university who commercialized an almost identical concept with the Lokai bracelets.

Into 2011, we continued gathering funds, shooting beyond 1.3, then a mind-blowing 1.5 million. Honestly, I was mildly surprised the global organizations, like Save the Children, USAID, or UNICEF, whose mandates include pediatric health, had zero interest in supporting our mission—even to grant a simple endorsement. The Clinton foundation did invite me to a health initiative, yet I was barred at the door and ordered to use the servant's and entertainments entrance to attend their event!

After numerous attempts, a UNICEF rep finally agreed to meet me in Nairobi. He opened the discussion by offering hope, "Eastern Africa does deserve its first public children's hospital. But we don't partner with unique developments like yours." At least they acknowledged the need.

When I emailed Raj Shah, the leader of USAID, he placed me in contact with his African health expert. She reported that Africa did not require a hospital for children and suggested I support existing smaller general clinics. I retaliated that Nelson Mandela completely disagreed with her view, which did nothing but severed that conversation. The contact at Save the Children was more direct, blatantly hinting I leave Shoe4Africa and join them.

Several times during these years, I received job offers. People who failed to believe I could shun an attractive salary. One executive boldly offered, "You hold dream contacts, bring in substantial funds, but work for free? Sweat for us and receive a salary. What will it take?"

What would it take? The truth? I loved my vocation way beyond money. Our operations were varied and vibrant, engaging, and exciting. I could be an integral part of every program—which other careers would allow such freedom?

I would be presently adding stoning to my rainbow resume. And that inexplicable incident happened in the act of distributing food. If nothing else, this work was diverse, dramatic, and never dull.

I had traveled up to Turkana, in the north of Kenya, to start a new program. Louis Leakey, the famous paleoanthropologist, claimed the area to be the cradle of humankind; it is where the ancient tools, dating to 3.3 million years old, have been unearthed. Turkana stands as the most underprivileged of all the Kenyan counties—figures state around 88% of the residents survived below the U.N. poverty level. As in most African countries, the capital received the lion's share of international aid, rumored to swallow 90%, and the rest trickles out, with pennies reaching the far desolate borders.

The idea would be purchasing foodstuff in Eldoret to distribute to the needy kids. City wholesalers offered a forty-percent discount in bulk buying over Turkana prices, so we hired a truck to drive the horrible thirteen hours required to traverse the rocky tracks labeled, misleadingly, as roads.

Pieter from the HATC camp volunteered to tag along with a man called John Kelai. John, born in Turkana, joined our Shoe4Africa ambassadors' team after winning the 2010 Commonwealth Games Marathon, and we could conduct a running clinic to encourage others from this area to follow in his footsteps. With air tickets at a bargain forty bucks, the three of us skipped the daylong trucking and flew to the county capital, Lodwar.

Disembarking from the twenty-seater plane, sand, rocks, and pale-yellow landscapes smother your eyes in a brutal Saharan-like setting. The sticky, sultry air felt depleted of all energy, and I immediately regretted promoting a sports event. John, who had sorted our sleeping arrangements, instructed our driver to head to the Nawoitorong Lodge to greet a team of athletes who had volunteered to assist with the project. Hearing of my Nordic ties, the driver mentioned a Swedish lady funded this community center. He added the woman also subsidized a local girl's education; that young lady, Ajuma, since matured into a Vivienne Westwood fashion model!

After the brief meeting to coordinate the function, I insisted on physically inspecting our truck. It was missing. John, born two hours thirty minutes' drive south of Lodwar, explained that the vehicle was parked at his village. Could we all leap in a van right now and host a small event? No, I declared. Rule number one is to never deviate from the blueprint. Neither Pieter nor I, after a two-hour journey to the Kitale Airport—with a four-hour flight delay—wanted to contemplate an additional five-hour road trip on bumpy dirt roads. Veering off-plan is ill-advised for reasons soon to become apparent. John objected, "People have been waiting since yesterday, and I told them Shoe4Africa is coming. All the kids will cry if you don't show up."

As visitors, against my intuition, I relented. Reluctantly, we clambered into a thirty-year-old rigid automobile and drove south to Katilu.

It was mid-afternoon when we departed, and, no exaggeration, the baked air glistened before our eyes. Glancing out of the window, I observed impoverished children hang by the roadside, hoisting empty plastic bottles high above their heads and pleading that we might toss out any empties we carried. I gazed at cloaked nomads, leading trains of heavily laden camels, trekking to God knows where.

Meantime inside the truck, we might have been wedged on a camel hump for the cushioning we received. Pieter, whose spine has rankled him for years, winced upon each rut the wheels climbed over. I sympathized because my healthy backbone cried like a hungry baby. Would the road smooth out? Nope, the barren scenery continued with scant variance as the convoy skimmed over the bleached packed dirt, till finally, we approached our destination, John's home.

The location was a diminutive center, and there to greet us blocking a road of no traffic stood a throng of drunken Turkana ladies.

High pitched ululations alerted the community that the local hero had returned. Awash with the acidic smell of homemade brew, the ladies—wearing only a loose-fitting robe knotted over one shoulder like a toga—advanced, gyrating without any restraint. Lost in a chorus of wailing, their hugs and hands treated us differently from any western welcome I have experienced. To the right, I could see in the closest scrub field a sizable crowd congregated around our food truck, and the women dragged rather than escorted us to receive the masses.

John, meantime, rightly enjoyed the adulation he received as the first man to put Katilu upon the map. Ladies wrapped the athlete in multiple strands of tinsel, parading him around the park like a pomp politician. I spied a band of rowdy drunkards standing adjacent to the food truck, and with the fast-approaching darkness, realized that the event had the potential of a ticking time bomb. Noticing civilians armed with AK-47's slung over their shoulders did not encourage me to relax in the slightest.

The reason offered for the guns focused on a constant threat of raids—people lived in continual hi-alert. The weapons functioned as protection and to ward off rustlers. Police stations are few and far apart. It can be hours before an officer would appear, and a bullet can save a life.

Lining up the children to collect their gift parcels, we offloaded supplies from the rear of the truck. After half an hour of sweaty but organized distribution, the scene turned hostile as impatient adults, now realizing nothing was designated for them, aggressively shoved the youngsters aside. Cramming close to the truck, as they could not snatch the kids' food parcels, about thirty adults tried storming the vehicle. More vultures stood by—the opportunists, not as brash, but who lingered for the dirty spoils.

The event had tilted off-script. Screams escalated, and I knew chaos was imminent. Sticks shot above heads, waving like truncheons in the air. The two cars, including the one I rode in, hightailed with Pieter and John onboard. I had a choice—chase after the fleeing vehicles or defend the castle.

Because I was a custodian of the American donations, I refused to abandon the trailer packing thousands of dollars of goods hallmarked for the kids. Yelling to the driver Eric, I urged him we too must leave. He shrugged as if to ask, what is the big deal? Our truck bed stood exposed after we pulled off its canvas covering but thankfully, the sidewalls were vaulted so the looters could not plunder as they so wished.

Only when the people began prying open the rear swing gate utilizing a crowbar did our driver, recognizing possible vehicle damage, react. He ignited the engine and finally stomped his foot on the accelerator. Unable to scramble out of the back, my volunteers and me fell over each other. Although bouncing like bobble-tops, nobody complained.

We followed no apparent path across the open fields until I noted the driver home in on an iron sheets barn.
One of my men bellowed, "Here is secure, and we can leave food for the area chief to hand out to kids in the morning after church. The place belongs to the Administration Police."

I agreed—if the men acted speedily. Sacks of maize, flour, sugar, and the offloading of cases of orange juice, boxes of tea, oil, and fats, began, but not fast enough. Five minutes later, running across the field, I noticed the famished villagers had tracked us down. Oh, shoot, what now? My heart fluttered—why did I agree to this crazy idea?

Upon reaching us, the numbers had multiplied, and the hooligans once more tried clambering onto the truck. Meantime we continued, tossing the supplies to the armed AP on the left. Screaming commands at the top of my lungs, the workers understood the imminent trouble. A man on my team brandished a mean-looking wooden cane to smack on any heads, hands, or arms, climbing onto the truck.

Initially, the caning worked, and I thought we might succeed, even though the bolder ones kept trying and risking further thrashings. But the numbers increased, and the masses held the upper hand. I dismissed the possibility of further offloading and corralled the men to guard our foodstuff, but I could not convince stubborn Eric to flee. Leaning into his window, I blasted, "Go, this is irresponsible. There are too many people!"
"Relax," the driver laughed, "calm down, it is nothing!"

My blood boiled; this foolish guy refused to open his eyes to the danger. Zing, I detected a metallic sound, unlike the lash of the stick. Goodness, stones are flying. Using my arms to shelter the head, I dodged the hurled weapons. I sidestepped when a woman ran forward and lobbed a rock the size of a grapefruit directly at me—there is gratitude for you. A worker at the rear of the truck raised a 90 kg (198-lbs) sack of maize to use as a shield.

Calling Pieter, my hands shaking, I asked where the heck John the host was, "Can you believe they are flinging stones at me? I am the only one desperate to leave."

Who volunteers for this kind of work? My assistants, all locals who recognized the food-grabbers, at first laughed and tossed insults at the vagabonds. The amusement ceased when the stone-pelting formed to a united mob effort. The majority of the tiny missiles rebounded off the metal frames, but more than a couple struck targets. A horizontal rain of stones was impossible to avoid, and even the brazen cane-bearer now cowered behind the maize sacks.

Across the field, the ruckus encouraged yet more people to join the hoodlums. I pointed the hazard out to the driver at the exact moment when a cabbage-sized rock hit a volunteer's head. Purple blood trickled from his wound, and the man slumped, stunned, unable to stand. Finally, the workers teamed by my side, shrieking for Eric to fire the engine. Fists slammed in fear against the cabin window, and now, realizing he stood alone, the motor turned over.

For twenty to thirty meters, the raiders—men and women—gripped on the tailgate, but the dried ruts in the field took care of them. Even clinging on to the trailer rails presented problems. We raced towards a center and intercepted a car to ferry the injured volunteer to a medical clinic. Unconscious, he did not look good—a gory mess. You could not condemn these malnourished pillagers. Had I resided in this village, where people barely owned a piece of clothing and an enticing food truck trundled into town, of course, count me in for plundering. When dire hunger howls, all reasoning disappears. Thankfully, no one fired a gun.

After reuniting alongside the team at Lokichar Center, dropping sacks with a local orphan's home, we returned to Lodwar. The lodge rang, "Goodnight, we closed the kitchens. We hope you don't need to dine, or are you heading to your lodgings?" Shoot, we required a couple of hours driving over the gnarliest of roads, and I had forgotten about food. Every time I participate in these projects, my stomach shrinks into a knot, and my appetite vanishes.

The next day's planned event ran like a dream. Children accompanied by their Sunday School leaders arrived in an orderly fashion. Busloads of kids streamed in from six a.m. till past four p.m. Entertainment complimented the gifting of food packages to the kids, and our training clinic boomed as a well-attended occasion with a spirited group run of enthusiastic athletes.

Hunger is not a math problem where you plug in numbers and discover a solution; you make do the best you can. And yes, our efforts seemed like one drop in the ocean, but from what I perceived, a worthy drop.

❦

One year later, I returned to Lodwar for another feeding project. This time, traveling alongside Ajuma, the Vivienne Westwood model. After touring the district, the few Turkana schools we visited broke my heart. Barren buildings lacked in every element, and most kids did not even possess pens or pencils.

Imagine sitting in classes, and only the teacher holds a book. Each formula, equation, and symbol must lock into your memory. Memorization is how schooling works, yet the brain typically requires a referral textbook. John Kelai mentioned he used a stick for a 'pencil' and the sandy dirt as a 'book' when he schooled in Turkana. Visualize the potential of a child from Lodwar who attains even a C grade. What and who would they become if thrown into a private Manhattan academy?

Rather than dwell on the impossibility of zapping all the kids over to America, we handed out books, pencils, and pens, at the feeding project. I always tell myself, doing something is better than doing nothing. You are not expecting gratitude in this work, but when a seven-year-old courtesies and whispers words in

English, their third language, it can bring a tear to your eye.

After the event, watching a rising pink moon with a trillion stars twinkling in the sky, I spread out on a reed mat cushioned by the sun-warmed sandy soil enjoying an ice-chilled Tusker beer. A ladies' empowerment group joined me, and I could have been relaxing in a chic New York coffee shop listening to friends' aspirations. We all strive to be productive, but a glaring omission burned a hole in this conversation, the same gap I noted at the local schools. The instruments required for these individuals were invisible to assist them in navigating and getting ahead in this world. In 2010, Hilary Clinton was spot on when she said, 'Talent is universal; opportunities are not.'

Around eight p.m., a child approached with a toothy grin; the locals call him Hustler. Although aged over five years, stunted from malnutrition, I swore he would pass as a three-year-old. Everyone, I mean everyone, in the community recognizes him, and only by the name Hustler.

Leaving his mother's shack at daybreak, he walks a mile (1.6 km) into town by himself. He turns up exactly when people are eating, hoping for food. No one I met has heard him talk, and no one remembered hearing him cry. For my brief three-day visit, Hustler acted like a magnet to my steps and shadowed me during each day. A guardian angel must hover over his path, for his mother is unaware of his whereabouts.

As we handed out gift bags earlier, Hustler was present. But, unlike the other kids, he did not giggle—push and shove—pressing to be the first in line. Hustler stood like a lone blade of grass on the periphery of the field, observing from a distance. Everything he did at this early age caused him to stick out.

When Ajuma ordered he should depart at ten p.m., he stumbled away without a protest. His silhouette faded until it became a smudge on the dark horizon—I felt lonely for his absence, longing to holler and call him back if only for my comfort.

His smiling face returned the following morning, gulping down an entire mug of steaming tea in stony silence. Soon after, he played with a parked bicycle. As he touched the machinery, another boy turned the pedal. The motion trapped his four stubby fingers between the front chain wheel and the metal links. The action churned my stomach, and Hustler yelped—like that of a kicked dog. He then fell deathly silent. I leaped forward to reverse the pedal and carefully roll his fingers out of the chain wheel. Four tooth hole-marks indented into his little fingers. Astonishingly, I saw no tears.
"Look at Hustler, not even crying. I would be bawling."
A woman sneered back at me, "Here, we do not waste tears. We do not have anything to waste. I am certain, living in New York under a nanny's care, he would be balling. But what is the point in Lodwar?" I looked around at a beautiful but spartan land of sand and stone, and I could not see any ladder leading to an easier life. How did people get ahead? By running and leaving?

On my final night, closer to midnight, a twenties-something woman flung off her clothes and draped herself naked on the bend of a rough road. Owning a skin as dark as coal, she hoped a hurtling car, steered by a careless, intoxicated driver, might claim her life. We visited this lady yesterday. She acted like Hustler—what was the point in crying if no one listens?

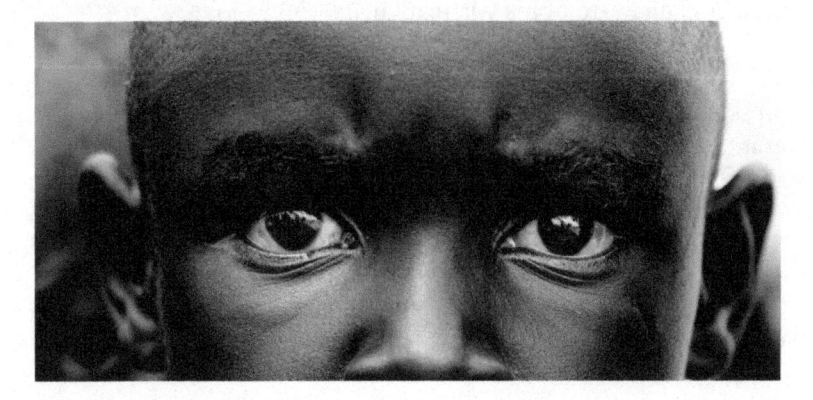

Chapter 21. 2011

PROBLEMS, PROBLEMS, AND SOLUTIONS

The best way out is always through. — Robert Frost

Seemingly every day, I appealed for charity help. If not for donations, then for favors. The latest problem: Pro-bono lawyers declared we should insert wording into our status regarding constructing the hospital instead of aiding health projects. Fair enough, that adjustment sounded simple. As they submitted the paperwork, the lawyers casually mentioned, "Don't fundraise or talk about the hospital as we file the paperwork...to anyone." What? For how long? "Well, there is commonly a backlog, could be six months or longer. Hard to say."

Right when I needed to spread the word and rally support, now I was handed an insurmountable roadblock of indeterminable time. Had I the energy, I would have collapsed on the law firm floor. Rather than vent my frustrations, I wondered what other options did I hold?

A month later, in Kenya, Mo & Tania Farah and I discussed the notion of launching a foundation in Britain. They also embraced the passion of uplifting the lives of the underprivileged kids in East Africa. The potential looked gigantic, as Mo generated immense publicity leading into his hometown Olympics. Sharing the idea with a friend, Dr. Millicent Stone, a physician residing in London, I scheduled for her to meet with Tania and Mo when they returned home. Meantime, I researched the British nonprofit bylaws. I hoped, if Shoe4Africa stumbled in legal formalities, then an English chapter, say Health4Africa, could complete the hospital. Cripes, I had to conjure up something as the lawyers informed me that a rejection from the charities bureau would involve reapplying for a 501(c)(3) status.

The timing of the law firm was not dreadful but hideous. Hugh Jackman, a renowned Australian actor, had agreed to compete in a half marathon to garner media for our cause. When attending an event in New York, whispers circulated that a famous guy was present. Appreciating the value a celebrity can draw to a tiny charity, I planned on bumping into this man.

Glancing around the room, I recognized a dapper man attracting the focus who, I deduced, must be the performer. I swanned straight up, questioning, "What are you doing on the second Sunday in March?" Staring at me as if I resembled a space cadet (it was October), Hugh laughed and repeated, "What *am* I doing?"

I inquired if I could train him to partake in the NYC half marathon. Sure enough, five months later, we raced through the streets and finished the run in a commendable two hours. Hugh had quizzed, "Is there anything you want me to do press-wise?" Yet respecting the lawyers and biting my lip till the blood almost seeped through my teeth, I smiled, "Can I save your help for another day—let's run and just enjoy ourselves."

Anthony meanwhile anchored in two actor friends, James LeGros, who competed with us in 2009, and Tom 'Flash' Cavanagh, presenting a sizable media opportunity—what a fiasco.

Unrelated, but over the last two years, a couple of generous donations floated east from another actor, Rosario Dawson, and she inquired if her hairdresser could join our squad. Too bad Rosario had conflicts, or there was the entire cast for a Hollywood blockbuster.

Meantime, I received a call from CNN producer Trish Henry. Would I like to sit for an interview with the Emmy award-winning chief medical reporter, Dr. Sanjay Gupta, regarding my hospital dream, in a program to be beamed over the world? ARGH!

When Sanjay jetted to NYC, all we could discuss was old shoes! How frustrating; all these media attracting folks, but hey, do not mention a snippet about the hospital. Ironically, five days, five flipping days after Sanjay's interview, the lawyers shone the greenlights to resume hospital mentions.

The media presented an arena where I could have improved. I mean, who says no to America's most popular sunrise television show? A Good Morning America producer, Ameya, emailed. He wondered, did I have the interest to appear on the program but to highlight non-Shoe4Africa angles? The Montel Williams Show also expressed an invitation. But any media leads, I always requested they feature Anthony. I figured if a viewer recognized Goose, he would seize their attention better than I might. Amanda, an associate producer of Montel Show, like Ameya disagreed; their audiences, she noted, wished to learn how ordinary individuals stepped up. Here, the problem might have been me.

Various problems also arose attached with solutions. A question came from a member of one of New York's most famously philanthropic families,

"Kenyans become the beneficiaries, so are they putting skin in the game?"

I never fundraised in Kenya, and the inquiry caused me to rethink. Eddie Stern, an accomplished runner, had posed the question when I solicited him for funds at a five km race I organized. Although we just met, his reputation preceded him; his generosity is well-documented. I am always eager to hear why a person helps particular charities and knew Eddie had supported an obscure foundation in Kenya. The amount was substantial, half a million, and I wondered what drove his altruism. The answer surprised me when I had stated,

"You must really like Kenya."

"Well, I have been to Nairobi only once," Eddie replied, "so it is hard to say. But being robbed there was very unpleasant."

Oh, no—I anticipated dire news when requesting his support. But Eddie considered the bigger picture. He delivered a challenge. Find a Kenyan donation, and he would match their contribution up to $50,000.

Therefore, before my subsequent trip, I googled millionaires + Kenya, discovered a name, and secured an appointment. Manu Chandaria's industries looked impressive—national and global—would he match Eddie?

Hearing I sought funding for a public hospital, Manu's nose shriveled up. He adamantly had no confidence in the national sector.

"Private healthcare is the way to go for this country." He cited the example of an acquaintance of his, Dr. Gikonyo, who received tax exemptions, donations, and loans to establish a private facility in the upmarket suburb of Karen, Nairobi. He mentioned their specialty centered on grown-ups, and an ancillary pediatric center could work upon the same principle.

"This private hospital generates healthy profits—a great model to replicate," added Manu.

Wait, permit me to reset the needle. My aim was not to earn money from this venture. I drew upon research and discussed how Kenya, with an estimated population of fifty million, had a tiny splinter able to afford private healthcare. I asked, "Have you been to Eldoret?" He had not. The people owning the majority of the healthcare plans were ex-pats, UN staff, foreign charity workers, parliamentarians, and the rich, residing in Nairobi or Mombasa.

Never had I enjoyed private healthcare, and how does a person receiving a dollar or two a day prepay the premiums?

(a UNICEF report at that time noted 42% of Kenyans live below the poverty line, defined at $2 per day).

Several discussions took place at Manu's spectacular residence in Muthaiga but raising a donation without strings attached proved to be impossible. However, I like to believe our talks touched his heart, as four years later, his name appeared on an Eldoret building when Ruth Lily's foundation aligned with Indiana University funded a Chronic Disease Outpatient center. The team required a final ten percent of bankrolling, and, I heard, Manu stepped in.

Reverting to google, I discovered Kenya's most successful enterprise to be the telecom giant Safaricom. Although the majority shareholder is Vodafone UK, I guessed the company would support a public children's hospital…like Eddie. I arranged a meeting with the CEO, Bob Collymore, yet again failed to gain financial aid. Contacting their foundation, I received instructions to apply for a $200 community grant, but that likewise received the reject button—Gosh, Eddie would have broken out in laughter settling a 200-dollar match!

Eddie's offer swung in front of my eyes like an unclaimed lottery prize, but nobody stood up. Other meetings produced identical results, and I believed I would never claim a penny from Eddie. However, back in America, the fund thermometer inched higher. Now, against the odds, we sailed over 1.85 million dollars. How could I surpass two?

Solutions? The following idea spun from threads. Labels can boost a scant piece of cloth's worth through the ceiling. Fendi, an Italian brand, peddles cotton T-shirts for up to $850. Yank off the tab, and honestly, what is the worth?

In New York, I briefly greeted two sisters who launched a successful fashion house. They kindly created an exclusive T-shirt design for Shoe4Africa that we call The Charity T-Tux. Commonplace in NYC are glamorous galas held at high-end establishments to serve any number of African causes. The entrance ticket, to offset the expensive costs of hosting, can be $1,000 or higher.

Invariably, you sit in a ballroom sipping champagne and scoff a platter of Kobe steak and asparagus trimmings. You then view a video of the CEO who donned their 'I'm in Africa' cargo pants and jetted over to an impoverished site on the continent (do not worry as tonight they will dress like you). The charity has shot emotional and evocative footage designed to open hearts and checkbooks. Somehow, the irony of you dining like a King as underfed mortals struggle to survive slips by you. Do not get me wrong, I enjoy a good party, but after watching starving and impoverished people—or anyone suffering in difficulties—the concept appears twisted. Regardless, when Jeanine described the frugal tale of Shoe4Africa's efforts to the sisters, I observed the artistic minds turn.

The Rodarte design for Shoe4Africa presented the ultimate boycott of the gala excuse. The concept was elementary: Purchase the T-shirt, skip the party, and *100%* of the proceeds will channel directly to constructing a hospital for the sick kids. The tuxedo and a bow tie sketched out in black ink on white cotton became an instant classic. Familiar names like Keira Knightly and Michelle Obama don and desire the Rodarte label—I was certain we had scored a winner. Anthony and Jeanine kindly fronted the funds for a print of 3,000 of these limited-edition shirts. One of their kids wore the garment to a NYC Chanel reception, and the congregation adored the concept. I began to imagine a video promo clip, 'Fah…fah…fah…fah-sion' (For-A-Hospital).

I wondered if I might coax Manhattan resident David Bowie to allow usage of a five-second stanza from his iconic ballad and request his wife Iman to model the T-shirt for a spectacular launch? Okay, slim chance but timely as I now partnered with Iman's Cosmetic line to hand out make-up kits in Kenya.

For the last three years, promoting the women's empowerment projects, we invited models like Ajuma, and Miss Kenya, to teach make-up tips as we hosted beauty events in the slums. The results proved remarkable and inspirational. Generous souls like Iman and the Kevyn Aucoin company sponsored the package of products we distributed. Naturally, the kits, each worth over $100, are not lifesavers, but they added dignity, a huge smile, and lasting memories. Employing a fashion photographer—once spiffed up—we furnished the ladies with stunning resume shots. Therefore, to request Iman for an additional favor was not as far-fetched as it might at first sound.

Meantime, in the fall of 2011, another group of runners would participate in the NYC marathon. Charity running exploded in the past few years, and seventy runners ran to raise funds for the cause. At our pre-race party, Geoffrey Mutai, who, in April, clocked the world's fastest marathon at the Boston event, attended with other famous athletes to greet our fundraising heroes. Can I claim it was our homemade *ugali* powering Geoffrey to set the—still-standing—course record at the next morning's event?

The ever-kindhearted Jeanine and Anthony hosted at their copious Park Avenue apartment, meaning zero expenses for Shoe4Africa. One partygoer mistook the energetic-looking Ms. Portman for a professional athlete. He snapped her photo and quizzed in a text message, "Which marathon has the slim lassie wearing the dark blue won?"

The running community provided such a robust venue to fundraise that I opted to host a Manhattan five km. Our annual women's event in Iten thrived, with over one thousand competitors each December. Giving out free T-shirts, shoes, prize money, and general costs had to be underwritten—a New York experience would be the opposite and create profits.

Securing a race permit for an event sixteen days away, I began selling entries. We promptly sold out and raised $60,000 in sponsorship with help from 'Mr. Schools' banking connections. Running *and* good friends was the force pulling us forward to establish this hospital.

Unexpectedly, an African donation surfaced to complement Eddie's generous pledge. Dr. Aruasa's email exchange invariably evolved to regular in-person meetings to finalize our designs as the private to a public partnership with Moi Teaching and Referral flourished. Recently, a new CEO joined the MTRH, and Dr. Kibosia arrived, holding an impressive resume. He mingled with high rollers in the business world and introduced a friend who agreed to match Eddie's generous premium.

Then another amazing solution materialized, appearing in the form of a simple email. Just a dear friend offering an incredible donation—our most substantial to date—and her single stipulation was anonymity. Satisfaction, energy, and relief all rolled into one emotion. We surged forward during a day I yo-yoed back to the States. And boom, just like that, we surpassed the construction funding goal. Phew, talk about a weight off my shoulders. On the plane, a passenger patted my arm, asking my purpose in Kenya. She gushed about a trip of a lifetime, enjoying an outstanding safari and spotting the big five wildlife. I could have replied, preparing to launch a hospital or returning from the slums after supporting the abused ladies' program. Or I could allude to the upcoming health empowerment race with one thousand women. What about mentioning our Kimani Maruge 'oldest schoolboy' peace festival success hosted at his former school? Or cite the opening of our second school in Nandi County. But, I retorted, 'Yeah, safari.' I did not lie as the word translates as 'on a journey.' I continued on the odyssey that began by boarding a plane to Africa in 1995 when all I desired was to go for a run in Kenya.

Hugh Jackman and I, at the finishing line. Photo by NYRR. And Chelimo, slipping on the Rodarte Charity T-Tux, more about her soon.

Chapter 22. 2012

WITH A LITTLE HELP FROM A JCB DIGGER

What you do makes a difference, and you have to decide what kind of difference you want to make. - Jane Goodall

A recent addition to our board, Jim Wilkinson, received an exciting job offer. Accepting the role of an Executive V.P. at PepsiCo, he roped in a three-year sponsorship for Shoe4Africa. Wow, PepsiCo promoted icons like Michael Jackson and Madonna, and now Shoe4Africa? The affiliation dug deeper than just a donation—the food giants assembled a team to develop the partnership. Hosting events, placing a co-branded video on their web, and dressing up booths at the marathon expos—I am not sure why but to be accepted by a global player made me feel we, as an organization, had arrived somewhere.

And just on the verge of arriving, Hurricane Sandy, traveling at 90 m.p.h., smashed into NYC at the tail-end of October. This storm wreaked havoc in the eastern states, but particularly in New York. In Staten Island, water flooded and washed out entire buildings, destroying those flimsy houses constructed of wood and plasterboard. Drenched possessions, like shipwrecked boats, lay strewn in the street gutters.

At this time, I was planning our December five km race in Manhattan, and it would represent our final push before the groundbreaking—in short, every penny counted. Already we suffered a financial beating with the cancelation of the city's Marathon. However, I knew I should transform the event into a moneymaker for the individuals affected by the storm.

I switched the purpose and organized a run for NYC Kids affected by the hurricane. Stacey, who now served as our treasurer, purchased hundreds of Christmas gifts for the youngsters. She needed to hire storage with lifting and loading apparatus because the bulk was so immense. The race and the drive proved an enormous success. In seven days, we collected $85,000. Completing this improvised fundraiser in America made our event in Kenya all the sweeter at the end of the month.

※

In Eldoret, on the penultimate day of the year, I climbed inside a greasy JCB digger. I would drive forward, yank two of the hydraulic levers, and hopefully select the ones to engage the metal trough to churn the field. Along with the ink on the contracts, we would scrape away the soil to 'break ground' for the new hospital.

Phew, from an emotionally charged hair-brained dream in 2008 to a concrete reality. It was my mother's seventieth birthday, with my father's seventieth to follow in five days. Over in England, my siblings had organized a party in Cornwall for the celebration and did not understand why I was continually absent at family functions.

One area where I failed is to be there, in person, for my relatives. Who knows, maybe leaving home so early has its repercussions, but the contract stated I had committed to breaking ground before the end of 2012, and unavoidable delays pinned me down to this date. Fortunately, my elders, unable to travel, understood, and this event, they told me, was a heck of a birthday treat for them.

The function, held in a car park, was typical Shoe4Africa style. Scrimping and saving, I invited no one, bar doctors, nurses, and medics employed at the close-by general hospital. Several of these professionals would relocate over the road to our hospital following the two years necessitated for the construction.

The event did not go as planned. I had expected this day to be a joyous occasion. By contrast, people voiced grievances. Medics complained about office designation if they did not receive their own personalized space, as other grumbles surfaced. Even moans arose about toilets in the new building, despite our designs for fifty-four units.

Why listen in, I thought as one nurse stepped forward and berated me, "Go back and tell your people to pledge more money. We need the fourth floor to hold another department for..." And I forget the rest of her speech. When you embark upon a public project, an element will always bother at *least* one person.

Ever since the early days, I annoyed folks and periodically received complaints. Anonymous souls mentioned problems in the States needing addressing, and each criticism arrived as if the author transmitted the voice of a nation. Shoe4Africa told a story about losing a shoe—it did not state a directive. Our programs and donations had traveled the world to Russia, Ukraine, Sri Lanka, Ethiopia, Tanzania, Morocco, and should my haters have inquired, New York City. The same week of receiving another disgruntled email, I dispatched one thousand pairs of brand-new shoes to a public school in Manhattan for a Secret Santa program. Another one thousand new pairs were gifted to an organization where I sat on the board of Directors, the Achilles, hallmarked for local distributions.

I typically either labored for or subsequently owed big favors for these contributions. I volunteered time and donated annually to domestic charities, but to mention such matters to your haters is futile. If I took to heart each comment or criticism, I would have retired in my first year—a charity beggar should lose all personal feelings. Well, most of the time because everyone deserves a little love.

Chapter 23. 2013

LOVE IS. A NANDI ELDER, & POISON

In dreams and in love there are no impossibilities. – János Arany

Twice, I sprinted up the stairs of the Empire State Building—both times clocking eleven minutes for a measly vertical dash of less than 400-meters. If the skyscraper could communicate, she would remind you lightning does indeed strike twice. Despite breaking ground, I pressed the pause button. Although eager to commence with the construction, the general elections approached on March 4th. Reminiscing too clearly the troubles of 2007, I stalled the project till the Spring season turned to Summer, and the new government formed and settled in.

༺༻

For a decade, John Legere was a prominent name in the American telecommunications industry. A couple of years before elevating T-Mobile beyond what must have been their wildest dreams, he posed a question, one of the best.
"How can I help you?" We quickly became friends, and he joined our board of directors. I believed it played as a loss for Shoe4Africa when he shuttled from Manhattan, out west to the company headquarters in Seattle.

On July 1st, John called, requesting the location of our hospital. He was chatting to a woman in Bellevue, inside a T-Mobile store. Being a hands-on CEO, he habitually interacted with and listened to his customers. Why was she in the store, and did she have a problem? And in conversation, he discovered she hailed from Kenya. John replied his friend was establishing a hospital in Kenya. She asked whereabouts, and when he responded Eldoret, her eyes widened. No, she was not a Kit Carson fan—Eldoret happened to be her hometown. She expressed a wish to view the construction site. I mentioned to John, "Anytime, but right now, there is nothing to see." By an odd coincidence, or not, she would fly to Kenya in fifteen days, and I traveled in twelve.

Chelimo Saina first set foot in the States back in the nineties, initially to study at the University of Missouri. Over an email exchange, I asked did she fancy attending the ceremony to lay the foundation stone. Answering yes, she requested I picked her from the Eldoret Airport. But as last-minute paperwork surfaced, I postponed the function. I emailed, suggesting we cancel, but she refused, "No, I want to visit regardless." Later she confided, "I had to see who this crazy white man was building a hospital in my hometown!"

In the arrival hall, she commanded the attention of the airport. Like a drum major and two bountiful strides ahead of the other alighting passengers, she marched forward bearing a huge smile. "Hi, Toby," she cried in an unexpected British accent.
Driving to the site brought no awkward pauses despite her witty comment I might make a decent *matatu* driver.

Chatting to her was akin to reuniting with an old friend. Her accent reflected a childhood spent at a British boarding school in Kaptagat, and it told both in her voice and colorful jargon. Who today calls a person a 'good egg?' She indeed possessed charm.

Parking outside the acres reserved for the project, Chelimo remarked she was born half a mile from this spot and grew up half a mile in the opposite direction. A coincidence, but I thought little of it. Although the area, a scrubby field, was empty, hints of development—like the uprooting of stomps and the arrival of construction machinery—promised exciting development. Gazing at the dirt, I could already imagine children playing in landscaped gardens, healing with love and laughter.

When it became the time to leave the field, Chelimo beckoned Kimani—my site manager—requesting he capture our photo. Her long hair brushed against my chin as she offered instructions on varying angles, and I felt invigorated by sensuous energy. She wore a discreet scent, far from overwhelming, but one that drew you in closer. And as our legs, hips, and bodies touched, side by side, mysterious energies flowed between us.

Since acquainting myself with Chelimo, I have discovered, time after time, people constantly gravitate to her confident and engaging personality. Her site visit passed swiftly, but she made a charming impression.

Dropping Chelimo in town, I presumed we would not meet until a subsequent visit—if our timing coincided. She had other plans, "We can have dinner tomorrow night. I am flying to Nairobi the day after. Shall we say seven-thirty?"

Seldom do I drive at night in Kenya because if you have issues, and my truck is over twenty-seven years old, there is little assistance on the rural roads where I work. The car, purchased last year, suffered from mechanical hiccups, and I wondered whether the trip presented a wise idea. Yes, I wanted to see Chelimo, but no, I did not want to break down in the dark hours.

Motoring into Eldoret, my phone rang, and Chelimo, ten minutes before our appointment, requested if I might delay an hour. Having driven for fifty minutes and unwilling to linger in the car for an hour, I decided to cancel. Our destiny almost never happened. But before I swung a U-turn, she changed her mind, "Actually, why not just come now." She had no idea I was driving from Iten.

Arriving at her family home, Chelimo stood dressed in figure-hugging jeans with a cut orange blouse, and the clothes embellished her natural beauty. She had selected a local restaurant, and walking into Mamma Mia's, an elderly couple lounging at the nearest table glanced up, delighted to recognize Chelimo. Friends of her late parents, they at first greeted us in English, then slipped into the Nandi ethnic tongue. "Ooh, what a nice pair you make. Please notify us when you celebrate your engagement."

Chelimo whispered in Nandi, "No, no, I met him yesterday." But she blushed. Then, the man, an established elder, rose from his chair. Offering two hands, he profusely thanked me for Shoe4Africa's community work. Great, I mused, excellent timing.

Close to midnight, back on the roads, I deliberated over the series of coincidences. Chelimo bumps into John in one of the thousands of T-Mobile stores, John mentioning this project, and although the proposed building is 10,000 miles away (16,000 km), the location sits in her hometown. The detail that her vacation date overlapped with my travel plans. Then, the construction site centers half a mile from the spot where she entered this world and half a mile from her childhood home. I again pondered, was a life a string of coincidences?

If I needed proof that these events overstepped happenstance, a bizarre, almost unbelievable twist occurred on Chelimo's following trip.

Naturally, over the summer, our relationship developed with both intimacy and passion. Upon her next visit, she wished to travel to the remote birthplace of her late father, a site she had last visited twenty-five years earlier. He was born in a mud hut, long since destroyed, located in a nondescript cornfield. She narrated her father lived in abject poverty and was sixteen years old before he first attended school. But in time, he thrived, becoming a member of parliament representing Eldoret North.

Leaving by the main road and motoring beyond Eldoret—passing the county limits—we entered the province of Nandi. Soon, we skirted by a town called Mosoriot (Good Hope), and after driving for over an hour, the car veered off the tarmac and onto the dirt roads. The nature was captivating, with corridors of verdant tea fields and bursts of the odd flowering jacaranda or Nandi flame trees bordering the trails. When the mud track narrowed, the green bushes brushed and scraped like iron fingernails over a blackboard against each metal flank of the car. We had arrived at that place known as the middle of nowhere. Being forced to slow on the rutted pathway, Chelimo found it surprising when the kids, racing to see our approach, appeared to recognize the driver. By a strange coincidence, just one thousand steps from where I established our first school four years ago, marked the birthplace of her father.

Chelimo and me, photographed by Mike Kobal.

Driving back to Eldoret and laughing about the connection, Chelimo explained, "These coincidences never surprise me. My family clan is deeply rooted in this territory; I am related to a renowned Nandi called Koitalel Arap Samoei, who believed strongly in the powers of destiny. My father was known as an *Orkoiyot*, a wise man predicting the future. Being a runner, you may know of my relatives Patrick Sang and Eliud Kipchoge?" Yes, I trained alongside Patrick in the nineties, and I had known Eliud since the early 2000s. Fast forward, Eliud, now my in-law, became our first hospital ambassador in December 2015, four years before the world recognized him as the first man to break through the two-hour barrier in the marathon distance.

※

August 21st would be the rescheduled day for the laying of the foundation stone. Due to the hospital symbolically rising from the ashes, I invited religious representatives to commemorate the occasion. A Christian reverend, an Indian priest, an Imam, and a Catholic priest attended to utter bindings of unity. Regrettably, traffic stalled the arrival of the Jewish Rabbi. Around forty of us gathered as I placed a lettered plaque onto the foundation stone, *'Our dreams can come true if we live them'* because, in reality, I was living my dream.

I had done it—an enormous weight floated off my shoulders. Witnessing thousands of stones layered up to a roof would be a joy. I began imagining a glorious opening day in twenty-four months. Being onsite became my number one wish—better than any vacation.

To the workers, I hindered progress more than I helped, but I insisted on taking part wherever I could. My presence and participation always beguiled the staff—none had seen a white man on a construction site partaking in manual labor. They already presumed me a madcap—he lives inside one small rental room, yet to construct a house, but wants to build a national hospital for children in a country where he does not belong.

Hawk-eyed, I examined and vetted everything. Even cement mixing, I checked the ratios, and for cable cutting, at what length and thickness? Was this the brand paid for or a cheap knock-off? When elements out of my control arose, like the national power company refusing to alter the cables dangling over the site, I sat at their office for two days pestering till they deployed workers.

Every day, I chatted with Kimani to receive real-time updates. Staff knew my digits for Kenya and New York, enabling me to be reachable whenever needed. I turned up at odd hours, late into the evening or before breakfast, to monitor progress. The team must understand if one bag of cement went missing, it was akin to blood sucked from my veins. I spent as much time with the wheelbarrow pusher as I did alongside the quantity surveyor. Like a hobgoblin maniac, I interfered wherever possible.

One day, lounging with the crew over a lunch break, a woman attempted to grab my attention. About one hundred full-time laborers worked onsite, but she looked strangely familiar. Dressed in shapeless tatty work overalls, her skin showed an ingrained discoloring of cement dust. I nodded in her direction, and she at once shuffled forward. "You do not recognize me, do you?" She murmured in a husky tone, resisting eye contact. "Yes, life did not turn out well since we last met. Not every runner captures the gold."

Goodness, it was Naomi who had lodged at the camp during the clashes. Standing steps away from the foundation plaque, I cringed—so much for the living our dreams lingo.

֍

At long last, I scheduled a visit to the historic fig trees attending a cultural lecture at Koitalel's mausoleum in the Nandi Hills. The community near the first school had nominated me a Nandi Elder*, and I wished to learn more about the traditional customs. Among other tales, I gathered the Nandi state if a man is performing an act of worth, the deities will not pluck that person from the world—until he ceases being useful.

The concept sounded as if I possessed a monopoly get-out-of-jail card, at least whilst the hospital construction continued. The idea matched the same ethos Simon insinuated after we climbed Kilimanjaro—it was the mountain that permitted the success of our adventure due to the cause of the mission. Therefore, it came as a shock when I subsequently fell feverishly ill.

Circling outer Eldoret, I had joined a member of parliament, Oscar Sudi, to vet charity projects. Tired, splattered in mud, following his swish Range Rover sinking in a swamp, Oscar suggested an impromptu visit to a prominent business mogul.

Mr. Lagat was indeed home and retiring to a long mahogany dining table. Fork in hand, he welcomed us to join him. Being a millionaire, I hoped he might donate to the hospital, but like de Klerk, he butted in first, 'Could I build a school for his tea farms?'

*An Elder is an honored, venerated person of the clan.

That evening and through an interminable night, my stomach churned as if I had swallowed three buckets of engine oil. I figured it was a passing germ, nothing harsher. The next day, after morning coffee, my all-purpose medicine, I drove to the hospital.

Upon arriving, as I routinely did, I ordered four crates of sodas for the workers. Walking to the site and lugging two cases, faintness struck me like a hammer through glass, but I blamed the beating sun. I began staggering from left to right. As I did not want the employees to witness this weakness, after delivering the drinks, I retreated to the shade of the closest café. Tony Kirwa, a friend stationed at a local morgue, sat dining, so I pulled up a chair to join his company. Did he mumble, or were my ears mincing his words? I labored to digest his speech. Suddenly, blackness overflowed my eyes—I feinted.

When I roused, I wondered why a waitress knelt by my bedside, muttering Kalenjin words. Needless to say, I lay on the stone floor of the café in the arms of a confused manageress as Tony hollered for help. Coming to my senses, he recommended that I had my vitals checked, but I had no interest in visiting his office!

The following morning, I concluded my final task on this trip with a journey entailing three hours of off-road driving on muddy and bumpy dirt roads to Kibugat, southern Nandi. Lodged in the rear seat, over the ridged axle of an old pick-up truck, I groaned upon each bump and tried to distract myself by listening to the radio.

At the top of the hour news, I discovered both Mr. Lagat and

Oscar Sudi lay in a hospital—the report noted suffering from poisoning. The rumor surfaced someone required someone out of the picture. Plausibly, because the three of us consumed food intended for one, that might have saved us. Who knows the truth, but even standing at the Kibugat function presented a problem, let alone digging a ceremonial shovel into the hard dirt for the official groundbreaking. We had pledged to construct classrooms, aided by Caroline & Jason Palmer-Myers, for a dilapidated government school far off the beaten track.

Poison yikes, what next, I mean, seriously? What dragon must I slay to reach the castle? Stupidly, I boasted to the principal that no forces could stop me from completing the hospital—I sailed under the Nandi Gods' protection. If I taunted fate, I practically paid the price one month later.

∽∾

September found me darting to New York, scrambling to initiate meetings and cover jobs. Work on both sides of the ocean meant I covered two time zones eight hours apart. Furthermore, for the six weeks in Kenya, I spent five in America—not a suitable equation for my hands-on coaching programs. A friend, Jon Lang, supporting similar training ethics to me, volunteered to help coach the Shoe4Africa marathon team. Having gone back and forth, I presently understood delegating would be a wise move.

2013 turned out to be a transitional period for the organization. I know I had exasperated the patience of my board. Gathering the folks for an hour, three or four times a year, proved impossible. Half of the members failed to return a simple email. The magic had vanished. Time for fresh blood, and I knew Jon could rise above the role of a coach. I received a call from a friend, Dave Siegel, and he asked if he could become further involved with our mission. Dave survived on pure energy, an optimistic spirit, and as a proven generous fund-raiser, he seemed ideal. We arranged to meet, and that day is one I can never forget.

The Siegel's. Dave transpired to be a fantastic board member, along with his wife, Zeynep, who founded our Aces4Africa tennis fundraiser in 2016.

Lindi (my stepdaughter) in Nairobi & Seattle. Aged seven, she opened a school, at ten, hospital playrooms. Lindi is predestined for a wonderful future as she shares Chelimo's (her mom's) big heart.

Chapter 24. 2013-14

FLAT OUT ON FIFTH

Whatever good or bad fortune may come our way we can always give it meaning and transform it into something of value. – Hermann Hesse

October 7th broke out as a dull, dreary autumn day. Midafternoon, I unplugged the computer, placed my coffee mug in the sink to soak, and cracked open the window to air the apartment. Confirming the time, I carefully carried my bicycle out to the street. The bike is the easiest way to navigate New York. Rain or shine, sleet or snow, my primary transport, for a lifetime, has been pedal-powered. In a quarter of an hour, I would reach central Manhattan, whereas a taxi took far longer for this three-mile traffic-laced route. Moreover, my budget never allowed such luxuries. NYC taxis are abnormally expensive, and even when helping other charities—and offered to expense items—I have never once hailed a city cab in two decades.

On the schedule were four appointments to conclude the day. The first, at five p.m., involved coffees with Dave at his office near Times Square. Next, I must whip over to the Cornell Club on 44th St. for an Achilles International board meeting. Being a Vice President of the organization, it did not reflect favorably to arrive late, but too bad. The ensuing function at seven p.m. would see me scooting to Brooklyn. Team Lifeline, a subsidiary of Chai Lifeline, hosted a social event, and as the head coach, I should be there. My last engagement switched back to Manhattan for drinks with a doctor at a quarter to nine. I must be on time here because I had requested a four figured donation.

As I pedaled down Fifth Avenue, the rain fell, but it arrived as a placid refreshing mist. The type of drizzle that cleans the city of its dust and dirt. After the following set of lights, I planned to pull over and don my jacket so as not to arrive like a drenched cat at Dave's office. Ahead, I spied two police officers, decked out in dark blue, leaning on the construction scaffolding of a building at the crossroads—I double-checked the lights shone green because there is a seventy-dollar fine for running a red.

My goodness, barreling the wrong way up Fifth Avenue and against the flow of traffic, raced a black car. Crazy, the police are jailing this lunatic for sure. What is the driver thinking?

I glanced over my shoulder, eighty-odd meters behind, three rows of cars charged south like metallic battering rams. I presume the motorist observed the danger because he accelerated at full throttle, gunning the engine as a drag racer might, aiming for the closest cross street. Oblivious to my presence, he steered straight into my path. Bam, upon the impact and seated higher than the car's low-slung hood, I catapulted up into the air twisting out of control. Crashing down, I landed square on my head with an agonizing thud. Lying in a fetal position in the middle of Fifth Avenue during rush hour, I found myself unable to move. A massive headache pounded my skull with a jackhammer's repetition.

I figured the police, not twenty meters (21 yards) away, would rush over, halt the traffic, detain the driver, and dial an ambulance. They did not—instead, they continued yapping as if the event never occurred. My confidence I floated through life, guided by some transcendental force, vanished, and evaporated on the cold, wet tarmac. Lying still and unable to move, a car slowly maneuvered around my fallen body. Would the next driver not notice and crush an outstretched limb? Desperately I tried reaching into my breast pocket for my mobile to call 911, but I could not budge my arm.

Unable to move, I glared at the cops, spitting out a pitiful cry to gain some attention, but the police acted as if I did not exist. I wondered if they recognized the driver else, why am I ignored? Thank goodness one hero did step forward.

"How are you—are you OK?" The man peering down—Dan Dailey—said he had been driving about five cars behind. He watched as my body twisted to the height of the traffic lights. Like with the Tanzanian nurse, I pleaded for positive news, "The injury's not bad, is it? Can I make a five o'clock appointment? And my bike? Hey, I must meet Dave as he is waiting."

"Well, you won't make your meeting but, you are not looking too bad," he responded, then kindly added, "and your bike is close by, do not worry."

"And my six o'clock meeting? I am…"

"Hold up. You are not making any meeting today."

I doubted this, but I kept silent. I heard Dan holler to the car driver, parked thirty meters away, to stay put. An unknown lady stopped, thoughtfully placing her umbrella over my head to shelter me from the elements. Someone suggested I keep still. Ha, I had tried standing but was incapable.

Dan dialed for an ambulance, and when the medics arrived, a discussion arose as to where I should go. What a luxury, two world-class institutions to choose from within one mile. I collapsed in the right place, not like in Zanzibar. The ambulance staff recommended Harlem Hospital, but Dan, an expert in the medical field, advised Mt. Sinai. I chimed in, preferring Harlem because of the half a mile proximately to my apartment, and I could wheel the bike home after receiving a bandage or two. The ambulance men nodded, "And Harlem specializes in head traumas." So, Harlem won.

The police, no doubt realizing a report needed filing, had now sauntered over and watched as the medics affixed my skull to a support frame before stretchering me into the ambulance. I felt awful, experiencing the same blinding headaches I suffered at Charing Cross, England. I drifted, in and out, out and in of reality—as if a candlemaker dipped me into a vat of scalding wax. Shooting pains darted inside my skull like a released pinball. Dan was correct; no meetings for me, but I would attend a 6 a.m. coaching session tomorrow.

Sirens blaring, we raced to the hospital. Red lights, blue flashes, medics conversing all whirled together inside an imaginary blender before I found myself at the medical center. Helpless and immobile, I was wheeled into a corridor of a huge building. Lying silent, I felt an urge to abandon this hectic life, incessant travel, and stupid charity work. I wondered, what am I doing? Why not secure a regular job, God forbid, receive a paycheck? Why not live in one place and take annual vacations like a normal person? If life walks a spirit towards a destiny, then why this dumb accident halting me in my tracks? The irony: I send shoes to Africa, then almost lose my life in a fight for one shoe—I start constructing a hospital in Africa, and I end up in the hospital.

Soon, all those muddled thoughts became a dreamy concoction of confusion, and I realized four or five nurses stood removing my clothes. One man garbled strange words. I must inform him the lights were too dim, and he should brighten the room to inspect the injuries.

Amed Rawanduzy, the senior neurosurgeon, was headed home after a strenuous day when he received an urgent text, "There is a critical case. Please. You must return." A fellow doctor, examining my cloudy scans, had given little hope for my survival. He later delivered a chilling report, "You are fortunate that Doctor Rawanduzy came back. He undoubtedly saved you. I have never witnessed such a messed-up head. Blood everywhere, and what the hell caused the old skull wound on the other side of your brain?"

Dr. Rawanduzy, applying skills acquired and practiced for decades, performed his miracles. Once more, doctors extended my days in this beautiful, beautiful world.

By good fortune or another miracle, after flying up high, I came crashing down and landed upon the left side of my skull. Over time, the plates on the damaged right-side had slightly shifted, weakening the cranium—the impact there, I heard, would have spelled lights out.

One question people asked was, "Why were you not wearing a helmet?" I own two, but helmets caused pressure on the prior fracture leading to dizziness, so I rode without a helmet—that is why I seldom straddled a motorbike.

Later, when visiting me in hospital, Dan related, "The way you hit the ground, the height, on your head, I was certain you had died. I have seen accidents like this, but driving past, I noticed your eyes open. You blinked. Of course, I stopped." Dr. Rawanduzy and Dan Dailey rose up as my Samaritans.

I felt betrayed by the police officers on duty, but I understood maybe other incidents occurred that I did not fully comprehend. What stung was reading their accident report. The account stated I rode illegally, heading south on Madison Avenue, and the car driver was faultless. Digesting their statement felt like a boxer punching me in the upper stomach. It is inconceivable that the police would neglect such a detail as my actual location.

Initially, they adamantly stuck with their story stating I suffered confusion and broke the law. But the two police officers were unaware of my witness and his phone video camera—unaware the witness remained in touch with the victim. Months later, months, and after legal assistance from my friend Mike Sharp, the cops altered the paperwork. Yet, the driver never has received even the slightest reprimand for his illegal actions that almost killed me. If I perished and if not for Dan stopping, the story would be, 'He pedaled against the oncoming traffic on Madison and died.'

I woke up following the surgery twenty-four hours later in a solitary ICU like I did thirteen years before, surrounded by the same clutter of IVs, tubes, and beeping machines. Back then, a nurse smiled, 'Welcome to your second life.' Is this the third? Had I seen myself, I would have been shocked—half a shaved head exposed a large surgery scar with forty-two-inch-long metal staples pressed into my skull. My brain, looking through fuzzy eyes that gazed forward and saw no mirrors, did not register any signs of concern. Today, if I roused and could not lift a right arm or leg, I might freak out. Heavily sedated, such issues did not raise an eyebrow.

In Zanzibar, a slow bleed granted eleven days to reach a center of excellence. In Harlem, the hemorrhage flowed like Niagara Falls, yet I collapsed between two excellent hospitals. Untreated, Dr. Rawanduzy confirmed I likely had 120 minutes left to live. "Life, it is all about timing. You suffered a massive bleed," and the doctor then recalled a story of a hiker who grazed his head on an overhanging rock and died within an hour.

"But you, Toby, fly to the traffic lights, crash down, land on your already damaged skull, and somehow survive?"

I healed in the cubicle of the ICU ward closest to the control station, where the most critical cases lie. Doctors and nurses, monitoring my condition, barely allowed a moment of peace. I, who should be working on the hospital project, lay grounded. My mind raced, and it fretted about the prospects of this accident stalling construction. Watchdogs, auditors, quantity surveyors, and a commissioner vetted the checks and balances, but being the sole guarantor—on both sides of the ocean—meant without my signature, progress would stop. I must be in Kenya soon to clear an upcoming invoice. I must clamber out of this hospital bed.

A nurse arrived, requesting a contact number, a relative if possible. Disliking pity and dreading visitors, I played the dumb foreigner—works with my accent—and lied, saying I had no friends in town. She informed me an emergency contact was mandatory. Thus, I submitted Chelimo's name. I had no idea they must call her, so I begged for a compromise, "OK. But mention to her that I am fine." Over in Seattle, Chelimo did not buy the story.

"In the ICU, but he is fine? Then ask him to walk to the phone." Her elder brother, Ian, had died in a terrible car accident, and she related feeling her bones bend on the verge of a breakdown hearing the news. She promptly phoned Anthony requesting a truthful update, and soon he and George Hirsch, the NYRR Chairman, arrived at my bedside. The plan of silently recovering backfired. When Anthony appeared, Chelimo dialed again, informing him she had booked a flight.

"I am fine," I whispered, not wanting her to hear my feeble voice, "she should not inconvenience herself as I'm checking myself out tonight," which I genuinely believed.

Anthony nodded and delivered a convincing speech. He winked,

"Done. I am a good actor. Dr. Mark Greene knows how to sound like a doctor!"

Therefore, the next day when Chelimo strolled into the cube, I could not believe my eyes. Adored by all, cementing friendships fast, she was the only civilian authorized to stay, 24/7, throughout the week on the ICU ward. She and the staff bonded like glue. Obtaining nurse's scrubs, you could have mistaken her for a medic. Our room transformed into the community drop-in and story-telling hub—seemingly half the staff migrated from Africa, and we traded Green card sagas and immigration gossip.

On the third day, did I see worms crawling from a visitor's head? I surmised mind-warping medication might be to blame. Dr. Rawanduzy assured me it was safe to quit the painkillers, but could the body tolerate the ache? That I coped in Tanzania meant yes. Besides, I had a big red help button to push as a safety net. Chelimo later reported my face puffed bright crimson, and for two days, I writhed in a bath of a couple of inches of body sweat. Yet, convincing myself that painkillers delay the healing processes by reducing the fever symptoms, it was critical this illness burned more intensely to knock out the infection, so I could recover and jet straight to Kenya, back to work. Staying in Harlem wasted time. Not tying in with this belief, Chelimo considered requesting the nurses to feed the drugs intravenously into my system. She did not follow my reasoning. Somehow, my plan worked, and I forced the fever out of my body. I concluded this was step one if I wished to return to Kenya.

Dan kindly continued visiting, and discussing my condition with the physiotherapists, heard that I might suffer mobility impairments. At once, I freaked out, believing this would nix any travel plans. Directly I began implementing leg lifts or any other strengthening exercise possible and started an in-bed boot camp.

On the sixth day, showing improvements, I earned a promotion out of the ICU—not home, as I hoped, but to the thirteenth floor. Whoa, what a surprise, one bed instead of eight sat like a throne in a spacious, converted luxury ward boasting three enormous television screens, polished dark hardwood floors, two writing desks, a kitchenette, and a private bathroom. A plush red leather sofa bed sat placed for Chelimo. Staff dubbed this room the Presidential Suite. Goodness, what had I done to deserve the royal treatment? I later heard that unknown individuals had mentioned the works I performed in Africa to the management.

During this period, I gained a lot of appreciation for healthcare and friendship. Despite developing a relationship with Chelimo, at the drop of a hat, she immediately flew six hours to stay by my side for a week. And John Legere, the man introducing me to Chelimo, stepped up generously.

Having visited on occasions, he knew I craved to go home, but the medics adamantly opposed the idea. Knowing I lived alone presented too high of a risk, but the doctors countered they might approve a supervised place with medical support. The chance for complications like seizures and falls was too high. John, who worked out of Seattle, not only offered accommodation at his Manhattan apartment but to hire a twenty-four-hour nurse for a fortnight. I could not accept his kindness, but his thoughtfulness touched my heart.

Instead, I concocted a scheme, why not prove myself worthy of a release date? Attempting to walk presented an obvious move besides, how would I ever leave this joint? Seizures struck sick people who spiraled downward—I was recovering and needed to rocket straight back to Eldoret.

Imagine my glee on my initial training pass when I accomplished three circuits of walking the room. The next day, I exercised a total of two hours' worth of steps. The physiotherapist who had chatted with Dan passed by, pausing in shock. She cried, "Amazing! Is this you?" Base fitness from running, I know, healed the body faster. The following day, I completed loops around the thirteenth floor employing the nurses as timekeepers. Each lap, I aimed to set a course record for the circuit, rewarding myself with bananas.

So, as in Charing Cross, I discharged myself a week early. From the hospital's charity bin, I scavenged ill-fitting clothes because mine ripped in the accident then after collecting a bag of belongings and my bicycle, I checked out—but how quickly the wall of confidence used to defy the doctors' crumbled like a sandcastle when I stepped onto the streets. They were right—I needed more recovery.

Petrified that I might stumble, I shuffled both feet for better stability along the sidewalk. People resembled cruise missiles, and I became terrified of being hit again, only this time by the pillar of a pedestrian. I realized that I could barely walk from Lenox to Fifth Avenue, let alone the four blocks south. Should I turn back?

Forcing myself onward, I whispered, you must keep going if you really want to fly to Kenya. Yet, the task of arriving home was too daunting. Rather than achieving street blocks, I focused on reaching a lamppost to the next lamppost plan and concentrated on the miniature goals. Each time a person approached, I froze, and a cold sweat trickled down my back. The pavement lay flat, but pushing the bike resembled a workout. Weak and feeble, I did not realize the buckled front rim jammed the tire against the framework.

When I should walk over 135th street, I waited for two light sequences to gain enough courage to attempt the crossing. On the third time the sign flashed to proceed, I set off at my fastest clip. Midway across the double-lane two-way intersection, the lights switched. Car drivers blared their horns, guessing a madman wandered loose. Was I to be knocked again? I did not know what I should do and experienced an overwhelming urge to curl into a ball and cry in the middle of the road. A car driver slowed, I hoped to allow me to cross, but he lowered his window only to scream a cluster of abusive words. His acceleration nearly sliced off my toes. Why me, I mean, cars never travel the wrong way up Fifth Avenue, and the first vehicle choosing to do so drives straight into me?

So, if you trust in meanings, what does this represent? Read the tea leaves; It means STOP. You tried. Step aside, let another person take responsibility—it does not mean you have failed. Friends advised you to stop, rest, and recover. But no, and now look at you, whimpering in the road insisting you must pick up the hospital project as if your life depended upon it.

Heaven knows how, but I made it home—overwhelmed, relieved, and soaking in sweat. I concluded I must hit the pause button and hibernate for a month or two. Who cared if I suffered penalties for non-payment? Let me follow the medical advice and back off any work. My personal health stood at risk.

Inside the building, I let out an exaggerated groan remembering the cupboards were bare. Why didn't I ask at the hospital for a meal? The notion of detouring to the supermarket felt like scaling Mt. Everest. Instead, I flopped on the bed—the exhaustion of the half-a-mile journey had knocked me sideways. I disappeared into darkness for twenty hours straight.

Sleep shifted every no to a yes. Slumber had bolstered my confidence, and yesterday's doubts vanished into the yawns of my forgotten dreams. Stall the project—are you absurd? The thought of paying late fees provided a shuddering jolt. In my mind, donations to Shoe4Africa materialize from a fictitious grandma dwelling in a low-income apartment. She dips her wrinkled hand that has toiled with decades of backbreaking labor into a small, knitted purse and fishes out a ten-dollar bill—it is the last of her funds before next week's pension check. She wonders, should she include sausages in her meal or help impoverished kids in Africa? Instantly, she drops the bill inside a donation box, recalling an incident in life she never forgot. That fictitious grandmother stays by my side whenever I disburse Shoe4Africa donations.

Although I dreaded the idea of stepping outdoors, an all-consuming hunger prompted my exit. At least this time, I did not have to haul the heavy bike. However, returning from the supermarket—chewing on a bagel—my confidence grew. Take small victories, Toby, step by step.

Following breakfast, I connected to the Internet for the first time in two weeks. It was like adding color to a black and white print; I had forgotten how much I relied on connectivity to breathe. With a feeble right arm, I used one left-hand finger to type replies to a hoard of unanswered mail. Then, in a bout of optimism, I booked a flight to Kenya for November 4th.

The following day I wondered, to hasten the recovery, could I run a mile? Considering myself as an expert at head injuries, I adopted the post-Zanzibar plan. A day later, I upgraded to a three-mile jog (3.1 km). By day five, I progressed to six miles (9.6 km)—the achievement made me ponder, how many more miles could I run? Not only did Kenya call, but I had gathered hundreds of pledges for the upcoming marathon—especially as the fund-raising rolled over from 2012's canceled event. Donors allowed me another year, but if I failed to compete again, people might request refunds. Why not attempt to finish? I could brisk-walk if needs be.

On Sunday, with one week to go before the race, I devised an ultimatum—achieve double figures in a training run, and you can enter the marathon. However, I endured a difficult day and struggled to seven miles (11.2 km) before stopping, half exhausted, to breakfast with a friend, Kevin Freeburn. Granting a proviso, I deduced a quick snack mirrored a pause at an on-course marathon water station—after eating, I could run on and complete the mileage. Yet a weird dizzy spell struck in the restaurant, so I accepted Kev's offer on a ride home. Best to play it safe besides, I did clock double digits in kilometers!

That evening, John Legere phoned, kindly checking in. John is a facilitator, and, quite animated, I explained a project where I hoped he might partner. Ending the call, I fell into a fog of dizziness. The ceiling, like ocean waves, rocked before my eyes and keeping objects in focus presented a problem, but I did not panic. Logically, this could not be happening. It must pass.

Lying on the bed, I counted to ten before opening my eyes. What the heck? Believing my arms swelled, I hurried to rip off a wristwatch, but the strap hung loose. Little made sense, especially the room swaying like a disco dancer. With a heaving chest and shortness of breath, I kept glancing at the clock—soon, I will call for help.

After fifteen minutes of no improvement, I waddled to my neighbor using both hands for support. Diahan, more rational than I, rang for an ambulance. Checking in to the ER, two doctors recognized me, and hiding a smile, reprimanded my decision of checking out of the hospital early.

Ten hours later, Diahan, still graciously by my side, and I returned home at dawn after tests and screenings. What caused the problem was unknown but resting up was the doctor's order.

At a respectable hour on the West Coast, I rang Chelimo, who immediately phoned George Hirsch. An avid runner like me, eighty-year-old George jumped into his running shoes and dashed a mile to monitor my condition. Chelimo, hearing George's report, boarded the next flight to New York. Defeated, I paused the running-for-recovery theory and presumed rest would be sufficient. But troubled days hid right around the corner.

On November 3rd Chelimo and I eagerly awaited the runners on marathon day. Our apartment stands thirty meters from the course, so if I could not run, I wanted to cheer, especially the Shoe4Africa heroes who had gone out of their way to solicit funds for this hospital's construction. But when the time came to leave, standing upright became difficult. Full of disappointment, we streamed the event on a tablet.

Tuning in, I recognized the weathered and thorny face of the Kenyan Julius Arile, jostling for the lead alongside our friend Geoffrey. What a story. Trading his AK-47 gun purposed for stealing cattle and thievery to own a pair of used running shoes, Julius played out his wildest dream. A Canadian, Anjali Nayar, documented Arile's journey, and her movie—Gun Runners—

should conclude with this marathon. Yet race officials rejected his request for an entry. But begging is my forte, so I pleaded with Mary Wittenberg to take a gamble and grant him an elite bib number. Incredibly, Julius placed fourth and won sufficient money to transform his life.

Chelimo, shattered from nights of irregular hours, fell asleep delighted that fellow Kalenjins—Geoffrey present at our pasta party and Priscah Jeptoo trained by Claudio—captured the wins. Unable to rest, I chose to type thank you letters as not a single donor requested a refund despite my lack of participation. But today, lifting a finger over the keyboard felt like running a marathon.

"What is this thread?" Chelimo, having woken, somehow hovered behind my chair. Pulling on a purple suture protruding from my skull, she queried,

"Should this string be here?" Distracted, I had not heard her rise and dismissed the thread because it was the least of the problems. Why could I not complete even a single email letter; that remained a bigger problem. But she persisted,

"Something is wrong. The hospital is so close. Let us ensure it is nothing."

No, doubting my strength was admitting a weakness. I did not require a hospital, but recognizing concern in Chelimo's warm eyes, I relented. Throughout my life—bar head accidents—I enjoyed excellent health. I was seldom sick, rarely a cold, or even a cough, but regarding brain injuries? How many more blurry hospital visits must I endure?

Briefly explaining my history to the hospital receptionist earned a fast-track appointment. In an examination room, the doctor acknowledged this was not a dissolving thread. So, did it matter? He stood at the remote end of the room chatting with Chelimo, and I sat upright, legs dangling over the side of an examination stretcher.

Clamping my hands upon the table, I underwent a weird sensation believing I might slump downwards. Blackness blocked

out both pupils. Like at the café, I could not see anything. Even my lips, numb, seized when I attempted to speak. The intensity of opening my mouth felt like a gym session,
"I think I am..." and boom, I passed out, tumbling to the floor.

The doctor later confirmed I suffered a seizure because my eyes rolled backward. When I awoke, I honestly imagined I sat in the audience at the Merlin Theater. Stage left, Chelimo bawling, head bowed, and wailing out words in Nandi. Stage right, the doctor, bellowing for backup. Instantly, medics rushed forward, clasping resuscitation clamps held in the stance that boxers display their gloves. Meantime I observed the drama in creepy slow motion, frame by frame, unable to operate. But am I still here? Move Toby, show them you are alive. Little surprise, I woke up back on the wards.

For the following few days, I endeavored to slow down and be patient. But the burning desire to press on itched like a rash. Somehow, we hosted another sold-out five km race boasting a T-Mobile sponsorship, thanks to John, who entered himself and almost won the event! But the hospital project—the albatross around my neck—disturbed both sleep and every waking thought.

Remembering there is a two-week grace period following a payment's due date—and with a couple of days to spare—I decided to fly to Kenya, wearing a hospital fall-risk armband, to reconcile the bills without a penalty. Did I learn a lesson to take it easy? Of course not.

Moses Kiptanui and I toured the dirt roads in his heavy-duty Toyota truck for a day. The man drives as he ran—nobody goes faster. Chickens scuttled, lethargic milking cows fled, and villagers darted from his path. His legend in Kenya is for his rally car antics, not the world running records he cracked. My head bounced like a bobble-top from dawn to dusk and ached terribly, but since it always did, I thought little of it.

We were finishing off a school construction following a generous donation from Wendy 'the angel' Martin, who has been a godsend for Shoe4Africa for years; I needed to monitor the progress before agreeing to release the final payment. Since time permitted, or Moses created time, why not check all the schools? Limping home just prior to midnight, I set the alarm to rise early because the Daily Nation planned an interview at eight a.m. for a full-spread hospital story.

Early morning, chatting to the Editor Elias Makori, inky clouds swirled inside my eyeballs. Slumping against the nearest wall, I staggered to prop myself upright. Reflecting, I think I stressed and worried too much.

I fretted concerning issues in America and Kenya that covered countless diverse tasks. And on both continents, I did not maintain a team or even an assistant to offload unwanted problems or menial jobs. Running a charity, building a national hospital, schools, and maintaining numerous programs is a ton of work. Furthermore, navigating business in Kenya is radically different from the straight and smooth lines of America.

2014 proved to be a challenging year with a sluggish recovery and an inability to conduct my coaching programs. Suffering from multiple head pains and sliding dizziness, I swam in a precarious position. The plan of trusting in fate had obvious flaws. After the second near-fatal accident, I recognized the risks—what if I was permanently bedridden?

Lying as an invalid on Fifth Avenue marked the clincher—I had flung my life into this work like a tightrope walker without a safety net. Although the construction funds were complete, in truth, these projects would never end. The recent accident struck as a reminder of life's vulnerabilities. Believing in karma did not consider the actions of one lunatic car driver. Now, unable to lead the early morning and evening coaching sessions, was it time to re-evaluate my welfare?

Shoe4Africa operated umpteen diverse programs, constructed schools, and this hospital without providing a single salary. People in Kenya, observing our impact, assumed we were an established business, with an office, company cars, and an employed staff. Would they believe the untold story? Since packing my bags at sixteen, boasting little more than one hundred dollars to my name, I played on my wits, not my pocket, and never sought a career.

Moving forward and now entering into my twentieth year of volunteering for this cause, perhaps I should finally accept a wage and eliminate one stress?

Honestly, I tried my absolute hardest to avoid this moment but conveying a request to the board, I proposed the following year, in 2015, to commence deducting a $48,000 after-taxes salary from my fundraising efforts. Somehow, I omitted to include healthcare. Remembering the typical person that we assisted earns around a dollar a day, the amount did cause me to blush.

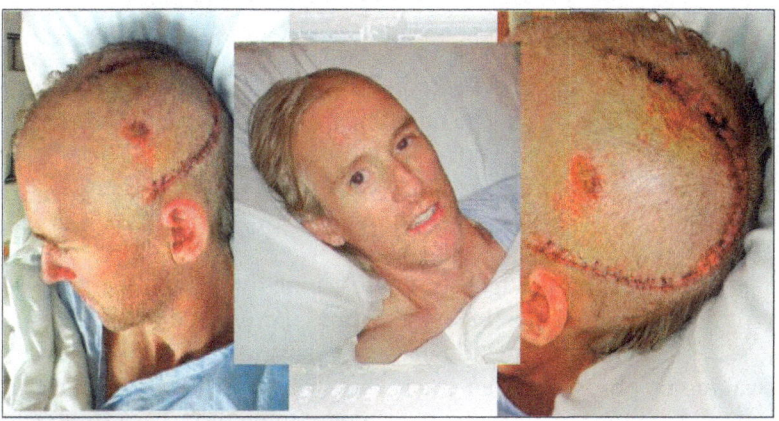

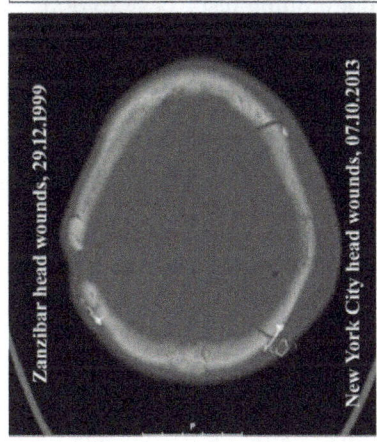

Both times, waking up after head surgeries, my appreciation for life heightened beyond measure. Here I am, feeling truly thankful to be alive after cracking each side of my skull on two separate continents and, somehow, surviving the incidents.

331

CHAPTER 25. 2014-15

NO FINISHING LINE

What we think or what we know or what we believe is in the end of little consequence. The only thing of consequence is what we do. – John Ruskin

Cats, the myth suggests, possess nine lives. Well, I outdid Felix the feline. Low and behold, I crumpled under another seizure, this time in Seattle, collapsing in a bathroom and waking up observed by an emergency worker in a bedroom. In the urgent care for less than one hour, undergoing tests, cost $6,000 and—still in shock—I received a second bill. The payment did not include the doctor's fees!

When I begin moaning, it is timely to recall the poor who cannot even receive medical help, let alone a bill. That haunting statistic—eighty percent of the under-five kids who died in East Africa never had the chance to see a healthcare provider—sticks like thick glue in a thin throat.

And what of the lady I once encountered trudging over a Kenyan farm field, forcing a handmade wheelbarrow with the forks clogged in gooey mud. Tears streamed down her cheeks as water might pour over a glass whilst she struggled to push her unconscious child lying sick, unaware she meandered in one directionless circle. No ambulance glided along Fifth Avenue for her comfort. Self-pity for receiving a bill paled in comparison to the cruel realities of life for others. The only benefit of these forced medical visits appeared to be gathering improvement tips for our building. Like, when laying skyward on a stretcher in Washington, I appreciated the design of dome mirrors placed on the ceiling—so an approaching trolley might not collide around a blind corner. Understanding that seizures could continue indefinitely, I barely paused before flying to Kenya. Besides, one more school required opening, and the usual projects necessitated arranging, and, of course, bills needed paying.

In Eldoret, the hospital grew, brick by brick, layer by layer, floor by floor, and I continued to be on-site whenever possible. Trivial matters made me grin, like helping to place the initial window frame or fitting the first toilet. I cannot express how much I glowed to be a part of the real-time progress. With the fictitious grandma still perched on my shoulder, we would easily complete the project under budget. I studied the money market and monitored the strength of the shilling against the dollar. When the greenbacks rose, I telephoned our bank to negotiate for better rates to pay the bills. Ministers and Governors stopped by and marveled at our efficiency and cost-effectiveness.

Another aid organization presented a proposal for a general hospital in Ethiopia. Could I vet the paperwork and explain how we slashed their costs by millions? Several red flags flew, like their project manager planning to compensate himself with a seven-figure salary for a two-year contract. Our costs for the identical position? Zero dollars.

The highlight of 2014 was the roofing of the hospital, symbolizing the completion of the structure was close. Even suffering from wonky balance, I shinnied up on the ridge to nail in the first section of sheeting. Funding continued to roll in, hallmarked for the equipment, fittings, and furnishing budget. Again, I was indebted to all the people who made this mission possible—like Michael Chambers of the MCJ Amelior Foundation, who had supported us since day one. Without my donors, Shoe4Africa would constitute nothing.

2015, my invisible health conditions became familiar and predictable. Upon waking, I suffered crunching head pains and unsteadiness. If shutting my eyes for a second when standing, I perceived myself falling, and if I tilted the head, my vision swung like a pendulum. Nausea and dizziness would then confuse me for a good ten minutes. In the subway stations of New York, I was meticulous in not standing near the train tracks, and walking the stairs, I required two handrails for support. Earaches persisted with a relentless hum each evening, and my right arm, to this day, endures nagging nerve damage. However, I marched onward, pretending I scored a miraculous recovery, all the while praying I would not undergo a seizure as I solicited a donation. No one, bar me, knew of my suffering. I kept silent because the golden truth of fundraising is nobody throws donations on a sinking ship.

Finally, the journey to create this healing center had reached its conclusion. I am ending on the glorious morning of August 12th, 2015. Among a crowd of people, Chelimo and I celebrated the opening of a fully staffed and serviced public children's hospital complete with two operating theaters, ICU, Surgical, burns wards, laboratories, imaging, and much more. The entrance displayed a covering of daffodil-yellow ribbons for the dignitaries to cut, and a marching band jazzed up the unforgettable occasion. Ministers, Governors, parliamentary members, clergy, doctors, nurses, parents, children, and friends combined to create a memorable day. I love the unique design and cannot find a building like it. Its profile, striking out against its peers, is a giant Y-shape to allow maximum airflow throughout each ward.

The architectural plan reduces the crossbreeding of airborne diseases and takes advantage of Eldoret's invigorating climate allowing additional natural light into the building. The yellow aluminum windows paired with matching interior paint raised eyebrows for the lack of conformity. The exterior walls are shaped with a taper to deceive the eye, making the height less imposing for a small child's approach. Why not construct a box-shaped design like most public buildings people queried and save considerable money, and why yellow? Yet, how many adults consider a kid's thoughts on how to design a hospital? The healing should begin when a youngster approaches our compound, and the impressions of a safe, friendly, and welcoming center are crucial.

Delivering a brief speech, I intended to touch upon some highlights of the implausible story that brought about this building. However, my list of people to acknowledge gobbled every second of the talk. The structure represented a milestone—the first public children's hospital in the region of East & Central Africa. A unique kids-only kids rule complex; no sick adults allowed in either the main building or the nine-acre compound.

In the next couple of years, not many, but we would treat patients from as far as Tanzania, Rwanda, Uganda, Southern Sudan, and Burundi. Monday to Friday, students from Moi University's medical school would utilize this facility for practicals. Two years to this morning, combining in and out-patients, 427 kids would be the daily average (circa 155,000 per year) receiving treatments here. We did it; we created a healing community. Yes, there was a meaning *why* I came to Africa—Doctor Mehta, you were correct. You knew when I harbored doubts.

Steps from the hospital entrance, a stone podium sleeps like a sentry embossed with a bronzed plaque. Thereon lies a quote summarizing this book's adventure, 'A dream project begun founded upon little more than an optimistic spirit.' My saving grace has been a soul tempered by steel endurance. But how did I get here? That is a running story and *Running with Destiny* was my way.

The End.

Epilogue

EVER ONWARD

Legacy is what you leave behind, but that others can use. – Diane von Fürstenberg

Chelimo, considering she had slouched for six hours against a Plexiglass window of the red-eye from Seattle, appeared in cheerful spirits when I collected her at the bustling La Guardia airport. In two days, she would enter her debut marathon.

"Now that I am here, I might bump into some NYC celebrities," she jested. Huh, slim chance, on a weekend trip for a marathon? Tonight, we should attend a Runner's World function, and tomorrow the day began with breakfast at Jerry's running store on Madison Avenue to meet with our team. Following this, we would partake in a remembrance celebration for Shay Hirsch by a lake in Central Park. Next, skedaddle to collect our bib numbers from the race exposition before attending Lou Adolfsen's Shoe4Africa pasta party at the Wooly, his chic club off Wall Street. Lastly, we should drop by the Hilton to wish Mary Keitany the best of luck for her title defense. On Sunday? Run 26.2 miles before darting back to catch the evening flight to the west coast.

Pre-dawn, early on the race morning, Chelimo and I stepped onto a marathon bus for a fifty-minute journey to Staten Island. Who boards and sits two seats behind but Alicia Keys. I would have missed the artist had it not been for her branded T-shirt. She politely smiles, saying hi. Few others arrive, and no one places themselves between Alicia and us. Our vehicle departs three-quarters empty. I nudge Chelimo, "Bingo, ask, and you will receive." But Chelimo yawns, preferring to doze. I, too, fell off the boil. The musician's foundation focused on Kenyan health initiatives, an ideal and obvious conversation starter for a boring bus ride.

Around this time, a gentleman called Steve—who sat for years on a board where I served—became the CEO of Beyonce's entertainment company. Do you think I even hinted at my fabulous plan to rebrand the Shoe4Africa hospital? Nope. Leads surfaced, but they all floated away in the wind. What happened? Had I lost the mojo? Nowadays, my energies resembled embers, no longer the Cuban festival drum. Or did I relax after the hospital project's completion? Either way, in 2018, *everything* would change.

I could not believe my ears, was it true? After reading a 'Bright future' pamphlet, boasting the battle against childhood cancer in America stood at its best-ever level—kids currently celebrated a ninety percent survival rate—I crashed down to earth hearing the African variant.
"The exact opposite," stated Dr. Kibosia as he stroked his chin, "Exact opposite. In Kenya and sub-Saharan Africa, ninety percent of the kids diagnosed with cancers will die."
Kibosia continued, "Imagine if you can, there is not a single kids cancer hospital, private or public in sub-Saharan Africa—that's well over one billion people. Ironically, here is the world's hotspot for pediatric cancers, but we are still waiting for a person to establish the first one." Now, his eyes locked upon mine, "You, Toby, could construct it for around three to four million dollars. Build it next door, in your complex."
Each expert in Kenya reinforced the claim concerning the dire need for a dedicated pediatric cancer center. Dr. Adamali, a Nairobi oncologist, predicted that cancer cases would cause as many if not more deaths than the Aids pandemic. Outside Kenya,

the Texas Children's Global Hope program backed up Dr. Kibosia's claim, '80 percent of children with cancer live in the developing world, with a substantial portion living in sub-Saharan Africa. In sub-Saharan Africa, 100,000 children per year develop cancer, and up to 90 percent of these children die.'

Meg O'Brien, M.D. for the American Cancer Society, laid it out in black and white, "In America since the 1960s, we've turned cancer from this frightening, inevitably deadly disease into something very fightable. That human triumph has not crossed the border in Africa yet. I was just blown away because so little attention was being paid."

Terry Vik, a professor of pediatric hematology-oncology from Indiana, informed me, "If you construct a hundred-bed facility, you will immediately start saving over 350 lives in your first year."

Dr. Vik, highly qualified, has traveled to Kenya for two decades to heal patients, and his estimates come from hands-on experience. If we increased to 150 beds, that would result in a minimum of 500 lives saved per year. Then, as the majority of cases—eighty percent—go undiagnosed in this region, according to the experts at Indiana University's Ampath program, if we added screening and preventative health, those high mortality numbers would plummet.

When Dr. Kibosia recited the horrific nine out of ten stats, I tasted vomit at the back of my throat. Nine out of ten? What chances are we allowing those kids? Shouldn't we duplicate the path the west took decades ago? Wasn't the construction of a children's cancer center the initial step? Access to healthcare is the answer, or am I overlooking something?

This dreadful story must be headline news—could I rally support? I called two American donor advisory services specializing in African aid. Both organizations informed me African Pediatric Cancers are not global priorities. I could not help myself, "Are you waiting for fatality rates of nine out of ten to rise to ten out of ten?"

The second African expert chimed in, "Ped cancers aren't on

our radar yet. The latest buzz is cash transfers to random people in Kenya. Our donors praise this model." When I replied that the Kenyan President practiced and promoted those methods forty years ago, the expert admitted ignorance to African-tried and tested ideas. Memories of hearing that 'Africans do not need a children's hospital' popped back into my mind.

I really did not fancy the notion of launching another substantial project alone. This hospital should be referred to an alternative organization, one associated directly with cancers. Besides, I executed my part—we built a twenty-eight-bed oncology wing at our hospital that delivered better odds. I could tick the contribution box. Furthermore, Shoe4Africa developments continued, and we were busy placing the final stones into our fifth school.

Using the wonders of hindsight, we can glance back—for example, with Gandhi, the occasion when he got tossed like a disused cigarette butt from a South African train—and declare, 'Aha, so that is one of the key moments why he did, what he did in life.' Well, New Year's Eve 2018 remained such a time for me.

We planned to host a soccer match at the hospital to launch the laying of an Astroturf pitch—kindly donated by Harrison and Shari Pire and friends. Sports and recreation are critical factors in rehabilitating a child, and the dream was to turn the children's compound into a health center of fun activities. Seven days ago, we had proudly opened a full-sized basketball court. Now, for the football, we arbitrarily selected youngsters from our playrooms to form a kid's hospital soccer team.

By coincidence, as patients announced their ailments, ninety percent of the squad suffered from cancers. The number struck hard, reminding me of that horrendous nine out of ten statistic. With tears swimming at the back of my eyeballs, I underwent a nightmare scenario. The whole team, bar one child, died on the field because their heinous crime was being born into poverty. Kids, already disadvantaged, presently fighting a terrifying disease, and left to wander among the wreckages of an unjust world. Who fought to make sure this finale did not play into a reality? Certainly not me.

Beryl, the captain, a zestful eight-year-old, who never stopped smiling, should have returned home a week earlier for Christmas when her chemo treatment ended. Yet she went on strike, refusing to leave her agemates over the holidays. Beryl and her friends stick together. These unfortunate children could not fly to Europe, as I did, for healthcare. Nor can they jet to India or the Americas like several prominent Kenyan officials and a former minister of health, and indeed the minister of medical services, when falling seriously ill. Beryl and thousands of kids are grounded, seeking what little the public services can offer. But what could I offer?

I knew a cancer ward nestled inside a congested children's hospital with hundreds of germs floating around was not the best scenario for a child with a compromised immune system. I understood our space was overcrowded and insufficient. So, could I cling to the courage to follow my heart? I would need a miracle. Nevertheless, I pledged to construct sub-Saharan Africa's first dedicated children's cancer hospital on the day.

Two weeks later, in a wintry climate, visiting dear friends Doug and Kim, a miracle materialized. That marvel arrived in the form of a suntanned unshaven man. Doug had returned from a soul-searching vacation in Mexico, with days spent combing for the bigger answers. He knew my history and kindly offered to partner on a project. Did I have any unfunded plans?

Easy-going but hard-working, Doug is a generous, big-hearted man who journeyed three decades with an inspiring lady called Juli Anne. Tragically, Juli lost her fight against cancer in 2010. Despite giving back his entire life, Doug desired to give back more. Providence—his substantial six-figure donation would be perfect for a cornerstone to initiate the launch of a 152-bed public children's cancer hospital. So—God help me—the upcoming struggle of fundraising commences.

Of course, true to my character, as with the first hospital, it should be accomplished as we fundraise and construct our seventh school, a health dispensary in Southern Nandi, and a second, and perhaps third, dormitory building.

Propelling forward two years, against extreme odds due to Covid-19, when donations for overseas aid all but came to a standstill, the construction funding for the cancer hospital is pretty much complete. Our little foundation has done it!

So how could I unveil this spectacular landmark project? Naturally, the inauguration must encompass a run. The Latin word *aequator* translates as to make equal, and since first hearing that 1/10 versus 9/10 stat, I yearned for the balance to shift towards equality by awarding the Kenyan kids with a fighting chance. Why not launch *on* the equator—fifty miles (eighty km) from Eldoret—and run to the construction site to highlight the gross inequality? Maybe invite friends and introduce a relay concept? I called Paula Radcliffe, and she kindly agreed to help. One by one, others stepped up, like William Tanui, the Olympic champion who chauffeured me to Eldoret in 1995, and Kip Keino, who I bumped into upon arrival. Like Moses Tanui, a runner from that crazy first morning Kenyan jog. Everyone who listened to my ramblings pledged to partake in this historic Great Equator Run.

Then, as we all stumble, jog, or limp the final leg, we will unite with a gathering of cancer patients from our hospital for a unique groundbreaking. Paula's fourteen-year-old daughter, Isla, a cancer survivor, will pitch in the first shovel alongside a Kenyan patient from our Shoe4Africa cancer ward for an emotional finale.

On the day, I know I will shed a tear for Beryl's memory. But I shall focus on that —after completing this project and the Sidekick Foundation donating a fifty-bed kids burns unit—I believe no pediatric center on the continent will serve more children than at our complex in Eldoret.

My thoughts will fade to that overcast morning when listening in horror to Grace's story, then picking up the proposal at Moses's café. Back then, it would have been so easy to say no and pursue the lucrative Manhattan Marathon project, but saying yes proved to be the correct answer, not just for me but for an uncountable number of children.

If our hospital fosters any problem, it is the disease of suffering from overcrowding—no child is turned away. Removing spacious, stylish beds and utilizing smaller and simpler models, and demolishing sinks in the wards to accommodate further patients felt bittersweet. And still, the numbers continue expanding for kids to receive quality treatment offered from our remarkable team headed up by Dr. Aruasa and the MTRH Management.

Daily, the staff hears heartfelt remarks of gratitude and appreciation from parents. Firsthand, countless mothers have spoken up and repeated one piercing sentence that makes this whole journey—which at times has been lonely, punishing, and rough—worthwhile, 'Was it not for Shoe4Africa, my child would be dead today.'

Donors, *thank you,* I am forever in your debt.

The Shoe4Africa Children's Hospital. Please contact me if you wish to help in any capacity with our mission of uplifting Health, Education, and Women's Empowerment: visit us at our hospital, or drop me an email, toby@shoe4africa.org.

AN INVENTORY OF ACKNOWLDGEMENTS

The period of 1995 – 2015, for me, signifies a calendar blur. I closed my eyes, and chunks of life drifted by the window way too quickly. Countless times, friends mentioned I must document the journey as it passed. So, I did. I scribbled a manuscript in 2010 titled Doubles, referring to how I lived in two different worlds but tossed it aside. I asked for help, became disappointed, and found frustration. I stopped. I picked up and put down stale words. Did I want what at times resembled a rocky jumble of memories mixed into print? No, but the cause that drives me to write overrides all the above; to shine a light where light has failed to shine on sub-Saharan African kids suffering from cancer. 9/10 is an abysmal, shameful statistic. *And* this book needs to offer acknowledgments to the multiple people who have stepped forward to make this journey possible.

Words fail to express the depth of gratitude I hold for the support I have received. I start with my parents, Colin & Jennie, for fashioning my life and being wonderful, caring souls. To my wife, Chelimo. When friends ask Chelimo how, for the first years of our relationship, she coped with my crazy travels, she describes it as being wed to a military man. Fortunately, she embraces our mission—along with my thoughtful, sweet stepdaughter, 'Windy' Lindi. To my brother Liam and sisters Lisa and Saskia; I wish I could enjoy our childhood again; it rushed by too soon.

Thank you to Anthony Edwards & Jeanine Lobell, Michael & Tina Chambers, for giving great support and encouraging me from day one. To Stacey & Hal Kelly; you are the best, to George

Hirsch and John Legere, and Wendy, Ben, KT Martin & family, and Mason Haupt, for exceptional schools' help. And, of course, to Dr. Wilson 'Daktari' Aruasa, Dr. Kibosia, Atogo Odhiambo, & Selah Peplan. Thank you, Dr. Rawanduzy, and Dr. Peterson, and your teams from Harlem & Charing Cross Hospitals. Thanks to Birju Patel, Ivan & Kim Zinn, to Rene Admiraal & Kristof Van Malderen, and the All4Running.nl team. A shout out to today's Shoe4Africa Board: Chairman Dave & Zeynep Siegel, Jon & Summer Lang, Alex Green, Amy Zhen, and Sherif Moussa, not forgetting all the previous members.

Thank you to Hedley Matthew, to Shmuel & Anat Harlap, Ásgeir Halldórsson, Rodney Cutler, Eddie Stern & Stephanie Rein, Chris & Mark Bilsky, Mary Darling, Mary & Derek Wittenberg, Catherine and Jon Howell, Brad Gerdeman, Michael Suchenski, Dick Traum, Melina 'Marathon Star' Terranova, Loredana Delucchi & her 500 knitted teddies. Thanks to Pieter Langerhorst & Lornah Kiplagat for accommodating me in Iten and keeping Shoe4Africa expenses at a minimum; you rock!

To Doug, a genuine superstar, & Kim—the *whole* 'Perry Team' for keeping this story running. To Josh & Hadley Ott and Joy Dushey, Nina Greisman, Victoria & Peter Farago, Marty Levine, Tom Cheslik, Caroline & Jason Palmer-Myers.

To Ivar Trausti Josafatsson, Jerry Macari, Tom Labreque, Matt & Janet Gordon, Bernd Erpenbeck, and dear friends Claudio & Claudia Berardelli, and not forgetting a thank you to the many anonymous donors. Thank you, Julian Wolhardt, Lara Tabatnik, JP & Natascha, Dalhia and Alegra, Reinhold. To Harish Menon, Wael Rammo, Jayson Petersen, Frank Schlepers, Manuela Scollol & Frank Bollen. To Lisa Nelson and Gavin Gee. To Markus Johansson for playrooms help, and to Ashley Ault for her drive to bring classrooms to the hospital. For the Kitchens, thanks to Michael Kugler and Urban Bettag. Thanks to Harrison & Shari Pire. To Joe Benun with Team U, Tom Bark, and Kevin Freeburn. Thanks to Marc & Michelle King Davis, to Diahan Walker-Sealy, and to the Daily Nation for promoting this story in Kenya, particularly to Elias Makori, Jared Nyataka, and their team of intrepid roving reporters. Thanks to Ambassador Lou Adolfsen, and all our running ambassadors. Gracious thanks to the eminent folks who offered support in various capacities; Kristine Froseth, Cara Buono, Ben Ahlers, Cristiano Ronaldo, Billie Jean King, Ryan Reynolds, Tom Cavanagh, James LeGros, Sarah Jones, Kim Alexis, Hugh Jackman, Natalie Portman, Rosario Dawson, and to the outstanding MCJ Amelior Foundation, to Pepsico, T-Mobile, and Omega. Thanks to the New York Road Runners who have been instrumental throughout this story, and to all the amazing individuals who have run marathons or hosted events to help us, the people not mentioned here. To thousands of kind donors—I am thankful for your extraordinary support. I know I have omitted names, and I apologize in advance; your kindness is chiseled in my heart. Lastly R.I.P. to my dear father, Colin, who climbed up to entertain the angels this year.

The foot's note – our copyrighted logo resembles both the continent and that of my bare foot, running along the shores of Zanzibar. Created in 2007, by the fabulous artist Susie Mendive.

In 2001, Noel (white T) landed in Kenya. The traffic rolled to gridlock on the main street of Eldoret, as we performed Rolling Stones songs to raise money for Kip Keino's Orphanage.

ABOUT THE AUTHOR

After living in five countries on three continents, surviving two brain surgeries on either side of the skull, Toby intends on settling down—soon. He is a philanthropist, coach, author/writer, former professional athlete, race director, and founder of Shoe4Africa.

Profiled twice on CNN, featured as a Humanitarian of the Year for Runner's World, with commendations by the Presidents of the USA and Kenya, he worked—unpaid—for two decades on charity projects. Most memorably to build East & Central Africa's 1st public children's hospital—mirroring Nelson Mandela's legacy dream. During this period, he constructed schools, hosted AIDS awareness, hookworm, & peace events, and re-gifted thousands upon thousands of pairs of used running shoes.

Toby has authored the books *Train Hard, Win Easy. The Kenyan Way*. First and second editions. *The Essential Guide to Running The New York City Marathon*. Also, *More Fire. How to Run the Kenyan Way* and now *Running with Destiny, An Odyssey of Mistakes, Machetes, and Miracles*.

He was a columnist and wrote for a variety of magazines and journals. Also writing and helping produce the Soundwalk audio running guides to NYC, Paris, London, and Berlin, and the NYC marathon's first audio guide.

Toby sat on the (NYRR) NYC Marathon's Board of Directors for fifteen consecutive years (named a lifetime honorary NYRR member in 2000) and was, among other roles, the Chairman of the Race Quality control. He functioned as a Board Director for eight years, then as the Vice President for a further eight years of a disability charity—Achilles International. He served on other charitable boards, and as a member of the Runner's World Coaches Advisory Board, also as a Commit to Fit ambassador for the global franchise SUBWAY.

Toby was the inaugural and head coach of what is today the NYC Nike Running Club. He coached four additional city running teams, numerous private individuals, and a handful of charity organizations teams. He coached at the iconic Fashion Institute of Technology, also for paroled prisoners and police cadets. He continues coaching for Team Lifeline. For thirteen years, he was the race director in NYC and in Kenya and directed one of NYC's most popular events; The Hope & Possibility 4-miler.

Toby resides between Eldoret, Kenya, and the USA with his wife Chelimo and stepdaughter Lindi.

Trivia? Although touted by the Scottish Balmoral Races as the fastest person ever to run a ten km race donning a kilt, Toby fails to, even once, outrun Chelimo, Lindi (house champion), or Fluffy, his pet highland sheep. His latest ambition is to construct sub-Saharan Africa's 1st children's cancer hospital.

A gallery of photographs accompanying each chapter are posted on the www.runningwithdestiny.com site.

Quotes.

"You hear stories of people who are mugged, not with a knife and a machete and a baseball bat, and not even injured very much, and all they'll tell you is how you should never go back there it's a dangerous place they'll never go back. Not only does the guy go back, he takes the thing that they were robbing him for and decides to give them to the community—I mean his brain's wired differently than most people." **Ali Velshi, NBC correspondent.**

"An unforgettable story from an unforgettable storyteller. Toby wanted to be an elite runner and seemingly had the talent and motivation. Yet on a trip to Kenya, he almost loses his life, amazingly recovers and goes on to change the lives of tens of thousands of people. When you finish this book, you will feel that every one of us can do more to help our fellow human beings. Truly inspiring!" **George Hirsch, Chairman of the NYC Marathon,** and founding publisher of New York, and the New Times.

"I became a member of a team running for a charity called Shoe4Africa. I assume you have never heard of them. I know I hadn't. Shoe4africa, founded by a former elite runner and a fascinating guy named Toby Tanser, works to improve the lives of impoverished people in Africa. Read Toby's story and the consequent origin of the charities name. As a teaser, the story involves a machete—as, I assume, all the names of charities do." **Joel Cohen**, **The Simpsons** Emmy Winning scriptwriter, and author of the wonderful book, *How to Lose a Marathon.*

"You choose fun stories to tell, then you tell them in an offhand, carefree way. It is very unusual. You write poetic prose." **Jeff Johnson, NIKE's** first employee.

"I commend you for Shoe4Africa's efforts to fight poverty. I also want to thank you for incorporating HIV/AIDS education into your program." **USA President, Bill Clinton.**

"You are making a fine contribution to the development of sport in Africa." **Sir Roger Bannister,** the world's first sub-four-minute miler.

"I am informed of the sacrifice you made to fund raise to build this facility. On behalf of the Government, I can not thank you enough for your contribution and unwavering support." **The Deputy President of Kenya, Hon. William Sameoi Ruto.**

"It is admirable work you are doing embracing the poor and needy of Kenya. Keep it up." **President of Kenya, 1978-2002, Hon. D. A. Moi.**

"Thank you Toby Tanser for giving your support to the children of Africa, I can only express my gratitude to you and to all who support you in this life-saving endeavor that is giving our children a better chance of survival. Bless you." **Edna Adan, Former First lady of Somaliland,** and founder of the Edna Adan Maternity Hospital.

"We are honoured to work with and help in some small way Shoe4Africa in the amazing and vitally important work that they do." **Paula Radcliffe and Gary Lough**—the 'royalty' couple of the Running World.

"SHOE4AFRICA has become a powerful agent for change." **NTV (Kenyan National Television).**

"Toby has done a lot more for a lot of people in his life than most folk would even attempt to do in a lifetime." **Liz McColgan**, World Champion, Olympic medalist.

"I thought Toby's run was amazing. It has never been done, and he's not doing it to be the best or to just do something, he is doing it for charity, to help other people." **Sir Mo Farah, four-time Olympic champion.**

"Although he almost died, it was a chance for Toby to find his calling." **Sanjay Gupta, CNN Emmy Award winning medical reporter.**

"Toby was not a white savior who started a charity to *Save Africa* (and himself). He was not burned out by corporate life, seeking a 'worthy' career-choice to save himself from a bankrupted life. No, he was driven by his heart. For two decades, he worked tirelessly without pay to change Africa, to bring jobs, education, and healthcare for others with seemingly little care for himself." **Lorna Chelagat**, Blogger, Kenya.

"We celebrate Toby because of his natural–born talent, mixed with his compassionate spirit, his courage and determination as a beacon and living example that we can all be extraordinary when we truly believe in something and persistently work at it." **The Xtraordinary.com**

"This is God's work." **Steven Spielberg**, speaking about the building of the Shoe4Africa Children's Hospital.

"Your writing is amazing. You are a born storyteller. Your own personal story is a natural page turner. Running with Destiny is on par with Frank McCourt's "Angeles Ashes."" **Andy Kelley Harding**.

"An adventurer's story of navigating life with few of the conventional qualities found in other explorers, but with better results for mankind." **Michael Zhan**.

"Toby's passion and commitment to helping Africa's children is infectious," **Robert Zoellick, President of the World Bank,** (2007-12).

"Fun and Intense." **Nelson Farris**, Nike's Chief Storyteller.

"I'm supporting Toby and Shoe4Africa so much, because he is doing something from the bottom of his heart. He lifts up others before himself." **Marathon World Record holder, Mary Keitany**.

"I have not seen any person, or politician in Kenya, do more good than what I have seen what Toby Tanser has done." Member of Parliament, Boston Marathon winner, **Wesley Korir.**

"The next time you go and do a crazy run, tell me, I am coming!" Two-time New York City Marathon winner, **German Silva.**

"This is one single man who has come to Kenya and struggled to do the work of a government. Who builds a national hospital and a series of public schools?" **Moses Kiptanui**, Three-time World Champion.

"Another classic from the author of Train Hard, Win Easy. That book, in Kenya, is the runner's bible!" **E. Tanui**, N'gong, Kenya.

"Toby has many other achievements under his belt, but more than anything, he shows us how one person can make a huge difference in the world." **Claire Bartholic, RunnersConnect.com.**

"Unlike the other mzungu's who occasionally come to Kenya to try and train with a group of the world's best runners, Tanser is not there in search of secrets to help end the medal drought in countries outside of East Africa. Not anymore, anyway. He's there to help a continent." **Duncan Larkin, The Competitor.**

"(Shoe4Africa) has done a great deal to raise AIDS awareness and inspire thousands of people to follow in the footsteps of their continent's tremendous distance runners and begin running themselves." **Awareness.com, Kenneth Cole.**

"Toby Tanser brings new meaning to 'life adventures' as he shares his incredible up and down experiences, opportunities, and life lessons." **GoBeMore.com**

"Thank you also for being an inspiration for all of us. You have such a positive outlook, and you are so supportive of us back-of-the-pack runners." **Supreme High Court Judge, Denny Chin.**

"This book is great! It's like my black and white writing in technicolor!" **Dick Traum**, author of, A Victory for Humanity, and Achilles Founder.

"For many years, Toby has played a major role in nurturing Kenya's athletic talents." **General J. Tuwei, President, Athletics Kenya.**

"Toby is one of the running ambassadors of our time." **Tina Muir, runningforreal.com**

"Shoe4Africa came into being in the craziest of ways, but its founder has seen it grow to embrace the whole of East Africa." **Nzino Mutune—Daily Metro.**

"Shoe4Africa initiatives are making a real change to the lives of people across Sub-Saharan Africa." **UK African Minister—Hon. Bellingham**.

"I will forever support Toby and Shoe4Africa, because I have seen the wonders they've achieved." **Abel Kirui**, 2x World Marathon Champion.

Made in the USA
Coppell, TX
28 March 2024